James Ernest Caldwell

Debates relative to the affairs of Ireland:

In the years 1763 and 1764 - Vol. 1

James Ernest Caldwell

Debates relative to the affairs of Ireland:
In the years 1763 and 1764 - Vol. 1

ISBN/EAN: 9783337728083

Printed in Europe, USA, Canada, Australia, Japan

Cover: Foto ©ninafisch / pixelio.de

More available books at **www.hansebooks.com**

DEBATES

RELATIVE TO THE

Affairs of Ireland;

In the Years 1763 and 1764.

TAKEN BY

A MILITARY OFFICER.

Sit mihi fas audita loqui.   *Virg.*
What I have heard, permit me to relate.

To which are added,

An ENQUIRY

How far the RESTRICTIONS laid upon the Trade of IRELAND, by *British* Acts of Parliament, are a Benefit or Disadvantage to the *British* Dominions in general, and to *England* in particular, for whose separate Advantage they were intended.

WITH

Extracts of such Parts of the Statutes as lay the Trade of *Ireland* under those Restrictions.

VOLUME I.

LONDON:
M.DCC.LXVI.

TO THE

RIGHT HONOURABLE

WILLIAM PITT,

THESE

DEBATES

Are Humbly INSCRIBED

WITH THE GREATEST

Veneration of his ABILITIES and VIRTUES

AS AN

ORATOR and STATESMAN

BY HIS

Moſt Obliged,

and moſt obedient

humble Servant,

J. C.

PREFACE.

IN the Beginning of the Winter of 1763, when the Parliament was about to meet for the firſt Time after the Concluſion of a long War, when the Cultivation of the Arts of Peace had been recommended from the Throne, and the Attention of the Legiſlature would be naturally turned upon the Redreſs of Grievances, and the Eſtabliſhment of public Oeconomy, I felt an Inclination to be preſent at the Deliberations of ſo auguſt an Aſſembly, at ſo critical a Time, and on Subjects ſo Intereſting and Important.

I therefore attended in the Houſe of Commons, from its firſt ſitting till the Receſs at *Chriſtmas*, without Intermiſſion, except one Day, when a Breach of Privilege was complained of, by a Member whoſe Letter had been charged by an Officer of the Poſt-Office, being that Day confined by Indiſpoſition: after the Receſs, other Avocations rendered my Attendance irregular.

PREFACE.

During this Time the great Queſtions concerning the Grant of Penſions on the civil Eſtabliſhment, and the Sums neceſſary for the Military Eſtabliſhment in time of Peace, were debated. A Debate alſo came on, concerning an Addreſs to his Majeſty on the Peace, the Report of the Committee appointed to enquire into the Inſurrections in the North, the Reſidence of the Clergy, the Publication of a Libel, and ſeveral Others, which were Objects of a very intereſted Curioſity.

By theſe Debates, carried on with the deepeſt Penetration, the moſt extenſive Knowledge, and the moſt forcible Eloquence, I was ſo impreſſed, that, after I had left the Houſe, the Voice of the Speaker was ſtill in my Ears, and the Sentiments I had heard excluded all others from my Mind. I was impelled, as it were, by an irreſiſtable Impulſe, to commit to Paper what was thus forcibly retained by my Memory, before it ſhould be mixed with other Ideas, or in any degree obliterated by them; when I made the Attempt I found the Taſk ſtill eaſier than I had imagined, my Attention was more fixed, and

the

PREFACE.

the deliberate Recollection which Writing made neceſſary, brought back the Ideas in a ſlow but regular Succeſſion, and generally in the very Words which had been uſed to expreſs them.

I had, indeed, upon former Occaſions, experienced that my Memory was not unfaithful with reſpect to Sentiment, but that with a mere Succeſſion of Words, or Sounds, it was not always to be truſted. I could, very early in my Life remember the Principles of an Argument, and the Events of a Story, but I found it difficult to retain mere Words, when I was to learn a Language, or the Succeſſion of mere Sounds, when I applied to Muſick.

Why ſome Perſons remember Words and Sounds, who cannot remember Principles and Events, in a regular Series, I ſhall not here enquire; but as, when we think, our Ideas occur to our own Minds in ſome Terms that would expreſs them to another; ſo when we recollect Ideas that have been communicated to us under certain Terms, thoſe Terms naturally occur with the Ideas, rather than any other, being already aſſociated with them.

PREFACE.

This seems to account for my having been able to recollect the Words, as well as the Sentiments, of those whom I heard speak in Parliament, without possessing that mechanical Kind of Memory which can retain Terms, not as Symbols but as Sounds, and which sometimes distinguishes those who discover scarce any other Faculty of the Mind; for there have been Persons, who, though they could repeat a Discourse of considerable length delivered in a Language they did not understand, after once hearing it, yet could not have comprehended the meaning of it, if it had been delivered in their mother Tongue. I do not, however, pretend that I have always done Justice to the Speakers, either with respect to Language or Sentiment, whatever is amiss, therefore, in either, must be imputed to me, though the Honour of whatever is excellent must undoubtedly be theirs.

When I had succeeded in recording these Speeches, so much to my own Satisfaction, I could not help wishing to communicate the Pleasure I had received. I considered, that nothing could be a more interesting Object of Curiosity than the Sentiments of those who have been selected by the Suffrages of their
Country

PREFACE. v

Country to compose the Supreme Council of the Nation, with respect to the Laws which are there formed for its Government; and that it must afford the highest Satisfaction to every Individual to see the Reason and Foundation of those Acts on which Property, Liberty, and Life depend.

I considered also, that, except some faint and imperfect Attempts in *England*, this Service had never yet been rendered to the Publick; a Desire therefore of obtaining Honour to myself, concurring with that of benefiting others, both self love and social determined me to make public what I collected only for my private Amusement and Satisfaction.

It is true, indeed, that the Subjects debated, in the Parliament of *Ireland*, are not of the same Importance with those of her sister Country, on which the Fate of a Constitution, that is the Admiration and Envy of the World depends, and which in some Degree involve the Interests of all the States in *Europe*; yet they afford a sufficient Field for the Patriot and the Orator, and they affect, not only this Part of the *British* Dominions, but have some relation to the whole.

The

The Parliamentary Debates, however, of this Country are interesting, not only on account of the Importance of the Subjects, but the Abilities of the Speakers. Our House of Commons consists of Gentlemen who have eminently distinguished themselves in every learned and honourable Profession; and, upon this Occasion, I cannot but observe, that there is scarce one Native of this Country in the Parliament of *England* that is not a Speaker of some Distinction. Let me add, that, in my Travels through many Nations, during an absence of seven Years from my Country, I came into no Kingdom where I did not find Natives of *Ireland*, in every Profession, and almost in every Art, who had been preferred to eminent Stations merely by their Merit, having entered the Country under all the Disadvantages of Aliens, without Money, and without Friends.

I flatter myself that these Debates, notwithstanding the Injury they may have suffered in my Hands, will discover Abilities in the Speakers, that would do Honour to any Age and any Nation; and that, notwithstanding their different Situations and the different Circumstances

in

in which the Bufinefs of Parliament is tranfacted, their Speeches will not fuffer by a Comparifon even with thofe of the Senate of *Great Britain*.

In *Ireland*, as I have obferved before, the Debates are confined to Subjects that principally relate to its interior Intereft: The Parliament affembles but fix Months in a Revolution of two Years; an indifpenfable attendance on the Courts of Law prevents many Members from being conftantly prefent, and the whole Number is comparatively few.

Thefe Circumftances confidered, the Spirit of the Debates now offered to the Publick, will do yet greater Honour to the Speakers, both with refpect to their Principles and their Abilities; and it may fafely be left to the World to determine what a figure they would make in an Affembly where their Eloquence would be prompted by every Motive that can influence the Human Mind, at the fame Time that they would acquire all the auxiliary Powers of Habit, by long and frequent opportunities of Exertion.

Upon

Upon the Whole, I flatter myself that these Debates will not be found wholly unworthy either of the Subjects, or of the Speakers; yet as they were written entirely from Memory, where some of the slighter Traces may have faded away, I hope the Publick will regard them in the same Light as they would a capital Picture somewhat injured, and here and there retouched by an inferior Hand, yet so as nearly to imitate the Colouring, and always to preserve the *Contour*.

In this light I would also submit them to the Gentlemen by whom they were delivered, and who I hope will do me the Justice to believe that I have never wilfully deviated, either from their Sentiments or Expressions: This is all the Merit I claim, and all the Attonement I can make for such Imperfections as they shall discover in the Work, except, that I did not take any Notes, or procure any Notes to be taken.

I must also, in justice to these Gentlemen, declare, that not a single Syllable of the following Speeches has been shewn to the Person supposed to have delivered it, nor have I had the least Communication with any Member con-

concerning them, either by Letter or Conversation, immediately or by Proxy. The particular Interest of *Ireland* as a separate Nation, and its general Interest as Part of the *British* Dominions being frequently discussed in the following Debates, and mention being made of several Restrictions laid upon the Trade of *Ireland* by the Laws of *Great-Britain*, an Enquiry naturally rose how far *Great Britain* is benefited by such Restrictions. As the Subject of this Enquiry is of great Importance, and has never yet been examined, it is hoped that an Attempt to examine it will not be thought an improper Sequel to this Work, and that such Defects as may appear in it from the Author's want of sufficient Knowledge and Abilities for so important an Undertaking, will be supplied by those who are equal to the Task.

The present Situation of *Ireland* is such as renders it absolutely necessary that some Persons of the greatest Experience and Abilities should make it the Object of their serious and most mature Consideration, particularly as to its Defence, when another War shall break out; its Government, with respect to Popularity and Resources; and, above all, its Trade in its

present

present and most deplorable State, when the high Price of Land, and consequently of all the Necessaries of Life, is starving at least one half of the few and miserable Inhabitants of the Country. Where hereditary Property is so unequally divided, Trade only can feed the Hungry and cloath the Naked: And I hope it will not be thought Presumption in me to say, that if a proper Attention is not given to these Particulars soon, it will be too late, and the Consequences will be fatal.

DEBATES

Relative to the

Affairs of *IRELAND*.

TUESDAY, March 11, 1763.
FIRST DAY.

A Copy *of the Lord Lieutenant's Speech.*

My Lords and Gentlemen,

IT is with the utmost Satisfaction that, in Obedience to his Majesty's Commands, I am now to meet a Parliament which has already given so many and such very distinguished Proofs of its Zeal and Unanimity in the Support and Service of the Crown.

I have it expresly in Command from his Majesty to declare to you his entire Approbation of your past Conduct, and to assure you that the whole Course of your late Proceedings

ings has filled his royal Mind with every Sentiment of Regard which can flow from a juſt and gracious Sovereign towards a dutiful and a loyal People.

It is with particular Satisfaction I communicate to you at the Opening of this Seſſion of Parliament thoſe great and important Events which have occurred ſince your laſt Meeting.

By the Concluſion of a general Peace, the Tranquillity of every Part of *Europe* is perfectly re-eſtabliſhed; his Majeſty's Dominions are enlarged; the Commerce of his Subjects is extended; and you are, at length, relieved from thoſe Burthens which are unavoidable in the Progreſs even of the moſt ſucceſsful War.

Intereſted, as you are, in the Happineſs of ſo excellent a Sovereign; and ſenſible, as you have ever been, of the ineſtimable publick Bleſſings which you have enjoyed under his illuſtrious Houſe; you will receive with Pleaſure, the Information of the auſpicious Birth of the Prince of *Wales*, and of the further Encreaſe of the Royal Family, by the Birth of a ſecond Prince: Events which promiſe mife fuch an Addition to his Majefty's domeftic Felicity, and fuch a lafting Security to our happy Conftitution.

Gentlemen of the Houfe of Commons,

I have ordered the proper Officers to prepare the feveral Accounts and Eftimates, that they may be laid, in due Time, before you: You will obferve, that although, from the Exigencies of feveral extraordinary Services, the Expences of the two preceding Years have confiderably exceeded what was ufual in Times of Peace; yet they are fallen far fhort of the Sums which were fo liberally voted in the laft Seffion, a great Part of which ftill remains unborrowed *: His Majefty having determined to make Ufe of the Credit given to his Government in no other Proportion than as the Neceffity of his Service exactly required. I confider it as extremely fortunate, that I enter upon the Government of this Kingdom at a Time when the Situation of publick Affairs

* This Word having been cenfured by fome without Doors as not a Denifon of our Language, it is not improper to obferve, that *un* is a Privative or Negative Particle, which is placed, almoft at Will, before Adjectives and Adverbs, and has been placed before *borrowed* both by *Dryden* and *Locke.*

will permit so very considerable a Diminution of the public Expence, and when I am commanded by his Majesty to thank you only for your past Efforts, without again having Recourse to the experienced Liberality of Parliament: I have nothing to ask but the Continuance of the Supplies for the Support of the ordinary Establishment, which it is hoped will not exceed the Produce of the ordinary Revenue, and I recommend to you a proper Attention to the Reduction of the public Debt.

My Lords and Gentlemen,

Not only my Duty, but my earnest good Wishes for the Prosperity of *Ireland,* oblige me to take this Opportunity of mentioning to you the only unpleasing Circumstance which has occurred since my Entrance upon this Government; the tumultuous Risings of the lower People, in Contempt of Laws and of Magistracy, and of every constitutional Subordination, must, if not duly attended to, be productive of the most fatal Consequences, they are a Disgrace to a Country of Liberty; they are ruinous to a Country of Commerce; and must be particularly fatal here, where the least Check to the rising Spirit of Industry is

so

so very sensibly felt, and so very difficult to be retrieved; no Means can serve more effectually to prevent these Disorders for the future, than the Encouragement of such Institutions as tend to impress on the Minds of the lower Order of People, early Habits of Industry, and true Principles of Religion: For this Purpose, your Protestant Charter Schools were established, to which I therefore recommend the Continuance of your Care, Encouragement, and Support: Your Linen Manufacture demands, and will reward every Instance of Public Attention; there is nothing which can more properly excite your future Endeavours, and nothing has more fully answered your former Expectations: This Manufacture has been, at all Times, the favourite Object of Parliamentary Encouragement; and I should be concerned that any National Advantage which has been cultivated under the Administration of my Predecessors, should be neglected under mine: Be assured you cannot take any Measures which will be more grateful to his Majesty; or, which I shall be more sollicitous to forward, than those which may in any Respect, advance the growing Prosperity of this very improveable Country: If, therefore, any of your Manufactures may be

further

further extended; if any Thing can be done towards exciting the Spirit, or, providing the Means of Induſtry: If any Improvements in Agriculture can be produced, upon wiſe and practicable Principles; and in every Thing that tends to the Encouragement of Virtue, or the promoting of true Religion, you will have, towards the Attainment of thoſe Ends, not only my zealous Co-operation, but his Majeſty's ſteady and willing Protection. I come to this Government with the King's expreſs Commands, and my own very warm Inclination to recommend and ſupport ſuch Meaſures: His Majeſty has the firmeſt Reliance on your experienced Duty and Loyalty; on your unbiaſs'd Regard to the Public; and he doubts not that this Seſſion of Parliament will be carried on in a Manner ſuitable to your own Dignity, and to the Unanimity of your paſt Proceedings.

If the moſt inviolable Attachment to his Majeſty, and Zeal for his Service; if a firm Adherence to thoſe Principles by which the Proteſtants of *Ireland* have ever been diſtinguiſhed, were Qualifications ſufficient for the Diſcharge of the high and arduous Truſt committed to my Hands, I might inſure to myſelf

an

an Adminiſtration not unacceptable to Parliament: And I ſtill flatter myſelf, that, as the only Ends I have in Purſuit are the King's Service and the Public Welfare, I may obtain the only Rewards I have in View, his Majeſty's favourable Acceptance of my Services, and your entire Approbation of my Conduct.

Mr *W— B—* moved, that an humble Addreſs ſhould be preſented to his Majeſty to aſſure his Majeſty that we ſhall be always ready to give him the moſt convincing Proofs of our Loyalty and Zeal for the Support of his Crown and Dignity. To expreſs our warmeſt Gratitude for the gracious Approbation with which his Majeſty is pleaſed to honour our paſt Conduct; and to aſſure his Majeſty that we ſhall in the Courſe of our future Proceedings, by our Perſeverance in the ſame Principles of Duty and Loyalty, endeavour to deſerve the Continuance of his Majeſty's royal Favour and Protection. To return our moſt dutiful and moſt grateful Thanks to his Majeſty for his paternal Care, in being graciouſly pleaſed, upon the Re-eſtabliſhment of a general Peace, immediately to relieve his loyal and faithful Subjects of this Kingdom from thoſe heavy Burdens which they chearfully bore, during the late fuccefsful War. To exprefs the Happinefs we muft feel from every new Acceffion to his Majefty's Dominions, and Extenfion of the Commerce of his Subjects. To exprefs our moft unfeigned Joy, upon the aufpicious Birth of a Prince of *Wales*, and of the further Addition to his Majefty's Royal Houfe, by the Birth of a fecond Prince; Events, which, as they promife fo great an Addition to his Majefty's domeftic Felicity, and fuch a lafting Security to our happy Conftitution, muft give the higheft Pleafure to a People deeply interefted in the Happinefs of fo excellent a Sovereign, and fo fully fenfible of the ineftimable public Bleffings which they have, without Interruption, enjoyed under his Majefty's illuftrious Houfe. To acknowledge it as a particular Inftance of his Majefty's tender Concern for the Welfare of this Kingdom, that he has been gracioufly pleafed to appoint a chief Governor to prefide over us, of whofe approved Fidelity to his Majefty, and fteady Attachment to his royal Houfe, we are fully perfuaded, and of whofe Honour, Juftice, Integrity, and other eminent Qualities, we have conceived the higheft Opinion. To exprefs our juft Senfe of his Majefty's great Goodnefs in having made ufe of

the

the Credit given to his Government in the laſt Seſſion of Parliament, in no other Proportion than as the Neceſſity of his Service exactly required; and to aſſure his Majeſty that we ſhall, with the greateſt Chearfulneſs, continue the neceſſary Supplies for the Support of the ordinary Eſtabliſhment, with a proper Attention to the Reduction of the public Debt. To aſſure his Majeſty that we have ſeen, with the greateſt Concern, the tumultuous Riſings of the lower People, in Contempt of Laws, of Magiſtracy, and of every conſtitutional Subordination, which, if not duly attended to, muſt be productive of the moſt fatal Conſequences, and which, we are fully ſenſible, are diſgraceful to a Country of Liberty, and ruinous to a Country of Commerce. That we are convinced that no Means can ſerve more effectually to prevent the like Diſorders for the future, than the Encouragement of ſuch Inſtitutions as tend to impreſs on the Minds of the lower Order of People early Habits of Induſtry, and true Principles of Religion; and for this deſirable Purpoſe we ſhall continue our Care, Encouragement, and Support of the Proteſtant Charter Schools, and ſhall have the ſtricteſt Attention to every Method by which our Linen Manufacture may be improved and extended.

tended. To assure his Majesty, that we shall be actuated by the same Principles of Duty and Loyalty, by the same unbiassed Regard to the Public, which recommended our Conduct in the last Session of Parliament, to the Approbation of the best of Princes; and to declare, that we consider the Continuance of his Majesty's royal Protection as the sure and solid Foundation of our Welfare and Prosperity.

Mr *B*——'s Motion was seconded by Mr *C*— *C*—, who expressed himself to the following Effect:

Mr. S——,

Although I am conscious that the honourable Gentlemen who moved for the Address, has expressed the Sentiments of the House in general, in which my own are included, in a masterly and pathetic Manner, which makes it impossible to speak after him, on the same Subject, without great Disadvantage, yet the Gratitude that I feel to the best of Sovereigns will not suffer me to be silent; and upon this Occasion I had rather be distinguished by the Warmth of my Heart, than by the Force of my Understanding, or the Elegance of my Elocution.

Elocution. The truly paternal Attention which his Majesty has shewn to this loyal, brave, and free Nation, ever since his Accession to the Throne, has inspired me with Sentiments too powerful to be suppressed; and the Declarations made, on the Behalf of his Majesty, by the Lord Lieutenant from the Throne, cannot fail to fill every Breast in the Kingdom with equal Gratitude and Joy; for who is there that does not only know, but feel his Interest in that delightful Prospect of Tranquillity and Happiness which these Declarations have thrown open before us? What can be more pleasing to a Nation, that has a lively Sense of the Blessings it enjoys in the full Possession of its civil and religious Rites, under the auspicious Government of the illustrious Family that now sits upon the Throne, than to find that our most amiable and truly *British* Prince has taken the first Opportunity of expressing, in the strongest Manner, his Approbation of the Conduct of its Representatives, his faithful Commons in the last Sessions, and of assuring them, that the Burden of those Taxes, which a just War made indisputably necessary, shall now be suspended. The Increase of the Family of such a Sovereign cannot but be regarded as

an

an earnest, that those Blessings, of which he is the Fountain, shall flow to us, and to our Posterity, in copious and perpetual Streams, which neither Change, nor Time, shall be able to divert or exhaust.

But there is yet another Instance of his Majesty's most gracious Attention to this Nation, which, I am sure, I cannot mention with greater Pleasure than it will be heard; he has sent over to us a Nobleman equally distinguished for his Abilities in Public, as for his amiable Qualities in private Life; a Nobleman, to whom, Nature and Fortune have vied in Liberality, and, to whom Virtue has vouchsafed still superior Endowments; his Generosity and Benevolence are equal to his Possessions, which, in his Hands, are no more than the Power of doing Good, intrusted with him, as the Delegate of Providence, for the Benefit of Mankind; but he does not stop even here, his Virtue is not only Genuine but Splendid, his Liberality is heightened by a Taste and Magnificence, which have been equalled by few, and excelled by none; by such a Disposition, joined with such a Fortune, he not only reflects Honour upon his Country, but gives it the strongest Pledge of

his

his Superiority to Temptation, and his inviolable Attachment to the Public Good; for what can influence him to betray his Truft, whofe fupreme Delight is to fulfill it, or what can feduce him to illicit Gain, who defpifes illicit Pleafures, and whofe Fortune already enables him to poffefs thofe which his Virtue prompts him to defire. In Governors, indeed, of whatever denomination, a fuperiority of Fortune feems to be a Requifite of great Importance, for, without it, the very defire of doing Good becomes fometimes a Snare to do Evil; the mere wifh of impotent Benevolence, though it is a kind, is a painful Senfation, and where there is not Ability to fulfill it, frequently creates a Dependance pernicious in its confequences, however fpecious in its intention.

It is happy for me, Sir, and for the Public, that I cannot be accufed of making my Court by a fanciful Panegyric. The Truth of what I have advanced is too well known, and too generally acknowledged; and his Excellency has given us an earneft of his Talents for the important Truft, that is devolved upon him, by his Speech from the Throne, which is now the Subject of our Confideration; he

has

has selected and recommended to us those Objects of National concern, that are indubitably most interesting to this Kingdom: He has recommended the bringing the deluded and unhappy People in the lower Class of Life, who have been drawing Confusion upon the State, and Misery upon Themselves, at once to a Sense of their Interest, and their Duty, which are eternally and inseperably united; as these Irregularities must arise either from erroneous Principles, or that licentiousness which Idleness never fails to produce, he has also recommended the Encouragement and Support of the Protestant Charter Schools, and the Linen Manufactory; and he has promised, in the warmest and most emphatical Terms, that he will heartily concur in effecting the good and important Purposes he recommends; as such are his Majesty's gracious Dispositions towards us, such is his Representative among us, and such are the Declarations from the Throne, I most earnestly second the Motion for an Address of Thanks to his Majesty for the same.

It was then resolved, *Nem. Con.* that an humble Address be presented to his Majesty to the Effect already mentioned, and ordered that

that a Committee be appointed to draw it up, and a Committee was appointed accordingly.

The R—t H——ble Mr *T— C—* then moved, that an humble Addreſs of Thanks be preſented to his Excellency, the Lord Lieutenant, for his moſt excellent Speech this Day to both Houſes of Parliament, and ſpoke to the following Effect:

Mr. S——,

After what has ſo truly, and ſo forcibly been ſaid in commendation of the Nobleman, whom his Majeſty, as a ſignal Mark of his paternal Care and Attention to his loyal and faithful Subjects of *Ireland*, has appointed to be Lord Lieutenant of this Kingdom, by the honourable Gentleman who ſpoke laſt, the Motion I have to make, that an humble Addreſs of Thanks be preſented, for his moſt excellent Speech, can be conſidered only as a neceſſary Compliance with the Forms of the Houſe; ſince I am confident that every one who hears me, feels already thoſe Sentiments in his Heart, of which, Thanks, in the warmeſt and ſtrongeſt Terms, are no more than the

the Expreſſion: The Speech itſelf, though one of the beſt I ever heard on the like Occaſion, is ſuch only as might be expected from a Nobleman, ſo diſtinguiſhed by every great and good Quality that can endear the Man, or adorn the Governour, ſo fit to repreſent a Prince, who is at once the Happineſs and the Glory of his People, whoſe Virtues are ſuch as convert every Wiſh, however luxuriant, into a well-grounded Hope, and promiſe reality and permanence to whatever Bleſſings Imagination can form; under ſuch an Adminiſtration, no expectations of Advantage within the Verge of Poſſibility are romantic, for it cannot be imagined that he, who has hitherto been ſo eminently diſtinguiſhed for Integrity, Honour, and Munificence, will loſe any Opportunity of diſplaying them with yet brighter Luſtre, and more extenſive Influence, by the Power which he derives from delegated Royalty, and a Character equally exalted and endearing, the ſubſtituted Father of a grateful People.

Mr. C—— having thus introduced, and made his Motion, was ſeconded by Mr. S-—— M——, junior.

Upon

Upon which, it was refolved, *Nem. Con.* that an humble Addrefs of Thanks be prefented to his Excellency, the Lord Lieutenant, for his moft excellent Speech this Day to both Houfes of Parliament.

WEDNESDAY, Oct. 12, 1763.

SECOND DAY.

THERE was a meeting of the Committee, appointed to draw up the Address to his Majesty, in the S———'s Chamber, when no Objection was made to it, as it was produced, except that it was proposed instead of the Words " congratulate * *with* his Majes-

> * The original Reading was right, *congratulate* is both an Active and a Neuter Verb, as an Active Verb, it signifies, *to express Joy for the good of another*; as a Neuter Verb, it signifies, to rejoice *in participation for a common good*, and is always used with the Preposition *with*; now the Birth of the Prince being an Event not only beneficial to the King, but to the People, the Word *congratulate* should have been used as a Neuter, not an Active Verb, and by making it an Active Verb, omitting the Word *with*, half the Complement is taken away, for it implies, that the Birth of a Prince is a good only to his Parents like a common Child, whereas, by making the Verb Neuter, and congratulating with the King, it implies a good to the People; *Swift* uses the Expression *congratulate with*, in his Introduction to Polite Conversation: In Defence of the Objection, it was said that *con* is *with*, but if this proves any thing, it proves too much, for if *with*, for this Reason, should not be used with congratulate, neither should it be used with condole or concur.

ty,"

ty," to insert " congratulate his Majesty," which was agreed to.

Mr. *W—— B——* reported from the Committee, appointed to draw up an Address to his Majesty, that they had drawn up an Address accordingly, which he read in his Place, and after delivered in at the Table, where the same was read, and is as follows:

CopY *of the* ADDRESS.

" *Most Gracious Sovereign,*

We your Majesty's most Dutiful and Loyal Subjects, the Commons of *Ireland,* in Parliament assembled, firmly attached to your Majesty's Sacred Person, royal Family, and Government, humbly beg Leave to assure your Majesty, that we shall be always ready to give your Majesty every convincing Proof of our Loyalty and Zeal for the Support of your Majesty's Crown and Dignity.

The Approbation with which your Majesty has been graciously pleased to honour our past Conduct, fills our Hearts with the warmest Sentiments of Gratitude, and lays us under the strongest Obligation, to endeavour by a conſtant Perſeverance in the ſame Principles of Duty and Loyalty, to deſerve the Continuance of your Royal Favour and Protection.

We think it our indiſpenſable Duty, to return your Majeſty our moſt grateful and ſincere Acknowledgments for your paternal Care, in being gracciouſly pleaſed, upon the Re-eſtabliſhment of a general Peace, immediately to relieve your loyal and faithful Subjects of this Kingdom, from thoſe heavy Burdens, which they chearfully bore during the Continuance of the late ſucceſsful War; and we humbly beg Leave to aſſure your Majeſty, that we feel the greateſt Happineſs, from every new Acceſſion to your Majeſty's Dominions, and Extenſion of the Commerce of your Subjects.

Permit us to congratulate your Majeſty, upon the auſpicious Birth of the Prince of *Wales*, and the further Addition to your Majeſty's Royal Houſe by the Birth of a ſecond Prince; Events, which, as they promiſe ſo great an Addition to your Majeſty's Domeſtic Felicity, and ſuch a laſting Security to our happy Conſtitution, muſt give the higheſt Pleaſure to a People deeply intereſted in the

Hap-

Happiness of so excellent a Sovereign, and so fully sensible of the inestimable public Blessings, which they have, without Interruption, enjoyed, under your illustrious House.

We acknowledge it, as a particular Instance of your Majesty's tender Concern for the Welfare of this Kingdom, that you have been graciously pleased to appoint a chief Governor to preside over us, of whose approved Fidelity to your Majesty, and steady Attachment to your Royal House, we are fully persuaded; and of whose Honour, Integrity, Justice, and other eminent Qualities, we have conceived the highest Opinion.

We are most gratefully affected with your Majesty's Goodness, in having made Use of the Credit given to your Government, in the last Session of Parliament, in no other Proportion than as the Necessity of your Service exactly required: And we shall with the greatest Chearfulness, continue the necessary Supplies, for the Support of your Majesty's *ordinary Establishment*, with a proper Attention to the Reduction of the public Debt.

We have seen, with the deepest Concern, the tumultuous Risings of the lower People, in Contempt of Law, of Magistracy, and of every constitutional Subordination, which, if not duly attended to, must be productive of the most fatal Consequences, and which, we are fully sensible, are disgraceful to a Country of Liberty, and ruinous to a Country of Commerce.

We are convinced that no means can more effectually prevent the like Disorders for the future, than the Encouragement of such Institutions, as tend to impress on the Minds of the lower Order of People, early Habits of Industry, and true Principles of Religion; and, for this desirable Purpose, we shall continue our Care, Encouragement, and Support of the Protestant Charter Schools; and shall have the strictest Attention to every Method, by which our Linen Manufacture may be improved and extended.

We beg Leave humbly to assure your Majesty, that we shall be actuated, in our future Proceedings, by the same Principles of Duty and Loyalty, by the same unbiassed Regard to the

the Public, that recommended our Conduct in the laſt Seſſion of Parliament, to the Approbation of the beſt of Princes; and that we ſhall always conſider the Continuance of your Majeſty's Royal Protection, as the ſure and ſolid Foundation of our Welfare and Proſperity."

The ſixth Paragraph, being read a ſecond Time, Mr *E— S— P—* got up and ſaid, that the Words *ordinary Eſtabliſhment*, ſeemed to include a Senſe which had intirely eſcaped him in the Committee, and that he muſt now give ſome Reaſons why he thought them improper; the Words he ſaid might be taken to imply the Eſtabliſhments hitherto granted, and would then include the Penſions, which he never could conſider as conſtitutionally neceſſary to the Support of Government, nor did he imagine it to be the Senſe of the Houſe that they were ſo; as he was therefore of Opinion that the Houſe did not mean to declare their Acquieſcence in the Continuation of the Penſions, and as the Words *ordinary Eſtabliſhment*, were ſo far ambiguous, as in the Opinion, of ſome at leaſt, to expreſs ſuch an Acquieſcence, he ſaid he thought they ſhould be changed for ſome other, the sense of which was more definite and certain; he said that it was not the Business of that Day to enter into a critical Disquisition concerning the Import of the Words he excepted to, nor was he just then prepared exactly to define them, but proposed, as an easy Expedient to remove all possible difference in Construction, that the Words *ordinary Establishment*, might be expunged, and the Word, *Government*, inserted in their stead, which he moved accordingly.

He was answered by the R—t H——ble F— A—, who said, that the Words *ordinary Establishment*, were a Parliamentary Expression, confirmed by long and uninterrupted Use, and inserted in almost every Address that had been presented from that House to the Throne; that they had never been known to serve as a Foundation, for any Claim not more explicitly admitted, and that, therefore, there was not the least Reason to suspect that they would now be perverted to serve any such Purpose; he observed also, that if any such Design should be formed, it would never succeed, because no Expression in an Address was obligatory, or even supposed to be so; Addresses being considered only as Things of course,

course, a general Expression of Duty, Loyalty, and Attachment relative to the Speech from the Throne; he added, that he was firmly persuaded his worthy Friend upon the Bench behind him, (Mr *P—*) would be the first Man in the House, to shew a well-timed Spirit of Opposition against any Person who should claim a Right to infer an Acquiescence of that House to any one Point, from an Expression in an Address; as the Words in Question therefore were justified by incontestible and repeated Precedents, and as changing them would shew an ill grounded and offensive Diffidence, without answering any one good Purpose, he thought they could not with Propriety be removed for any other, especially as his worthy Friend had declared that this was not a proper Time to examine critically into their Meaning, and had candidly confessed himself unable to assign it. If it had not been for this Concession, he said, he should have been tempted to have called upon him for an Explanation, but as no such Explanation was either given, or offered, and as a Change of these Words would render the Address singular, by departing from the Words of the Speech from the Throne, which it had been always the Practice to adopt in

Addresses from the House, he declared himself against the Motion.

The P— S——, and A—— G——, said, that, notwithstanding, the Words in Question were supported by Precedent, and truly Parliamentary, yet that the Change proposed was a Matter of so little consequence, that they did not think it necessary to take up the Time of the House in a Dispute about it, and therefore agreed to the Alteration proposed.

The S—— G——, Mr J— G——, then got up, and spoke as follows:

Mr S——,

I do not get up to oppose the Alteration suggested by my worthy Friend, which, however, I should certainly do, if I had any of those Suspicions which he seems to entertain, for if I thought that any Advantage would be taken of a Concession of this House, in an Address, I should certainly oppose the Insertion of the Word *Government*, instead of the Words *ordinary Establishment*, which, perhaps, more effectually than any other, preclude such Advantage, at least much more effectually than the Word proposed to be substituted in their stead;

stead; as a seeming Distrust has induced him to propose the Alteration, so, on the contrary, nothing but the utmost Confidence could induce me to consent to it, for we differ diametrically, as to the Force of the two Expressions. The Word *Government*, is surely liable to a larger Construction than the Words *ordinary Establishment*: The Words *ordinary Establishment*, if they have any Meaning, must certainly exclude something, whereas, the Word *Government* admits all; I would submit it to my worthy Friend himself, whether *Ordinary* does not necessarily exclude *Extraordinary*, and, whether he does not think many of the Sums granted last Year come under the latter Denomination, particularly, those granted for carrying on the War: The Words *ordinary Establishment*, therefore, if they can be supposed to include all the individual and specific Sums granted last Year, must be supposed to include what is not Ordinary, or else the Expences of a War must be supposed to come under that Denomination: Which side of this Dilemma then shall we take? Shall we say that the Expences of War come under our Ordinary Establishment? Or shall we say that the Words

Ordi-

Ordinary and *Extraordinary* mean the same Thing? If by *ordinary Establishment*, it is absurd to suppose all the specific Sums granted last Year to be included, why should we suppose it to include Pensions, merely because Pensions were granted, or continued last Year? It would be certainly much more easy to found a Claim of granting or continuing Pensions, upon the general Engagement to support his Majesty's Government, than, upon the specific and limited Promise, to support his *ordinary Establishment*, which is all that has been asked on his Majesty's behalf: To support *Government* it is frequently necessary to give very considerable Sums, as well by way of Pension as otherwise, for secret Service, of which the Crown is the sole Arbiter and Judge, and which, by the very Nature of the Thing, cannot be sufficiently disclosed to be particularly accounted for; it is, indeed, both our Duty and Inclination to support his Majesty's Government in the Just and Genuine Sense of the Word, but yet the general Expression of supporting Government, is more liable to be stretched into a Sense not necessarily included in it, than the Words *Ordinary Establishment*, besides, being in itself, and in its just and genuine Meaning, a

Word

Word of much more extensive Signification; in a Word, Sir, the Terms of the Speech could not possibly have been chosen if any Thing not openly and explicitly avowed had been intended; I conclude, therefore, from the very Choice of the Words, that there was no such Intention, and that as no Advantage was meant to be taken of us by the Words originally inserted, no Advantage will be taken of that now proposed in their stead, and, for that Reason, readily agree to the Alteration.

The Alteration was accordingly made.

The Right H—ble *T— C—* then read the following Address to the Earl of *Northumberland*, Lord Lieutenant General, and General Governor of *Ireland*.

" *May it please your Excellency,*

We his Majesty's most dutiful and loyal Subjects, the Commons of *Ireland*, in Parliament assembled, return your Excellency our most sincere Thanks for your most excellent Speech from the Throne; and we beg Leave to congratulate your Excellency on your Appointpointment to the Government of this Kingdom.

We are inexpreſſibly happy that our paſt Conduct has met with his Majeſty's Approbation; and we flatter ourſelves that by our future Proceedings we ſhall not forfeit that Regard, which his Majeſty has ſo graciouſly condeſcended to honour us with.

We beg Leave to expreſs our Satisfaction, that the Situation of public Affairs will permit ſo very conſiderable a Diminution of the Public Expences; and that your Excellency is appointed to the Government of this Kingdom at ſo happy a Period. And we aſſure your Excellency we ſhall moſt chearfully grant ſuch Supplies as ſhall be neceſſary for the Support of his Majeſty's Government, and ſhall give all proper Attention to the Reduction of the National Debt.

The Riſings of the lower People, mentioned by your Excellency, give us the utmoſt Concern; they deſerve, and ſhall have, our cloſeſt Attention; and we are fully ſenſible that no Means can ſerve more effectually to prevent thoſe Diſorders for the future, than the

the Encouragement of such Institutions as tend to impress on the Minds of the lower Order of People, early Habits of Industry, and true Ideas of Religion.

As we are fully persuaded that your Excellency will, upon all Occasions, be ready to forward the growing Prosperity of this very improveable Country; so we shall, on our Parts, be solicitous to demonstrate to the World, that we cannot more effectually serve our own Interests, than by endeavouring, through the whole Course of our Proceedings, to contribute to the Honour, the Ease, and Permanency of your Excellency's Administration."

Mr *H— F—* afterwards stood up and spoke as follows:

Mr. *S——*,

It must give every Member of this House the highest Satisfaction to reflect, that we now meet freed and disencumbered from the Apprehensions under which we suffered the Beginning of the last Sessions: We have also the Happiness of being acquainted with the Dispositions of each other, so that no Requisite

site is wanting for the mature Consideration of what may be most for the Advantage of our Country, independent of every other Object. It is, however, a melancholy Reflection, that those who distinguish themselves by their Independance, Disinterestedness, and public Spirit, those who make the Advantage of their Country their only Obeject, are too often branded by the Name of *Faction*, and under that opprobious Appellation held forth to public Obloquy and Reproach, merely because they will not concur with the mean, interested, and selfish Views of those who implicitly adopt the Measures of a Court, that they may themselves become the Objects of Court Favour. But whatever designing Knavery may pretend, or thoughtless Ignorance admit, the Word *Faction*, as a Term of Reproach, may be justly retorted upon those by whom it is so liberally bestowed upon others. Those are certainly a Faction, in this Sense, who unite upon any selfish or contracted Views, against the public or general Interest, whether they are many or few: Those who insidiously endeavour to extend the Prerogative, under the specious Pretence of supporting it, those who encourage the Exercise of unconstitutional Power, assumed by a Minister

ster under the Colour of strengthening the Hands of Government, and those who concur in the Distribution of pecuniary Gratifications to Individuals, at the Expence of the Nation, as a Compliment to royal Munificence, those and those only deserve to be stigmatized by the Name of *Faction*. It is certain, indeed, that they do not more mistake their own true Interest than the true Interest of those in whose Measures they implicitly concur; as the supreme and only real Happiness and Honour of the Prince, are derived wholly from the Freedom, Wealth, and Happiness of his People, so the Happiness and Honour of a Minister, if he is capable of any Thing that may be truly so called, are nothing more than the reflected Honour and Happiness of his Prince; so true it is that Providence has made the real Happiness of the Individual depend upon the same Conduct that produces the Happiness of the whole; that every Vice is manifestly a Folly; and he who sacrifices the Interest of his Country, its Freedom, Independance, or Wealth, to any private Advantage of himself, his Family, or his Friends, eventually betrays the very Individuals he would serve, by taking away what is of infinitely more Value than any Thing he can give

give; for what, in the Eſtimation of Honeſty and Reaſon, can be equivalent to a common Intereſt in thoſe invaluable Bleſſings that diſtinguiſh a free People! God forbid that I ſhould renounce or diſparage the forcible, yet tender Ties of perſonal Friendſhip, parental Affection, or ingenuous Gratitude; permit me to ſay, that no Man in this Houſe is more under the Influence of theſe Attachments than myſelf; no Man has more ardent Love for his Friend, a ſtronger Senſe of Obligation, nor warmer Paſſions; nor do I dream that any Man is bound to love thoſe whom he has never ſeen more than thoſe who are indeared to him by the Ties of Nature, and of Blood; much leſs that he can love the Public, who does not love his Relations and Friends, which muſt make, to every one not deſtitute of Humanity, the moſt endearing Part of it; but, I ſay, that he only purſues the true Intereſt of his Friend and his Relation, who concurs in every Meaſure to ſecure to them that upon which every other Bleſſing depends; that Freedom and Independance, without which neither Labour is profitable, nor Reſt is ſweet; without which Gold is not Wealth, nor are Titles Honour. The narrow minded ſelfiſh Court Sycophant, who,

in

in the Wickedness of his Folly, sacrifices the many to the few, does, in fact, sacrifice the few with the many; and does nothing more than involve those for whom he is willing to betray his Country, in the Ruin which his Treachery is bringing upon it; the Tool of Court Faction is, like those who employ him, the Dupe of his own Cunning, and the Scourge of his own Vice. The nameless Vermine, that court Sun-shine quickens in the Slime of Venality, will soon find that the same Influence which produced will destroy them; when the Moisture of that Dirt, in which they crawl, is a little farther exhaled, they will find it stiffening about them; they will first be deprived of Motion, then of Life, and the next Gale will sweep them away with the Dust in which they perished. It is not, indeed, strange that remote should be sacrificed to immediate Good, when the Temptation strikes strongly upon the Sense, and the Principles, both of Virtue and Wisdom, by which alone it can be resisted, are wanting; but it is strange, and not less deplorable, that, in this Country, many should be found who sacrifice their chief Interest to a subordinate one still more remote and precarious; who give away their Share in the public Prosperity, not for immediate Riches and Titles, but for mere Names and Shadows; for Promises never meant to be fulfilled; for painted Vapours, which appear solid only by their distance, which float in airy Regions, where they can never be approached, and which vanish for ever with the Light that gilds them; nay, in this Age of Vanity and Dissipation, Men are corrupted, even by less than a Promise, a trivial Complement; a familiar and a gracious Smile, or a Squeeze by the Hand, are deemed valuable Considerations for those inestimable Blessings which our Forefathers procured for us, at the Expence of Treasure, of Ease, of Health, and even Life itself. While this Infatuation spreads among us, and its Effects are proportionably more extensive and more alarming, it behoves those who are not yet circumscribed by the enchanted Circle, those who have still the Use of unperverted Reason, and who still Estimate the Blessings of Life by their just Value, to exert themselves in behalf of their native Country, and like its Guardian Angel "to watch over it for Good." They are deeply concerned in its particular Welfare, as distinct from other Parts of the *British*

Dominions, and they are acquainted with its true Intereſt, and know how it is to be purſued, which cannot be the Caſe with thoſe who honour us with their Company from the other Side of the Water: This tender, this jealous Vigilance is ſtill more neceſſary as it is not our Happineſs to have a native Prince to wield a native Sceptre among us, but muſt appear to our Sovereign as we are repreſented by others, and receive the Benefits of his Adminiſtration, not directly, but as it were by Reflection. As a means conducive to the good Purpoſe, which I have endeavoured to recommend, I beg leave to move.

"That the proper Officer do attend and inform this Houſe, whether any Patents, granting Penſions at Will, now in Being, out of the Revenues of this Kingdom, are Inrolled; and, if any ſuch Inrollments there are, that the proper Officer may lay thoſe Inrollments before the Houſe."

When Mr F—— had made this Motion, the S———r replied, that Patents, granting Penſions for Life were never Enrolled, and a Member replied to the S———r, that this

Circumſtance was known to the honourable Gentleman who made the Motion, and that he intended it ſhould by this Means come officially before the Houſe.

The Houſe then ordered accordingly.

THURSDAY, *Oct.* 13, 1763.

THIRD DAY.

C———— L————, M. D.

Mr S——,

I Rise up to remark a Defect in this Constitution no less manifest than important; the long Duration of our Parliaments; as the Evil of this Defect is self-evident, I might reasonable suppose all Arguments for the Proof of it to be precluded, and, as it is of the most alarming and fatal Kind, I might also, with equal Reason, suppose all Arguments for the removal of it to be superfluous; indeed, the Proof of what is already manifest, is no less difficult than unnecessary, for by what Form of Ratiocination could I prove the Light to shine at Noon-day, or demonstrate the Colours which the Objects round me derive from that Light? yet, because there may be some, who by shutting their Eyes, and involving themselves in voluntary Darkness, obtain a Pretence to doubt the Reality of what others intuitively perceive, I will endeavour to display what all who are *willing to see, do see,* in such a Manner as to make it impossible for those who love Darkness rather than Light, to suppose, or even pretend to suppose, the Light does not shine, and that the Figure and Colour of the Objects it makes visible, are the mere Illusions of Fancy.

To drop the Metaphor, Sir, it is impossible to suppose that Men in general will discharge their Duty with a Zeal, Steadiness, and Assiduity, when it is contrary to their Interest, equal to that which they will exert in fulfilling it, when their Duty and their Interest coincide; the Duty of a Member of this House is infinitely the most Important that can devolve upon a Subject, and his Interest must either be connected with it, or opposed to it, in Proportion as he is dependant upon his Constituents, or upon any Minister, who may have formed Designs, in which his Constituents could not possible concur. By the Defect, which I have remarked in our Constitution, a Member once chosen to sit in this House, sits in it for Life, or at least, for the Life of the Prince upon the Throne; a Proposition from which the following Deductions incontestibly proceed: He has nothing either to hope or to fear from his Constituents; but from

from a Minister his Expectations may reasonably be great; he will be tempted to oppose the Measures of a good Minister, merely, that he may be bought into his Service, and to sell himself into the Service of a bad Minister for the same Advantage; the Minister also may afford to bid high, when he buys for Life; so that a Degree of Virtue, which might resist a small Advantage, may be surmounted by the Minister, merely in consequence of his being in a Situation which will make it worth his while to offer greater. Time for this iniquitous Compact is also abundantly allowed, which, whatever might be the Inclination and Interest of the Parties, would not be the Case, if Parliaments, instead of lasting for Life, were, according to their primitive Institution, to last but a Year; or, according to a late Regulation, for three. A Representative who has a Seat for Life, may become an absolute Stranger to his Constituents, while he continues the Trustee of all that is dear and important to them upon Earth: He who, when elected, had a good Estate in the County, or City, by which he was chosen, may, by the Vicissitude natural to Worldly Affairs, be totally undone, and not have a Foot of Land in the World; his Interest, therefore, in the com-

common Intereſt is leſs, and his Dependance naturally greater upon thoſe who may poſſibly wiſh to ſubvert it. The Diſpoſal of Property will thus remain in one who has no Property of his own, and the Liberty of others depend upon one whoſe own Liberty, probably, depends wholly upon his Seat in Parliament; there is no Time in which he can be called to account for his Breach of Truſt, no Time in which a worthier Man may be choſen in his room; add to this, that the Sitting of a Member, once elected, for Life, is an Injury to thoſe who are excluded, and who ought to take their Turn; it is alſo a perpetual Check upon zealous and active public Spirit, for, as Man, the beſt Man, is a mixed Character, much will never be done for others, if ſomething for ſelf is not mixed with it; and our great Poet, and Moraliſt, has defined Virtue to be that Self-love which includes the Good of others; he, therefore, who might exert himſelf upon a public and important Occaſion, and avail the Public of his Parts, his Influence, or his Fortune, if he hoped by a well-earned Popularity, to obtain a Voice in the great Council of his Country, will, perhaps, either ſit wholly Inactive, or at beſt, make but a feeble Effort, if this Motive is wanting.

In-

Indolence, Sir, is the genuine Character of Despair, or of a State in which Hope has no Object; and how many would be actuated by Hope, if our Parliaments were limited to a short Duration, who are now likely to be torpid for want of that vital Principle, I leave every one present to determine. It is true, that now and then the Door of this House is opened for the Admission of a single Individual by Death; but all that is uncertain is, by a happy Instinct of Nature, deemed to be distant; and it being also doubtful in what Part the Vacancy will happen, the possibility is no more a Stimulus to one than to all; how different would be the Case if, at the End of a short Period, the Doors were to be thrown open for the Admission of our whole Number? How many Hearts would then continually beat with Ardour and Emulation, how many Assiduities would be practised, how extensive a Popularity acquired, how much our Constitution studied, and our Interest attended to, by those who now sink, with a supine Content, into the Oblivion of private Life, and sit, darkling and silent, in an obscure Corner of the Vessel, which they know they never shall assist to steer.

It would be very easy, Sir, for me to shew, by citing indubitable Facts from our History, that what I have endeavoured to prove *must be*, *has been*; that our Constitution has flourished, when Parliaments have been short, and declined when Parliaments have been long; that bad Kings, and corrupt Ministers, have made the Transition from short Parliaments to long, and good Kings, and upright Ministers, the Transition from long Parliaments to short; but to enumerate Effects as Evidence of their Causes, when the necessary Efficiency of their Causes has been demonstrated, would be like bringing Evidence to prove that a Man did not walk, and eat, and sleep, and transact his Business, after having already demonstrated that he is dead. Let it, however, be remembered, that the first who extended Parliaments to a longer Duration than three Years, was *Henry* the VIIIth, a violent and ambitious Tyrant, the Slave of every depraved Appetite, and equally impatient of Restraint from the Laws both of God and Man. As he knew that his arbitrary Will could not be gratified, but by gaining an Ascendancy over his Parliament, he first contrived to make his Parliament long, as the only Means of obtaining

taining that Ascendancy; and the slavish Obedience of the Parliament, when he had thus modelled it to his Purpose, is well known. It is also well known that *Charles* the IId obtained a long Parliament, which knew no Rule of acting but the Will of those who gave its Members their Pay; this Parliament obtained the Name of the *Pension Parliament*, and was, perhaps, the Model upon which some later Parliaments have been formed. But, to wave farther particular Instances, it is too notorious to be denied, that many dangerous Attempts have miscarried on the other Side of the Water, not so much from the Virtue of the Parliament, as from the Apprehension of an approaching Election; and of this Ministers have been so much aware, that the Close of a Parliament has always been deemed an improper Time to propose any Measure which is, in general, disagreeable to the People. In a Word, Sir, it would appear incontestibly, from the Reason of the Thing, unsupported by Facts, and by Facts without the Assistance of Argument, that the Prolongation of the Term of Parliaments weakens the Security of the People, and that nothing can make it safe to repose so great a Trust in any Set of Men, as the collective Body delegates

to

to its Representatives, but the Shortness of the Term for which such Delegation is made. But, if this is true of Parliaments in general, how much greater must be the Danger arising from the unlimited Duration of our Parliament, when we have no such Barrier against ministerial Influence as the Place-Bill in *England?* A Barrier which was thought necessary, notwithstanding the Limitation of Parliament to seven Years; and that it is less necessary to us, whose Parliament is unlimited, or that with it we might more safely suffer our Parliament for Life, than our Neighbours, is, I believe, a Compliment they are very willing to pay us, but which, I believe, no Friend to his Country would be ambitious to receive.

To conclude, as, at least, an Argument *ad hominem*, let me observe, that every Friend to the Revolution must, consistently with his Principles, declare in Favour of limitting the Time of our Parliaments, for how absurd is it to maintain that the People have a Right to make and change a King, and yet have no Right to change their Representatives, to whom they delegate their Power of keeping the King from being independant of his

People

People? I move, then, and I hope to be seconded by every Gentleman in the House, that leave may be given to bring in Heads of a Bill for limiting the Duration of Parliaments in this Kingdom.

"Ordered, that leave be given to bring in Heads of such a Bill, and that Dr *L—* and Mr *F—* do bring in the same."

" Ordered, that the proper Officer do lay before this House the Inrollments of the Patents, by which the Offices of the Chancellor of the Exchequer, Master of the Rolls, and Judges have been granted."

Dr *L—* then moved, that it might be an Instruction to the Committee that was appointed to enquire into the Risings in the North; to enquire also into the Causes of the Insurrections in the South: It seemed, he said, very extraordinary to him that the Indictments in the North were all laid for high Treason, and those in the South only for a Riot, and a Breach of the Peace. As the Crimes in both Parts of the Country were precisely the same, both in their Nature and Consequences, he was amazed, he said, how the

Prose-

Prosecution could be so different, except in the Pursuance of a particular and partial Instruction from above; he also threw out some general Reflections on the Conduct of the Judges who sat in the South.

He was answered by Mr *G*—, the S—G—, who said, he was greatly surprised that the honourable Gentleman had not been better informed, for that the Indictments in the South had, in many Cases, been laid for high Treason as well as in the North; and the Truth of this was so notorious, that several had even been executed upon the Statute; he observed, indeed, that in some Cases a Lenity had been shewn, but he said it was only when Reason and Humanity required it, when the Delinquent had been deluded, and, in some Measure, overborn by the Heads of the Insurgents, and that there was not the least Shadow of Reason to suppose that the Government had either Way interposed, or directed the least Partiality to be shewn in dispensing either Justice, or Mercy, on this Occasion. He added, that as the learned Judges, from the Nature of their Employment, could not sit in that House to defend themselves, he could not help answering for them, and should

think

think himself wanting, as well to his own Character as theirs, if he did not do them the Juſtice to ſay, that they had behaved through the whole of that unhappy Affair ſo as to deſerve the greateſt Honour both as Magiſtrates and Men.

To this Dr *L—* made no Reply, but, upon his Motion, it was ordered, that it be an Inſtruction to the ſaid Committee to enquire into the Cauſes of the Inſurrections in the South.

Anſwer of the Lord Lieutenant to the Addreſs of the Houſe.

" *Gentlemen*,

" I am extremely thankful for this very obliging Addreſs: The favourable Opinion you are pleaſed to conceive of my Intentions, at the Commencement of my Adminiſtration, will, I flatter myſelf, be confirmed in the Courſe, and by the Concluſion of it. It will be my chief Endeavour to merit your Approbation by my own Conduct, and faithfully to repreſent to his Majeſty the Loyalty and the Affection

Affection of Yours: Opportunities of doing this Act of Justice, so honourable to you, and so pleasing to me, I persuade myself will very frequently occur; and you may rest assured they shall be always very readily embraced, and improved to the utmost Advantage."

THURSDAY, Oct. 27, 1763.

FOURTH DAY.

MR. *R— F—* got up and said, that as many unavoidable Accidents frequently prevented the best-intentioned Subjects from qualifying themselves within the exact Time prescribed by the Act, and that, as the Act was never designed to distress such Persons, by taking Advantage of a Delay which they could not prevent, he humbly moved that Leave might be given, to bring in Heads of a Bill for allowing farther Time to Persons, in Offices or Employments, to qualify themselves, pursuant to an Act to prevent the farther Growth of Popery.

Ordered that Leave be given to bring in the Heads of such a Bill.

Mr *H—— L——*.

Mr S——,

As Liberty is the common Birth-right of Mankind, and, like Health, is that Blessing, without which no other can be enjoyed, it is cer-

certainly Matter of Regret, that, by the natural and neceſſary Imperfection in all human Things, the Liberty of Induſtry and Innocence ſhould, in ſome Circumſtances, be precarious, even in this Country, of which Freedom is the glorious, and almoſt peculiar Privilege, and in behalf of which our Anceſtors have been ever ready to expend the laſt Mite of their Property, and the laſt Drop of their Blood. As Juſtice is nothing more than Goodneſs, under the Direction of Wiſdom, which inflicts Puniſhment upon a Part for the Good of the Whole, Puniſhment, however merited, and however neceſſary, by no means excludes Pity: The Magiſtrate may, without Reproach, drop a Tear over the Criminal whom he condemns even to die, and feel the generous Struggle of Compaſſion in his Boſom when he denies Liberty, even to Idleneſs and Guilt; what then muſt be the Feeling of the humane and generous Mind, where the Law, either deceived by the Wiles of iniquitous Cunning, or the fortuitous Concurrence of ſpecious but deceitful Appearances, is found to have condemned blameleſs Simplicity, and laborious Diligence to a Dungeon, in which, like the Grave, " there is neither Work nor Device by which Man can profit,"

and

and which is crowded with all the Horrors that are the genuine Progeny of Misery and Guilt; and yet if no Man was to be committed to Prison, but upon full Examination, and incontestible Proof of his Guilt, what Offender could be secured? and if the Prosecutor, upon failure, in his Proof, was to become subject to the same Punishment, which the Delinquent would have incurred, what Offender would be prosecuted? At the time when Persons, taken up upon Suspicion, are committed by a Magistrate, the Proof of their Crime, supposing them to be really Guilty, is often known to be impossible, at least, it is always impossible where it is not manifest and self-evident, and where it is so, the Commitment is not an unmerited Punishment. And, as our Laws require nothing less than an absolute Demonstration of Guilt, by direct and positive Evidence, it would be Cruelty instead of Mercy to subject the Prosecutor, who has been already injured by the Crime committed, to suffer instead of the Offender, because he has not been able to demonstrate that the Person against whom there were reasonable Suspicions was he. What then is to be done? shall we admit more slender Evidence to convict the Accused, that it may be
equi-

equitable to punish the Accuser, if he fails in the Conviction? This, surely would be no Testimony, either of our Humanity, or our Wisdom; or shall we, instead of the Solemnity of a Tryal, by twelve disinterested Persons, the Equals, or Peers, of the supposed Offender, enable a subordinate Magistrate to determine finally of Life and Death, by such Probabilities as can hastily be brought before him, upon the first Apprehension of a suspected Person? Surely this would be still less eligible than the other Expedient. If the Evil then of sometimes committing an innocent Person to Prison cannot be obviated without bringing Innocence into yet greater Danger, and exposing it to yet worse Mischief, it is natural to enquire, what Methods the Legislature has taken to atone for the Wrongs which its own Imbecility makes unavoidable; when a Man, whose Poverty exposed him to the Imputation of Crimes, which the Wealthy could not be tempted to commit, has been kept a Prisoner till the Time of his Tryal arrives, and, when he is brought to the Barr, it appears that he is innocent, and, perhaps, that he has been the Victim of one of those Wretches, who make Perjury subordinate to every other Crime, or of some Villain, to whom

Day IV.] *Affairs of* IRELAND.

whom his Virtue or his Induftry rendered him obnoxious, and who, having by this infernal Revenge filled up the Meafure of his Iniquity, is fled the Country; when it appears that the unhappy Object of fuch diabolical Wickednefs has been languifhing in the Filth and Infection of a Prifon, the Affociate of Thieves and Murderers, that his Wife, and his Children, who received their daily Bread from the Labour of his Hand, have been expofed to all the Miferies of Want, imbittered by Grief, Anxiety and Terror; that his Reputation is fullied, his little Credit exhaufted, and Debts contracted, which, however fmall in the Eftimation of Affluence, are yet greater than he can ever difcharge; when thefe, and many other Inftances of his Diftrefs, and his Wrongs are become too manifeft to admit a Doubt, what Provifion has his Country made to alleviate them? what Fund is appropriated to prevent his being ftill the Slave of a petty Creditor, to maintain him in the Sicknefs and Debility, which he may have contracted in his Confinement, and to re-place him in the State from which he had been driven, by the erring Hand of hood-winked Juftice, or the combined Effort of Violence and Fraud? Methinks I am anfwered, by the Regret and

Com-

Compassion, which I read in your Countenances, "there is none." Alas! it is, indeed, too true that there is none; is the unhappy Sufferer then to be dismissed again into the World to surmount his Distress, and forget his Wrongs as he may? to this surely, no Heart can assent, without sighing over its own Inability to award him a better Lot; and yet this is infinitely preferable to the State, in which, after all the Proof of his Sufferings, and his Innocence, he is now abandoned by his Country. The Husband, the Father, the useful, yet injured Member of Society, whom twelve Men, upon their Oath have declared to have committed no Crime, or whom the Villain, by whose Machinations he was confined, dare not appear to prosecute, is dragged back to his Dungeon, where he is again confined, without Pity, and without Remorse, by the Tyrant of the Goal, till he has paid what is demanded of him, under the execrable, tho' specious Denomination of Fees. Who can speak, or who can hear it without Shame and Indignation! Is a Man to be mulcted by a Goaler, because, by the Wickedness of an Enemy, or the Fallibility of a Magistrate, he has already suffered, being innocent, a Punishment due only to the most atrocious Guilt!

Guilt! Is Innocence to be still punished, merely because it has been punished already? and are those, whom the Law is supposed to protect, to suffer more by the Extortion of its Instruments than by those whom it ought to punish and restrain? That we are at present under the Reproach of a Conduct so absurd, and so inhuman, so contrary to our Nature and Constitution, is not less astonishing than true, but, surely the Laws of God, and the Dictates of Conscience, every Sentiment of Humanity, and every Principle of Justice, require that it should be true no longer; how such a Practice, whether founded upon any Law, or whether merely countenanced by Prescription, was established, it is very difficult to conceive; it is more strange it should continue, and it is stranger still, that when a worthy Gentleman, whose Example I shall always think it the highest Honour to follow, brought a Bill into this House to set it aside, the Bill was, by some unaccountable Fatality, thrown out; happy is it for us, Sirs, that we are in a Situation so remote from the Distress I have described, that we can scarce believe it possible to exist: But if any Gentleman is inclined to visit these Scenes of Wickedness and Misery, the public Prisons of this Country, he will find the Number of those who are detained merely for their Fees, to bear a considerable Proportion to the whole; the Friends of suffering Poverty are soon exhausted, and he, whose daily Bread depended wholly upon his daily Labour, when once he is removed from the World to a Prison, is very soon forgotten by all but those who have it not in their Power to afford him pecuniary Assistance: The Legislature, Sir, should certainly interpose in this Case from mere Policy, supposing Justice, Humanity, and every more generous Motive to have lost its Influence; the Prisoner is necessarily idle, and, if a Miracle do not interpose, he will, at length become corrupt; the Public will be deprived of the Benefit of his Labour, while he is confined, and if, after long Confinement, he returns into the World, he will probably be the Pest of that very Society of which he was before the Support ; and, surely it is the Interest of Government, in every view, to prevent Mankind from thus starving and depraving one another : I flatter myself, however, that we shall not be prompted to espouse the Cause of suffering Innocence, of the

Poor

Poor, and "him that has none to keep him," by the mere frigid Senfe of Duty, and a Regard to political Principles; the very Indigence of the Sufferer, and our own Exemption from the fame Species of Diftrefs, fhould quicken our Activity, on this Occafion, and, I dare fay, every Gentleman prefent can lay his Hand upon his Heart, and with that Benevolence, which is at once the Honour and Happinefs of our Nature, fay to himfelf,

Homo fum, humani nihil á me alienum puto *.

I therefore, humbly move, that Leave be given to bring in Heads of a Bill for difcharging, without Fees, Perfons who fhall be acquitted of Offences, for which they are, or fhall be indicted, and for making a Compenfation to Sheriffs, Goalers, and Clerks of the Crown, for fuch Fees.

Ordered, that Leave be given to bring in Heads of fuch a Bill.

---

* I am a Man, and nothing by which Man is affected can be indifferent to me.

Mr.

Mr. R—— F——.

Mr. S—,

I rife up in Behalf of a Petition of the incorporated Society of *Dublin*, for promoting *Englifh* Proteftant Schools in this Kingdom. That a Difference of religious and political Principles, in any Country, is of the greateft Prejudice to the State, ftands in need of no Proof, nor can it be denied that this Kingdom has long, and does now fuffer all the Evils of fuch a Difference : I think, alfo, it will be readily admitted, that the Support of Schools, in which thofe, who would otherwife be Papifts, are educated in the Principles of the eftablifhed Religion of this Country, is a Meafure well adopted to remove thefe Evils, by gradually eradicating their Caufe; it follows, therefore, that, upon mere Principles of Policy and Intereft, this Inftitution fhould be fupported ; I hope, however, that there are other Inducements, of a more elevated, and a more amiable Kind, of which we all feel the Force. Every Proteftant muft neceffarily fuppofe that Popery, befides its Abfurdities, contains many dangerous Errors. To refcue the Children of the Poor, of thofe,

who,

who, "If in this Life only they have Hope, are of all Men moſt miſerable," from a State, in which they will implicitly imbibe Errors, that will at leaſt endanger their Happineſs, in a State of final Retribution hereafter, is a Work, that, where there is any Compaſſion for helpleſs Innocence, and for deluded Bigotry, any Regard for Virtue, any Zeal for Religion, will be undertaken from Feelings, and Principles, very different from civil Intereſt, and State Policy. But Motives of Compaſſion will not be wanting for the Promotion of this Inſtitution, even to thoſe who are inclined to ſet the ſpiritual or ſocial Advantage of Religion wholly out of the Queſtion; a Charter School is an Aſylum, not only from Error and Superſtition, but from Miſery; from Idleneſs, which enervates the Body, and depraves the Mind; and from Indigence, under which helpleſs Infancy frequently ſinks into the Grave; in a Charter School, the Principles of genuine Chriſtianity are taught, early Habits of Induſtry are formed, loyal Subjects are produced for the State, uſeful Members for the Community, and rational Chriſtians for the Church. It would be eaſy for me to enlarge upon this Subject, but as the good Effects of the Charter Schools have been ſo numerous,

and

and so manifest in the Neighbourhood of every Gentleman in this House, and are, indeed, so generally acknowledged, it would be taking up Time unnecessarily, which may be employed to better Purpose. I would now proceed to give some Account of their present State, but in this I am prevented by the Petition; I shall therefore only observe, that the Nurseries, for the Establishment of which Assistance is now sought from Parliament, are attended with Advantages yet greater than the superior Schools would produce alone; before Children could be received into those Schools, they would have arrived at an Age, when the strongest Connection is formed between Children and their Parents; by the Complacency of the Parent to the Child on one Hand, and, on the other, by the Affection returned by the Child to the Parent, in consequence of the Indearments which that Complacency produces; in consequence of this mutual Attachment, the Child, who, all the Time it is at School, remembers the Indulgence of parental Tenderness with regret, and pines with Desire to return Home, too often gratifies this Desire, as soon as ever it is dismissed, with an Impatience, and Ardour, proportioned to its Delay; the Intention of the School

School is thus defeated; the Influence of the Parent, and Relations, in conjunction with that of the Priest, enforcing the joint Precept and Example of both, precipitate him again into those Errors, which he had been taught to eschew, and the bad Habits essential to his chosen Situation inevitably recur; he is at length married among his Relations, and his return to Truth and Industry precluded for ever. But, on the contrary, Children are received into the Nursery at a Time, when they are rather an Incumbrance than a Gratification to their Parents, and, before they can be sensible of their Caresses; no tie, therefore, is formed, which can draw them back into the Delusion and Irregularities, from which they have been once delivered by the charitable Liberality of their Country; besides, the more early Habits of Industry are formed, and Precepts of rational Religion inculcated, the more strong and the more lasting both will probably be, and the more likely to produce their genuine Effects. That this Institution stands in need of Support, will appear from the Petition, the Allegations of which, if doubted, may be supported by incontestible Evidence; as the Support of it is, in every View, of the highest Importance, and as it has been, in a particular Manner, recommended from the Throne, I move that the Petition be referred to the Confideration of a Committee, that they do examine the Matter thereof, and report the fame, with their Opinion thereupon, to the Houfe.

The faid Petition having been prefented, and received, was read, fetting forth that the Society was incorporated by his late Majefty, in the Year 1733, and by the great Bounty of the Crown, repeated Aids of Parliament, the Subfcriptions and Benefactions of feveral Perfons in *Great Britain, Ireland,* and his Majefty's Plantations in *America,* has been enabled to erect, in feveral Parts of this Kingdom, forty-nine Schools, for the Maintenance and Education of about two Thoufand Children, as alfo a Nurfery, in *Dublin,* for the immediate Reception of fuch of the Children as are admitted here. That the Children in faid Schools are inftructed in the Proteftant Religion, and trained up to Induftry and Labour, in order to be apprenticed to Proteftant Linen Weavers, Flax Dreffers, Gardiners, Farmers, Tradefmen, and to Gentlemen for Servants. That the Society has been at a very confiderable Expence, in building feveral new Schools,

Schools, and has alfo accepted feveral other advantageous Propofals, which it cannot proceed to carry into Execution. That the Society, encouraged by this Houfe to build four Nurferies, one in each Province, for the Reception of one hundred Children under fix Years of Age, has fo far carried that great Plan into Execution, that Children have been fome Time fince received in three of the faid Nurferies, and that it has alfo purchafed Ground for the fourth Nurfery, but is at prefent unable to proceed further therein. That, by the great Number of charitable Inftitutions of various Kinds, both in this Kingdom and *Great Britain*, the annual Subfcriptions, and other Benefactions, to this Society have been greatly leffened; it is therefore under the moft urgent Neceffity, to make its Application to this Houfe, as the only effectual Refource, whereby it may be enabled to carry on a Defign, fo well calculated for promoting Induftry, and fo highly ufeful to the Proteftant Intereft in this Kingdom. And praying Relief.

" Ordered, that the faid Petition be referred, as by Mr. *F*—'s Motion."

The

The R—t H—ble Mr *A— M—* then moved that a Supply might be granted to his Majesty, and that, for the greater Freedom of Debate, the Houſe might reſolve itſelf into a Committee of the whole Houſe.

Mr *J— E—* then ſaid, that as the Penſions granted on the Eabliſhment of *Ireland*, were Objects moſt intereſting to the Nation, and moſt worthy the ſtricteſt parliamentary Enquiry, he was of Opinion they ſhould be made as public as poſſible, by being printed, that every Body might know by whom thoſe enormous annual Sums were received, in what Proportions, and for what Time, alſo in what Country the Penſioners reſided, that People might the better judge how far they were a national Advantage, or otherwiſe; he therefore moved for the printing the ſame.

" Ordered, that the Liſt of Penſions on the civil and military Eſtabliſhment be printed."

FRIDAY, Oct. 28, 1763.

FIFTH DAY.

The R—t H—ble Mr F— A—.

Mr S——,

I Take this early Opportunity to acquaint the Houfe with my Intention to bring in two Bills this Seffions, which, in fome degree relate to each other, and both which I think of the higheft Importance to the Religion, Morality, and civil Government of this Nation: The firft is a Bill for encreafing the Salaries of Curates; by the Statute of the 6th of *George* the Ift, it is enacted, that if any Rector, or Vicar, fhall nominate any Curate to the Ordinary, to ferve the Cure of fuch Rector, or Vicar, in his abfcene, the Ordinary fhall be impowered to fix, for fuch Curate, a certain Stipend not more than fifty, nor lefs than twenty Pounds a Year. And, by the firft of *George* the IId, it is alfo enacted, that it fhall be lawful for every Bifhop, at the Time of his licencing any Curate, or other Perfon, in holy Orders, to affift the Incumbent of any Parifh, by whom he fhall be nominated, to appoint a fufficient Stipend, to be paid at fuch Time as he fhall think fit, by fuch Incumbent, to fuch Curate; fuch Stipend not to exceed fifty Pounds a Year, nor fall fhort of ten; and, as both thefe Acts are taken from the *Britifh* Act of the twelfth of Queen *Anne,* the Ordinary is allowed to judge and determine all Cafes relative thereto, and the Curate's Salary is generally fixed at forty Pounds a Year.

Now, Sir, I think it muft be univerfally allowed, that the Salary of forty Pounds a Year was much too fmall for a Curate, even when the Act of the firft of *George* the IId was made, which is now fix and thirty Years ago; how greatly then muft it fall fhort, at this Time, when the Value of Money is fo much leffened, that Sums, which were then lent at Seven *per Cent.* are now lent at Four; at the fame Time that more Things are become neceffary, and every Neceffary is become dearer. I call thofe things neceffary, Sir, that Habit and Cuftom have affixed to the feveral Situations and Conditions of Men; the Refinements of this Age, and the Importation of foreign Articles, have greatly encreafed creased the Number of Particulars that are thus necessary; and, I believe, all things considered, it will be found that forty Pounds a Year, six and thirty Years ago, was, at least, equal to eighty Pounds a Year now; every Gentleman present, will, therefore, surely concur with me, in Opinion, that forty Pounds a Year is much too small a Pittance for one, who always by his Education, and frequently by his Birth, is a Gentleman; who receives new Dignity, from the sacred Function to which he is called; who would be degraded by associating with those whose Income in civil Life produces only a Pittance equal to his own; and who can preserve the Propriety of his Character, and the Respect and Weight, which alone can give Efficacy to his Ministry, only by moving in the Rank of those whose Revenue enables them to spend in a Month, more than he receives in a Year, which unavoidably brings many other Expences, under the Denomination of Necessaries of Life, with respect to the Curate, which, in another Situation, would not occur. I say, Sir, these things considered, I cannot suppose that any Gentleman present will think forty Pounds a Year a sufficient Stipend for those who perform all the Duties, for which, no less than one tenth

Part of the Revenue of the Country is allotted by our Ecclesiastical Constitution. If forty Pounds a Year is enough for those who perform these Duties, why is the Public taxed at more? Is it the Intention of Government to tax Industry for the Support of Idleness? Is a tenth Part of all that the Earth yields to the Husbandman, in return for the Sweat of his Brow, to be paid into the Purses of those who do nothing but pay back a small Pittance of it to a Substitute, who performs those Duties and Functions, which, in the Opinions of our Ancestors, make it requisite to possess the whole? Sure I am, Sir, that the Reasonableness of the Church Revenue can be supported by no Arguments, which will not prove that officiating Curates should have a much more ample Allowance than forty Pounds a Year. The very Appointment of Tythes is a Demonstration that the Founders of the Institution thought those who preached the Gospel, and administered the Sacrament, who were to admonish the Wicked, and encourage the Good, and to set an Example of Hospitality and Christian Benevolence, should have much more than the mere Necessaries of Life: And, as I am most sincerely of their Opinion,

Opinion, I would not have the Revenues of the Church lefs, but I would have them more equally diftributed; I would have thofe fupported in the Character, who render the Character fubfervient to the Duty, and not thofe, who with a Rank and Affluence, that would add Weight and Efficacy, both to their Precept and Example, leave the Labour of Inftruction, and Admonition, to thofe whofe Poverty and Dependance muft render both not only ufelefs, but contemptible. I will readily admit that a Gentleman, whofe Education has coft annually more than the whole Income allotted to the Function, for which he could no otherwife be qualified, who, with every private Shift, to maintain an outward Appearance fuitable to his Character, cannot hide his Diftrefs, whofe Body is harraffed by fatiguing Duty, and whofe Mind is depreffed by a Senfe of his Condition, ought to be regarded at once with Reverence and Compaffion; but the Queftion is not how he ought to be regarded, but how he is regarded; and, it is but too well known, that, againft the Contempt of Poverty, no Age has ever found a Remedy, no Ability a Defence, nor any Virtue a Cure; Poverty is not only an Evil in itfelf, but it is contagious too; it brings things into contempt, with which it appears to be connected. When it has rendered the Curate contemptible, it soon renders his Function so too, and when his Function is involved in his personal Disgrace, the Religion, of which he is the Minister, cannot long escape free. If Religion then is of any Importance to Mankind, it is of Importance to support its Ministers, in a State, in which Frugality, at least, may obtain Independance, and Virtue procure Esteem. But I have hitherto, Sir, considered the Curate of forty Pounds a Year as a single Man; if I was disposed to interest your Passions, as well as your Understanding, in his behalf, I would consider him as a Husband and a Father; I would describe the Distress of his Family during the Helplessness of Infancy, and the Langour of Sickness; the Distraction and Anguish of Mind which he must suffer, under a total and hopeless Inability, to supply what is requisite for the proper Nurture, and Maintenance of the one, and the Solace and Recovery of the other. I am sorry to say, there is too much reason to apprehend, that some may possibly be so illiberal and void of feeling, as to reply, with a Sneer, what Business have those Wretches to marry, who

can

can only pester their Country with a Progeny of Beggars? and who would consider a Curate, that should happen to have twelve Children, rather as an Object of Ridicule than Pity: It almost goes against me to offer a serious Answer to what deserves to be treated only with Indignation and Contempt; " increase and multiply," is the great, the general Law of our Omnipotent, all wise, and all gracious Creator, who has, in every Instance, made the public Good depend upon the lawful Indulgence of private Instinct; to encrease and multiply, is at once to enrich and to defend the State, it is to replenish the Earth, and to produce Candidates for Heaven; one of the most extravagant and pernicious Absurdities of Popery is the imaginary Merit of Celibacy; for, setting all political Advantages aside, that, which is Merit in one, would be Merit in all; the World then must subsist only by a Deviation from the narrow Path of Religious Perfection, the Saviour must, comparitively, have suffered in vain, and millions, upon whom everlasting Felicity would have been bestowed, as the Purchase of his inestimable Death, would never be produced to claim what he has purchased for them. Is Poverty then, among its other unmerited Curses, to preclude a Man from fulfilling the firſt and great Command; from continuing his Species, and anſwering the principal End of his Creation? If ſo, we are ſtill leſs excuſable, for ſuffering the Labourers of the ſacred Vineyard to want, merely, that others, who neither plant, nor prune, may abound; the Effects of Celibacy are an unſocial Mind, and diſtempered Body; an impoveriſhed Country and an enfeebled State; every Temptation to Celibacy ſhould therefore be removed, at once to avert both a private and a public Curſe; ſo that, in this View, the Argument for augmenting the Stipend of Curates will be ſtrengthened, and the Reproach, which is caſt upon thoſe, who marry, thrown back upon thoſe who lay them under Temptations to live ſingle; it muſt alſo, upon this Occaſion, be remembered that an Income, which leaves a Curate poor, will neverthelefs make a Labourer rich. Wealth and Poverty depend leſs upon the abſolute Poſſeſſions of the Individual, than upon their Habits and Station in Life; a Man, who is placed in the Rank of thoſe who ſpend four hundred a Year, will be expoſed to all the Diſtreſſes of Poverty with Fifty: He, who aſſociates only with thoſe, who get twelve Pence a Day, by manual

nual Labour, will procure the Conveniencies of Affluence with eighteen Pence a Day, which is not quite thirty Pounds a Year. If I am now afked, how I propofe to remedy the Evil of which I complain, I anfwer, that the Remedy lies farther than my utmoft Hopes will prompt me to afpire; I mean no more than to paliate, I know too well the nature of the Difeafe, to attempt a Cure; I do not propofe the compelling all who receive the Nation's Money, to perform the Duties for which it is paid; I propofe only that thofe, to whom the Duty is left, may be enabled effectually to fulfill it: But as, in order to this, it is not neceffary that the officiating Clergy fhould have all the Wealth that flows in upon the idle and voluptuous Non-refident, I only wifh that a fufficient Part fhould be paid them to anfwer the Purpofes of their Calling, and afford them the Comforts of Life: I am content that thofe, whom Merit or good Fortune, have put into Poffeffion of the original Revenue, fhould retain the Reft. A Contribution from thefe, comparitively fmall, would produce an adequate Revenue for the Curate, and, confequently, more good, both to Individuals and to the State, and would more promote both

the

the temporal and eternal Interest of Mankind than an hundred Times the Sum applied in any other manner; I do not, however, make any specific demand, and I mean no more by what I have said, than that Gentlemen of Ability may assist in forming Heads of a Bill for the End proposed.

The second Bill, Sir, that I have to propose will shew the Sincerity of my Declaration, when I said, that I did not wish the Revenues of the Church to be less; for it is calculated for the more easy and expeditious Recovery of Tythes; part of the good which I propose by this Bill, is, indeed, merely the removal of positive Evil. It is always of the most pernicious Consequence to suffer the Laws in being to be either questioned or eluded; great Care should, therefore, be taken, to have them clear and explicit, and that they should be neither oppressive in reality, nor appearance; if they are, in themselves, imperfect and ambiguous, they may be opposed without the Disgrace of factious Discontent, or a refractory Spirit: If they are oppressive, even in appearance, they will be opposed both from Motives of Interest and Honour, and, he that suffers, or appears to suffer, by their Execution, will be encouraged, and supported, by those who have no immediate Interest in the Question; Government will become odious, and, in some Circumstances, its Administration impracticable.

The Laws now in being, with Respect to Tythes, are so formed, as to enable the Parishoners to litigate the Payment of them with the Incumbent, to which they have frequent and strong Temptations; there is a universal, and very natural disinclination to pay that, for which, it is thought an equivalent Service is not done, the Rector being too often non-resident, and the Curate unable to discharge his Duty, by the Necessity he is under, of holding a Farm, or busying himself in some other Employment, to maintain himself and his Family: The Parishoners are often very justly provoked by the improper Behaviour of the Tythe Farmers, or Proctors, a set of People who are universally detested, and abhorred, by the very Nature of their Duty, and sometimes there are Discontents between Parishoners, and a resident Minister, arising, merely from the Difficulty of obtaining the Good-will of a great Number of People, of various

various Humours and Difpofitions, in Tranfactions, where Property is immediately concerned, and the pecuniary Intereſt of the Parties is oppofite. When the Caufes of Animofity are fo numerous, it can feldom happen, but that any one, who is fo far piqued, or offended, as to do all in his power to diſtrefs the Miniſter, may get many to concur in his Defign, who wanted only the auxiliary Motives of private Friendſhip, and Solicitation, to take the fame Meaſures before; this naturally brings on a Combination of the greateſt Part of the Pariſh, if not of the whole, to defeat the Law for paying the Miniſter his Dues. Among other Expedients, which have been found but too effectual for this Purpoſe, they all agree, to paper the Church, as they call it, the fame Day; that is, they give the Notice, which the Law requires, that they will all draw their Corn on the fame Day; for though they cut at different Times, yet they contrive not to have different Days of drawing: By this Means the Law is eluded, and the Miniſter diſtreſſed in the higheſt Degree; for, in a Pariſh of many Miles extent, and, but thinly inhabited, it is impoſſible for the Miniſter, to procure a fufficient Number of Horfes and Carriages, to draw, even a tenth Part

Part of his Tythes, on the Day appointed; for thofe, who combine to fummons him to draw them, combine alfo to deprive him of the Power of fo doing, by refufing to let to hire any Horfes for that Purpofe: It alfo, fometimes happens, that they refufe him a convenient Place to draw them to, the Confequence in both Cafes is, that the Tythes are left in the Field, and then, we all know what becomes of them. The Minifter, having no Remedy at Law, is therefore compelled to compound for his Tythes at, perhaps, one fourth of their Value, if his Parifhoner happens to prefer Intereft to Revenge; if not, which is no rare cafe, he will not compound upon any Terms, and fo the Tythe is entirely wafted and loft to both Parties alike. Thus, Sir, the Laws for the Maintenance of Minifters, with a View to eftablifh the Principles and Practice of Charity, do, at prefent, diametrically counteract their Intention; they are the Fountain of "Hatred, Malice, and all Uncharitablenefs," between thofe who ought to be connected by more than common Philanthropy, by filial and parental Affection, not " according to the Flefh but the Spirit," not founded upon temporal but eternal Things. I know it may be faid, and

with

with great Reason, and Truth, that Tythes will never be chearfully paid, till the Duty for which they are paid is performed; till the Minister maintains the Character of the good Shepherd among his Flock; and no longer leaves them a Prey to the Wolf, or to the Fox: But, it is also true, that no Virtue, no Piety, no Benevolence, however ardent, uniform and exemplary, would, as the Law now stands, always preserve that Union and Harmony, between a Minister and his Parishioners, which is essentially necessary to answering, in any Degree, the important Purposes of his Function: The Uncertainty and Defectiveness of the Law leaves room for Litigation, and every Litigation is founded, upon a Supposition, that the Minister exacts more than his due; if the Suit is determined in favour of the Minister, the Evil does not stop; the Minds of both Parties have been too much enflamed, during the Contention, to become cool when it is over; the Parishoner, though compelled to pay, will still want an inward Conviction, that the Law originally intended what it is now tortured to enforce; he will impute his ill Success to the Chicanery of the Courts, to the superior Influence of his Opponent, or to the Ignorance,

norance, or perhaps Perfidy, of the People, with whom he intrufted the Management of his Caufe; the Minifter, having endured every outrage that the fuppofed Sufferer by extortion could offer, will confider him as a malignant and inveterate Enemy, whom nothing can reconcile, and upon whom, therefore, all kindnefs and forbearance will be loft: At the fame Time, he, who by his Poverty is obliged to pay, without Litigation, what another Litigates, will imagine that Advantage is taken off his Inability to defend his Right, to infringe it; that he is oppreffed by an unrelenting Tyrant, who, under pretence of taking care of his Soul, is picking his Pocket, and making the Law itfelf an Inftrument of Cruelty and Injuftice: When once the Minifter, and his Parifhoners, come to be diftinguifhed by the unfriendly Appellations of Plaintiff and Defendant, or what is more hateful and bitter of *Premovent* and *Repugnant* *, there is an end of Paftoral Affection, of Efteem and Friendfhip, of Reverence and Duty; to addrefs them as " dearly beloved

---

* The Terms ufed for Plaintiff and Defendant in the Bifhop's Court.

in the Lord," becomes a Mockery and a Prophanation, and, I think, we may fairly conclude, that where Charity is wanting, there can be no Religion that is profitable to Man, or pleasing to God. It is to Animosities thus raised and fomented, that the late violent and unnatural Commotions are in a great measure to be imputed ; the mere Payment, of what the Law clearly and indubitably appointed, would never have raised such a Ferment ; it was produced solely by a Malignity that was gradually encreased by Disputation and Contest ; the principle Object of the Association, and of the Oath by which it was bound, was, Grievancies supposed to be suffered by the Act of the Clergy ; and, having mentioned this popular Resentment against the Clergy, I must add, from my own Knowledge, that the Distress of the Clergy in the Diocess of *Derry*, the Insults, the Persecution, the Cruelties that they suffered, would have been carried to an Excess scarce to be parallelled in History, had they not taken Refuge in that true Asylum of Distress, the glorious and ever memorable City of *Derry*, within whose Walls no Treason was ever suffered to enter, and within the Breasts of whose Inhabitants no Principle of Injustice, or Oppression, was ever known

known to lodge. At this critical Time, therefore, it seems to be the indispensable Duty of the House, to think of some Expedient, to put it in the Power of the Clergy, to fulfil the important Purposes of their Calling, by removing all Temptations to Strife, and Debate, "and to strike with the Fist of Wickedness;" and this, I think, would effectually be done, by enacting some plain, and explicit Law, by which, the Requisition of Tythes should be made wholly the Act of the Legislature, and not of the Minister; by which his Allowance, from the Parish, should be ascertained, beyond possibility of doubt, and the Manner of paying it, so determined, as to secure the whole to him at all Events, and leave no Power, either to Cunning, or Malignity, to defeat him of his Right. I should think myself happy, if Gentlemen would give their Opinion upon a Matter of so great Importance, and, if any Person present has Objections, I shall think myself greatly obliged to them, if they will afford me an Opportunity of attempting, at least, to remove them.

G Mr J—

Mr *J— H— H—*, P. S.

Mr S——,

It gives me the greateſt Pleaſure to find that the Sentiments, and Opinions, expreſſed by the R—t H—ble Member who ſpoke laſt, are exactly the ſame with my own; I am alſo happy that he has, in ſo maſterly a Manner, anticipated all that I could have wiſhed to ſay upon the Subject; he has left me nothing to do, but to bear my Teſtimony, that it is a Subject of the higheſt national Importance, and to rejoice, with every Friend to this Country, that it has fallen under the Conſideration of a Gentleman, whoſe Influence and Abilities are ſo extenſive, and diſtinguiſhed. If I can give him any Aſſiſtance, in ſo laudable an Undertaking, I ſhall eſteem it equally a Happineſs, and an Honour; and, as it has been ſome time the Object of my Contemplation, I ſhall watch for every Opportunity of ſo doing, and improve ſuch as offer, with the utmoſt Diligence, and Alacrity. If I can add any thing to what the honourable Gentleman has already ſaid, it is with Reſpect to the Combinations, that have lately

lately been formed againſt paying the Church Dues: Theſe Combinations, Sir, have been attended with Circumſtances more terrible and alarming than is yet generally known; I have, upon my Eſtate, in the Dioceſs of *Waterford*, many Papiſts, who are Tenants at will, and, whom, I can, conſequently, diſplace, to their great Diſadvantage, when ever I think fit. When I heard that theſe People were joining in a Combination againſt the Miniſter of the Pariſh, I directed my Agent to acquaint them, that, if they did join in ſuch Combination, I would diſmiſs them; they replied, that if I diſmiſſed them, they could not help it, it would be a Misfortune, but it would ſtill be the leaſt of two Evils; for they had better be diſmiſſed than have their Throats cut, which would be the certain Conſequence of refuſing to concur in the Combination, I was ſolicitous to prevent. A Combination, Sir, into which Aſſociates are preſſed by the Fear of Death, and, in which, therefore, many violate the Peace of the State, contrary to their Inclination and Intereſt, may in a ſhort Time ſubvert the Conſtitution, and defeat all the Laws that have been enacted to prevent public Evils, ariſing from the Growth of Popery. I am of Opinion, Sir,

that

that such a Law, as has been now recommended, would greatly tend to prevent these Combinations, by rendering them ineffectual, and by removing all Colour of Litigation, and Dispute. I, therefore, most earnestly recommend the Consideration of it to this House, and make this public Offer of such Service as is in my Power.

Mr R— F— said, that there was nothing he more ardently wished, than to have the Bill proposed, properly drawn up, and passed into a Law, and thought no way would be so effectual for that Purpose, as to appoint a Committee, in which, every one might give his Advice and Opinion.

A Committee was appointed accordingly.

Mr E—— M———.

Mr S—,

It will appear, by the Journals of this House, that an Order was made on the 13th of *October*, for the deputy Clerk of the Rolls, to bring in the Inrollments of the Patents, by which, the Offices of the Chancellor of the Exchequer, Master of the Rolls, and Judges,

Judges, have been granted. But I obferved, that he has obeyed that Order only in part; having brought in no more than the Inrollments of the laft Patents of the Mafter of the Rolls, and the Chancellor of the Exchequer; as it may be fafely taken for granted, that no Arguments are neceffary, to prove that the Orders of this Houfe ought to be punctually and fully obeyed, I might, upon this Occafion, content myfelf with obferving the Default, and, requiring that it may be amended, but, becaufe, I would not appear critically to remark minute and trivial Neglects, I muft obferve, that this Order was evidently made, with a View to a very interefting and important Enquiry; an Enquiry, Sir, whether judicial Employments, of fuch Confequence to the Kingdom, can be granted for Life, confiftent with the Laws by which it is governed, the leaft Violation of which may make way for a total Subverfion of our Conftitution; and, I muft freely declare it, as my Opinion, that, in order to determine this Queftion, and to difcover how, and, in what Inftances, the Grant of fuch Employments for Life is fupported by Precedent, all the Enrollments fince the Revolution fhould be produced; I fay, fince the Revolution, Sir, and, I fix that Period, becaufe, before the happy Event, which then took place, fcarce any regular Syftem of Government was eftablifhed in this Kingdom : *Britifh* Monarchs did, in many Inftances, and in both Kingdoms, " what was right in their own Eyes," an Evil, which the Revolution was brought about to prevent, by giving that Order, and Stability, to our Conftitution, which, I am perfuaded, no Gentleman here would be willing to have interrupted or fhaken. I would not, however, anticipate the Debate, which this Enquiry will necefsarily bring on, or prematurely throw out a Surmife, that the Crown had acted with Impropriety, or, even received erroneous Advice ; I think, however, that the Enquiry fhould be made, by confulting the Judges, the ableft Lawyers, and all the King's Servants, or rather, by bringing it in a judicial Way into fome of the Courts ; for Lawyers, confulted as to their private Opinion, may differ, and, we know, do differ, even when there are no Motives of Intereft to biafs their Determination ; but, in a public and folemn Enquiry, a public and folemn Opinion will be obtained, in which, perhaps, thofe who differed before, may, either convinced by Argument, or influenced by Authority of fuperior Weight, concur ;

cur; and, give me leave to say, Sir, that I think this House would be highly Criminal, tacitly, and implicitly, to acquiesce in any Act of the Crown, which might even be suspected of Illegality, without setting such an Enquiry on Foot, and availing itself of the Lights it would produce, and the Determination in which it should issue. As to myself, I confess, I am of Opinion, that the granting these Employments for Life, is illegal; an Opinion, in which, I know I am very far from being singular; this, however, I do not mention as being alone of any Weight to determine the Question, but only as a Reason for Enquiry, by proving a Difference of Judgement about it, and to put in a Claim, in behalf of myself, and those who concur in my Opinion, to our undoubted Right of having a proper and constitutional Method taken, to confirm our Sentiment if true, and confute it if false. I therefore, as a previous Step, move, that the proper Officer may be directed to fulfil, what I take to be his first Orders, which were to bring in all the Inrollments of the Patents of the Masters of the Rolls, and Chancellors of the Exchequer, since the Revolution.

Mr S——,

I do not get up, Sir, to oppose what that worthy Gentleman has moved for, no Person in this House being more desirous to have its Orders fully and punctually obeyed, more zealous to facilitate a strict and impartial Enquiry into the Legality of every Act of the Crown, or, more truly follicitous to maintain the constitutional Rights of this Nation, than myself; neither, Sir, do I rise up with any Design to anticipate the Debate, on this important Affair, which must take Place when the main Question comes regularly before us; but, I get up to declare, that, in direct Opposition to his Opinion, I most firmly believe, that, granting the Office of Chancellor of the Exchequer for Life, is neither illegal, nor unprecedented, as he has supported: This difference of Opinion, however, as he has justly observed, is the strongest Proof of the Expediency of an Enquiry, and, that such an Enquiry may be properly made, I think the Officer ought, punctually, to fulfill his first Orders. I think, farther, Sir, that not only all the Enrollments,

since

since the Revolution, ought to be laid before us, as neceſſary to that Enquiry, but all the Inrollments, ſince the Act of *Henry* the VIIth, relative to judicial Employments; for, I muſt take upon me to ſay, Sir, that Laws and Precedents, before the Revolution, have, and ought to have, their Force. It is true, indeed, that the Proceedings of the Crown, immediately before the Revolution, made a Revolution neceſſary; and I glory and rejoice in the happy Effects it produced: But, Sir, there were Periods before that Criſis, when our Government was in a reſpectable and honourable State; and, though it has been juſt ſaid, not to be the general Opinion, that the great Employments in queſtion have been granted for Life, yet, I am not aſhamed to repeat, once again, that, in my Opinion, it is legal ſo to give them; and, I know, that, in more Inſtances than one, they have been ſo given, ſince the Statute of *Henry* the VIIth.

" Ordered, that the proper Officer do obey his firſt Order, and bring in all the Inrollments of the Patents, by which the Offices of the Chancellor of the Exchequer, Maſter of the Rolls, and Judges, have been granted."

A Mo-

A Motion was then made by Mr R— L—, that an humble Addreſs be preſented to the Lord Lieutenant, that he will be pleaſed to order the Report of his Majeſty's Attorney and Sollicitor-General of this Kingdom, with Reſpect to the Legality of granting the Office of Chancellor of the Exchequer of this Kingdom, for Life, to be laid before this Houſe.

Mr J— H— H—, P. S.

Mr S——,

I riſe, up, Sir, to oppoſe this Motion, which, I conſider, as moſt improper and unprecedented, and pregnant with the moſt pernicious Conſequences. The Attorney and Sollicitor-General, Sir, are Servants to the Crown, and, it is their peculiar Office and Duty, to give the Crown Information, when conſulted, concerning the Nature, Extent, and Operation of the Laws, according to which the Government of this Kingdom is adminiſtered; this Information they are ſworn to give faithfully, and, according to the Beſt of their Judgment, ſo as neither to infringe the Rights of the People, in favour of the Prerogative

gative, nor the Prerogative in favour of the People; and what Right, Sir, have we to require their Opinion to be laid before us? It is given, in Confidence and Secrecy, to the Crown, by its own Servants, and is that very Service which they are appointed to perform: It is given, alfo, under the Sanction of an Oath, and what other Security will the Nature of the thing admit? If the Opinion, given by thefe Gentlemen to the Crown, was liable to be canvaffed in this Houfe, and to be made the Subject of Debate and Conjecture, perhaps of Cenfure and Invective, the Confidence and Secrecy, under which it is given, would be deftroyed, and they would find themfelves under fuch Influence, and in fuch a Situation, as would almoft, unavoidably, prevent that perfect Freedom, which, it is abfolutely neceffary always to preferve and encourage, in order to enable them to fulfill the Duty of their Office. But, Sir, I will venture to go ftill farther: I will fuppofe, that we had fufficient Reafon to conclude, that they had given an erroneous Opinion, and, even that they had willfully violated their Confcience, their Judgments, and their Oaths, in order to gratify fome illegal Defire, and juftify fome illegal Meafure, with a View to recommend them-

themselves, by so doing, to the Fountain of Honour and Preferment: I say, Sir, that, even upon this Supposition, we should have no Right to require them to criminate themselves, by producing such Opinion to this House; I say, themselves, Sir, for, I consider the Crown, and its Servants, as one; and, I will venture to say, that no Instance can be produced, in which such Requisition was made, even in Times, when, perhaps, the Rules of Justice were not so closely adhered to as they ought. Besides, Sir, what is now moved for, is absurd; and, for that Reason alone, if there was no other, I would oppose it; to what, Sir, does our Enquiry tend? We are to judge the same Question, which has been put to the Attorney and Sollicitor-General, we are not to judge them for judging it; and we are to determine, Sir, according to our Sense of the Law, according to indubitable Precedent, and according to our own Information, and not according to the Opinion of Lawyers, of what Rank, or Ability soever; I shall, therefore, give my Voice against the Motion as unprecedented, and, in every Respect, improper.

Mr

Mr E— M—.

Mr S ——,

"That the King can do no Wrong," is a Maxim well known, and, I believe, generally allowed; but, Sir, I cannot sufficiently exprefs my Surprize and Concern, at hearing Opinions advanced, in this Houfe, from which it muft neceffarily follow, that the King's Minifters, or Servants, can do no Wrong. We have been told, Sir, that the King and his Servants are one, and, that we have no Right to addrefs the King to acquaint us with the Advice given to him by his Servants, upon the Principle, that no Man is to be required to criminate himfelf; but this Doctrine, Sir, has the common Fate of Error and Fallacy, it overturns the very Principle it would eftablifh; that the King can do Wrong is true only upon a Suppofition that his Servants may; and that they may be called to an Account for fo doing: If they cannot be called to an Account for doing Wrong, it is of very little Confequence to us, whether their being liable to do Wrong is allowed or denied. What is it to us, whether

they

they can, or cannot do Wrong, if, when it is allowed they do Wrong, we have no Remedy? And how are we to have this Remedy, Sir, but by addressing his Majesty, upon any wrong or doubtful Measure, to know what Advice was given him concerning it, and who was the Adviser? Gentlemen have talked much of Precedents in this House, and have very justly supposed that Precedent implies a Right, and confirms it; and, if so, I am sure we have most abundant Proof that this House has a Right to address the Crown, to do, what is called criminating its Servants, and that the Crown has complied with such Address. We have Precedents, Sir, enough, upon Record, of corrupt Advisers of Kings, who have betrayed the public Cause, being given up to public Justice; and, are we now to condemn all these Precedents at once? to explode the Principle upon which they were formed, and renounce the salutary Effects they produced, by supposing, that the Crown and its Servants are one, and, that when these Servants are perfidious, and betray their royal Master's highest Interest, by betraying that of his People, he cannot be addressed to disclose their Advice, because a Man ought not to be required to criminate himself! I say, Sir,

Sir, to disclose their Advice, for, to favour the Supposition that the King can do no Wrong, he is supposed only to carry the Advice of others into Execution; the Servants of the Crown are answerable for every illegal or unconstitutional Act that passes the great Seal; yet the Act is not theirs, the Signature that makes it valid is not theirs, and the Order for passing it is not theirs; all these Acts are the Acts of the Crown; for what, then, is the Servant, or Minister, answerable but for his Advice, without which these Acts would never have been done? And how are we to acquire an Ability to judge of this Advice, but by addressing the Crown to lay it before us, with all that has any immediate Relation to it? I will venture to say, Sir, that thus to address the Crown is not only our Right, but our Duty and our Interest; and it is also the Interest of the Crown to comply with such Address: If its Servants have been faithful, the more strict the Examination of their Conduct, the more Honour they will acquire; if they have not, it will be equally dangerous both to the Crown, and to the Constitution, to screen them. It has been said, Sir, that if the Advisers of the Crown were to give their Opinion, under a Sense of their

their being liable to have it canvaffed in this Houfe, they would not be able to give it freely: I confefs, Sir, this is the firft Time I ever heard it advanced, that, throwing a Weight only into one Scale, was a likely Way to hold the Balance in Equilibrio; what is fo likely to prevent a corrupt Minifter from wronging his Judgment, and his Confcience, to gratify fome unconftitutional Purpofe in the Crown, as the Profpect of being made anfwerable for his Perfidy, and fubjected to an Enquiry of this Houfe? If, indeed, by *free*, Gentlemen mean an Exemption from all Ties, that reftrain Men from doing Evil, I will allow, that the Councellors of the Crown will be lefs *free*, under the Profpect of a parliamentary Enquiry, than otherwife; but, I believe, no Gentleman prefent will be an Advocate for fuch Liberty, either in them, or in any other Member of civil Society; to bring my Reafoning home, Sir, to the Cafe in Queftion, I fay, that the Chancellorfhip of the Exchequer is an Employment of the higheft national Importance, that your Predeceffor in that Chair enjoy'd it many Years with the greateft Honour, that it is now granted for Life, and, that if fuch Grant fhould appear to be contrary to Law, it is fuch an Innovation of

our

our Rights as those who advised it ought to be impeached for: Though I have mentioned only the Post of Chancellor of the Exchequer, I would not be thought to except that of Master of the Rolls, yet, by naming those Offices, I mean nothing personally against either of the worthy Gentlemen who fill them; I mean, only, that, what they enjoy worthily, they should enjoy legally; and, that, while we are adorning the Superstructure of our Constitution, we should not subvert the Foundation. I am persuaded, Sir, that there are many Instances of Impeachment parallel to this; Lord *Somers*, Sir, was impeached for the Advice he gave, with Respect to the Partition Treaty; others might easily be named, but, not to deviate farther from the Point immediately in View, I must declare myself an Advocate for the Motion.

The R—t H—ble *F— A—*.

Mr S——,

I am, absolutely, overwhelmed with Astonishment, to hear any Gentleman talk of impeaching two of the King's Servants, for giving their Opinion, to the best of their Judgment, upon Oath; I say, to the best of their

Judgment, for so we must suppose their Opinion to be, and are bound to act according to that Supposition; the Proof of the contrary, with Respect to Advice, properly so called, to do, or not to do, any certain Act in suspence, being impossible, before any Judicature but that of him whose Prerogative it is to search the Heart: " The Tree may be known by its Fruit;" and, a bad Intention may, in many Cases, be certainly, and therefore fairly inferred, from Advice to a bad Act: The Act, therefore, advised to be done, is the proper Subject of Examination; but, if Gentlemen would not suffer their Zeal to out-run their Judgment, they would see, that, in the Case before us, there is no such Thing as Advice; there is no Act performed by the Parties, of which we can take Cognizance, because there is no Act performed, concerning which we can possibly determine, whether, with Respect to the Agent, it is good or bad. The Opinion of the Attorney, and Sollicitor-General, Sir, which Gentlemen have affected to call Advice, is given, upon a Question relative to what *is*, and not to what *may*, or *shall* be. It relates, Sir, to the Tenor and Effect of Laws now in force among us, and which have long been

so;

so; and, are the Attorney and Sollicitor-General, Sir, anfwerable for what thofe Laws enable the Crown to do? or, for what the Crown may do, upon a Suppofition that it exerts no Power, but fuch as thefe Laws give? The Attorney, and Sollicitor-General, Sir, are, in this Cafe, anfwerable only for their Integrity, and, even for their Integrity, they are anfwerable only to God, as God only can know whether they are, or are not, fincere: As to the Cafe of Lord *Somers*, I can fcarce perfuade myfelf that Gentlemen are ferious, when they mention it as parallel to that in queftion: Lord *Somers* advifed the doing a certain Act, which was, then, a Contingency. The Attorney and Sollicitor-General advife no Act, but merely give an Opinion, with Refpect to what is, or is not, right by Laws actually in being. If this is Advice, Sir, a Man may juftly be called an Advifer, who tells another, according to the beft of his Knowledge, the Hour of the Day; in fhort, Sir, there is as much Difference between the Cafe of Lord *Somers*, who advifed the Partition Treaty, and, that of the Attorney and Sollicitor-General, who give their Sentiments, on a Point of Law, as, between giving a Man my Opinion of the Weather, and, advifing him to take a Journey. Besides, Sir, the conferring any Favour upon an Individual, is a Thing of so private a Nature——

Mr E—— M——.

—— So private a Nature! It amazes me, Sir, to hear that Right Honourable Genman, who was once so great an Honour and Ornament to the Law, make Use of that Expression; though the Object of the King's Favour be an Individual, yet the Favour conferred is such as interests the Public in the highest Degree; it is one of the first Offices in the Kingdom, and, the Power it confers, may be so exerted, as to be of the most fatal Consequence to the Public; but, waving this, Sir, the great Question is, whether the giving this Office for Life, be it important, or be it trivial, is not an Infringement of the Law? If it is not, whatever Danger may be incurred by it, it behoves us to submit; but if it is, I hope no Gentleman here will think of implicitly acquiescing in it, under a Notion of its being of a private Nature.

Mr.

Mr W— H—.

Mr S———,

I am under very great Obligations to the honourable Gentleman, who sits on the opposite Bench, for confirming my Sentiments, by declaring his own to be the same; and I assure you, Sir, that it has given me the highest Opinion of his Judgment, which I shall for ever honour and respect. My Sentiment, Sir, which has had the Honour of being thus confirmed, is, that Lawyers *do*, and that they *should* differ, in Opinions, upon Points of Law; I think, also, that it is very proper for Lawyers, upon some Occasions, not only to differ from one another, but from themselves; I believe there are many Gentlemen present, who have found the Advantage of it. If all Lawyers were to be of the same Opinion, what Subjects could there be for Litigation? If there were no Subjects for Litigation, there would very soon be no Lawyers; and, if there were no Lawyers, what would People do for Advice, and, to whom could even the Crown have applied upon the great and momentous Occasion that we are now considering? And, Sir, if the same Lawyer's Opinion was always to be the same in an Afternoon, as in a Morning, to what Purpose would Recourse be had to any of those cogent Arguments, which are now known to alter it? all Rhetoric, Sir, the most powerful Rhetoric would be useless, and that which could never be used would never be acquired; we should stagnate in Stupefaction and Inactivity, for want of Motives to act and to think; so that nothing less could happen from 'all Lawyers thinking like each other, and, from the same Lawyers always thinking alike, than what Gentlemen seem to have inferred from much less Injury offered to the Law, the total Subversion of our Constitution, and Ruin of the State. I cannot sufficiently admire and commend my worthy Friend's Opinion, that my Brethren of the Law ought always to be consulted, especially upon important and public Occasions; it is an Opinion from which great and manifest Advantages will result, if it should be adopted; and, I cannot but congratulate with my Brethren, that it is adopted in a very considerable Degree already. There are knotty Points, which, even those august Personages, the Lords, to whom we, in this lower House, look up with an humble Sense of our Inferiority,

ority, may, possibly, find it something difficult to discuss; they have, therefore, as it is very fit and becoming that they should, the Prime of our Lawyers for their Councellors; the Lawyer of a Lord, Sir, should not certainly be less than a Judge; and, accordingly, we see that our learned Judges, seated on the soft Wool Pack, and distinguished by the scarlet Robe, are always at Hand, in their House, to be occasionally consulted by them, to save them the Labour of thinking, which is, certainly, beneath the Dignity of Personages, so sublime and august. If it is fit, as my worthy Friend has advanced, and, as I heartily agree, that Lawyers ought *always* to be consulted, it is fit that we should have our Lawyers too, and, it gives me great Pleasure to see that we are not without them; look which Way I will, some of the learned Body are still in my Eye; and, this, being the Case, what need have we to look abroad? It would neither do us, nor our Lawyers Credit, to have Consultations, without Doors, to explain or determine what they are expected to explain, and we are to determine within. I humbly conceive, Sir, that this Affair, great, and solemn, and momentous, as it is, may maintain its Dignity in Parliament, as well

well as in a Court of Law; and be as skillfully discussed, and as wisely determined. As to the laying the written Opinion of the Attorney, and Sollicitor-General, before the House, I confess, I do not see what End it will answer. I have heard of a mechanical Philosopher, who, having spent many Years in the Discovery of the perpetual Motion, at last invented a Machine, consisting of a great Variety of Wheels, Levers, Pullies, and other Powers, which would draw a Cork out of a Bottle, very nearly as well as a Cork-Screw: We have the Attorney and Sollicitor-General here with us, and, instead of the round about Way of addressing to have the Opinion they were of some time ago, laid before us, instead of having Recourse to the Machine with Wheels, and Levers, and Pullies, let us ask them their Opinions at once, and draw the Cork out of the Bottle ourselves. There are, to be sure, many Objections against examining Persons *viva voce*. A worthy Gentleman, at the Bar, once told a Judge, that he had no less than twenty such Objections; and, being allowed to declare them, he said, that the first was, that the Man was dead. This was allowed to be satisfactory, and the other nineteen were not required. What they were, I cannot take

take upon me to say, but, Sir, as the Gentlemen, whose Opinion we desire to know, are not only living, but present, and able, and willing, to give the Satisfaction required, I do not think any one of the twenty Objections, whatever they were, can be supported against them. What their Opinion *was*, I cannot tell, and, if I could, I might be equally at a Loss to know what their Opinion *is*; as the Gentlemen, therefore, are ready to answer for themselves, I must, with the greatest Deference to the Opinion of my worthy Friend, declare myself against the Motion.

It passed in the Negative, 75 to 32.

SATURDAY, *Oct.* 29, 1763.

SIXTH DAY.

Mr *J— H— H—*, P. S.

Mr S——,

AS it is of the higheſt Importance, to prevent the Monopoly of Coals in this City, and the Extortion which a Monopoly never fails to produce, and, as an Act was paſſed laſt Seſſions for this Purpoſe, I think it is very proper, that we ſhould enquire how far that Act has been effectual, in order to continue it, or amend it, as ſhall appear to be neceſſary; and, I hope the worthy Gentlemen, who, by that Act, were appointed to carry it into Execution, will not think it amiſs, that it ſhould be the Deſire of this Houſe, that they ſhould attend, to give what Information they can upon the Subject, and inform the Houſe, in what manner they have fulfilled the Truſt repoſed in them. I, therefore, beg leave to move, that a Committee may be appointed to take into Conſideration, an Act to prevent the excessive Price of Coals, in the City of *Dublin*, and, whether the said Act is proper to be continued, and, whether any, and what Amendments be necessary, to be made therein; as also, to enquire into the Conduct of the Officers, intrusted with the Execution of the said Act.

It was then moved, that the Call of the House, which, by Order, now stands for next *Monday*, be adjourned till *Tuesday*, the Day following.

To this, Mr *H— F—* objected, and said, that he believed it was understood, that the very interesting and important Question, concerning the Pensions, was to come on, when the Call should take Place, and, he was both against deferring it, and losing a Day; he observed, that the House sat but six Months in two Years, a space of Time, which, if every Hour of it was employed, in the Business of the Nation, would be little enough to do it with the Deliberation and Attention it required, and, that, as a great Encroachment had already been made upon that Time, by late Meetings, and Recesses, he was unwilling

that

that another Day should be lost; he said, he feared also, that it might be made a Precedent to lop off a sixth Part of the Time, that it was their Interest, as well as Duty, to improve, which was his principal Reason against it, and that to the Motion, simply considered, he thought it scarcely worth while to object.

Day VII.] *Affairs of* Ireland.   111

MONDAY, *Nov.* 1, 1763.

SEVENTH DAY.

THE R—t H—ble Mr *B— B—* presented a Petition of *Henry Cottingham,* and *James King,* of the City of *Dublin,* Mercers, setting forth the Losses by them sustained, by the Journeymen Weavers, and Apprentices, of the City and Liberties, by cutting to Pieces many rich and beautiful Silks, and Velvets, then in the Looms of the Petitioners, and the Materials, Tackle, and Silk prepared for carrying on a Silk and Velvet Manufacture, all the Property of the Petitioners; and that the said misguided People (become sensible of their Injustice to the Petitioners, and of the great Injury and Damage they have brought upon themselves and their Country) have requested the Petitioners, to improve, and advance the Silk Manufacture of *Ireland*; which, the Petitioners, from their heavy Losses, are unable to do without the Aid of Parliament; and praying Relief.

The

The Petition being read, Mr *B*— moved, that it might be referred to the Confideration of a Committee, and, he was feconded by Mr *J— G—*, the S. G. as follows:

Mr S——,

As to the Allegations of the Petition, which the R—t H—ble Member has propofed to refer to the Committee, they are certainly the proper Objects of the Enquiry of that Committee, as they relate particularly to the Petitioners, but, as they are of a Nature that deeply affects the public Peace and Security, repugnant to all Duty, and fubverfive of all Order, they deferve the moft ferious and folemn Attention of this Houfe. It appears, by the Petition, that the treafonable Infurrections, which have fo frequently, of late, interrupted the public Tranquillity in remote Parts of the Kingdom, have now reached the Capital; infulted public Juftice on her Seat and fhaken the Government at its Centre; we are now called upon, not only to redrefs a private Wrong, but to affert the Caufe of an injured Nation: Not to reprefs the Violence here, by fome fignal Exertion of Legiflative

Au-

Authority, would be to encourage it elsewhere, for what will the Insurgents of remote Provinces conclude from the Impunity of those at the Metropolis, but, that the Government, conscious of its own Weakness, has surrendered at Discretion, and given up the common Rights and Privileges, which it could no longer defend, to the Mercy of a dissolute and outrageous Rabble? That I may not be thought to aggravate the Evil, by a rhetorical Display of imaginary Guilt, and imaginary Consequences, I will take the Liberty, Sir, to give you a plain Narrative of the Fact. A considerable Dealer in this City, who not only carries on a very extensive home Manufactury, but a respectable foreign Commerce, thought proper to import a large Quantity of *French* Silks, whether, as Patterns for weaving Silks here, or for Sale, it matters not; the Importation, with either View, is equally lawful; upon this, a Number of Manufacturers, taking it into their Heads to prohibit, as a private Injury to themselves, what the Law allows as a national Benefit, got together in a riotous Band, armed themselves in a hostile Manner, and, professing no less than Robbery, and Murder, beset the honest Trader's House, demanded, that

he

he should be delivered up to death, and, that his Silks, both those imported, and in the Loom, should be put into their Possession; when these Proceedings were opposed by a legal Force, under proper Officers, they flew in the Face of Justice, openly defied Authority, and, having overpowered the Magistrate, and his Assistants, they persisted in their Violence, to the Affright, and Confusion of the whole City: It has been observed, that in the Apparatus of Death there is more Terror than in Death itself; these Wretches, therefore, that the Murder they were prepared to perpetrate, might lose none of its Effect, carried a Coffin in Procession to the House of the Victim they had singled out, swearing, with horrid Imprecations, that they would carry off his dead Body in it: It happened, however, that he effectually secreted himself from their Fury, till it, in some Degree, subsided, but, they forced him to ratify such Conditions as they thought fit to dictate, by the most solemn Oaths; yet this, whatever Security they might think it, for his Behaviour in the Time to come, did not satisfy their Revenge for what was past; they, therefore, broke violently into his Work-shop, and Warehouses, cut great Quantities of valuable

and

and beautiful Silk and Velvet to pieces, broke his Looms, and, either, ſtole or deſtroyed whatever elſe they could lay their Hands upon. While this was doing, the unhappy Victim, his Family, and his Friends, were in an Agony of Conſternation and Terror; the City itſelf was ſtruck with a Panic, and no Man knew where the Violence might ſtop. It is a dreadful thing, Sir, for a licentious Rabble to wreſt the Sword out of the Hands of Juſtice, and to enforce, with Tumult, and Violence, the Execution of Laws which they apprehend to be eluded; but, it is an Evil that admits of no Aggravation, for them to impoſe Laws of their own, in Oppoſition to thoſe of the State; and, invade, not only Property, but Life, when they happen capriciouſly, to diſapprove the Conduct of thoſe, by whom, they do not ſo much as pretend any Law has been broken. I ſay, Sir, this is a Crime, which, with Reſpect to itſelf, can admit of no Aggravation, but with Reſpect to the Criminals, it may; if it appears to be committed not by the Ignorant and Thoughtleſs, but by the Knowing and Conſiderate; not by the Obſcure and Indigent, but by thoſe, whoſe Station and Property give Influence to their Example; not by thoſe who are in a ſubordinate and ſervile

State, but by "those that are put in Authority over them," how does the Guilt accumulate upon their Heads, and, of how much severer Punishment are they worthy? I am sorry to say, Sir, that this Guilt has been accumulated, and this Punishment deserved in the Case before us: My particular Situation, Sir, has acquainted me with the whole of this Transaction, from its first Cause, to its last Effects, and, I find myself, with inexpressible Regret, obliged to declare, that it appears with the strongest Evidence, upon various Examinations, that the Persons, who gave rise to it, are no other, than the Master and Wardens of the Corporation of Weavers, and, that the poor deluded Wretches, who, actually did the Mischief, were spirited up by them, acted under their Influence, and were little more than the Instruments of their Wickedness; yes, Sir, the Master and Wardens of that Corporation, who are intrusted by their Charter, with a very considerable Power, in confidence that they would use it for the Regulation, and good Government of its Members, have, in that very Hall, and in those very Seats, where, they ought to have exerted themselves "as a Terror to evil doers, and, a Reward to those who do well," per-

verted

verted their Inſtitution, and abuſed their Power, to the worſt of all Purpoſes, by ſeducing the Poor, and the Dependant, to Tumult and Rapine, Violence and Murder, the Ruin of Innocence, and the Subverſion of Government. It appears amongſt other Things, that the Maſter of the Corporation actually ſent Ambaſſadors on behalf of the Inſurgents, to Mr *Cottingham*, in order to bring him into a Capitulation with them, and prevail upon him, to give up the offending Silks, to be burnt, in compliance with their Demands, inſinuating, that there were no other Means to prevent more fatal Conſequences; upon theſe Facts I ſhall make no Comment, as, I am perſuaded, no Comment is neceſſary; the Expediency of taking the moſt effectual Meaſures, to prevent ſuch rebellious Inſurrections, for the future, is ſelf-evident, as they ſtrike, I had almoſt ſaid, at the very Exiſtence of our Conſtitution; if I have treſpaſſed long upon your Time, by an Endeavour to point out the Evils, that call aloud for a Remedy, in their moſt ſtriking Colours, I flatter myſelf, that I ſhall be excuſed, without an Apology, as I had no View in diſplaying the Malignancy of the Diſeaſe, but, that the Method of Cure might be vigorous and ſpeedy. As the End of War is Peace, so the End of Justice is Mercy: Whatever Punishment deters from Vice, prevents Misery; and, I am sure, I cannot more effectually exert my Benevolence, than by calling out the Terrors of the Law, against Practices which cut off Reward from Labour, and Security from Innocence; which, corrupt Poverty into Wickedness, and endanger the Vitals of the Constitution, by spreading a Gangrene in its Members.

The R—t H—ble *F— A—* then got up, and expressed his perfect Agreement with the learned and worthy Member that spoke last, with Respect to the Necessity of putting a stop, immediately, to the unbounded Licentiousness of the lower Class of People; a Licentiousness, which, he observed, was so different from the true Spirit of Liberty, that it was impossible they should subsist together; he said, also, that he could not, but greatly admire his pathetic, and animated Description of the Enormities of which he complained, and the various Distresses, which they produced: But, he said, he hoped to be excused, for differing a little from him, as he could not lay the Riot, wholly, to the Charge of his *Brethren,* the Weavers; (this caused a great Laugh,

Laugh, as he had juft been complimented with the Freedom of their Company) but, was rather of Opinion, that it was raifed, and carried on, by their Journeymen and Apprentices; efpecially, as they frequently entered into Combinations againſt their Mafters themfelves, demanding, in a clamorous and tumultous Manner, fometimes, the raifing their Wages, and, fometimes, the fhortening their Hours of Work.

Mr J— H— H—, P. S.

Mr S——,

I rife up to give my Opinion, that the Allegations of the Petition are an Object highly worthy of a parliamentary Enquiry; and, that as two worthy Members of Society have greatly, and moſt unjuſtly, fuffered by the illegal Proceedings of an enraged Mob, to the great Injury of a Manufacture, which they were carrying on, very much for the Benefit of the Nation, it is but juſt, that they fhould be redreffed, as well, upon their own Account, as upon that of the Public; I was alfo, the more ready to rife, on this Occafion, as, I over heard fome Gentlemen near me, make an Objection to the Petition, which it is in my Power to remove; they said, that a Petition of this Kind was a Novelty, and unsupported by Precedent; but this is by no means the Fact, for, I remember, among other Instances, a parallel Case, that happened in a neighbouring Kingdom, in the Year 1715: At that Time there were great Riots among the Woollen Manufacturers, and great Damage was done, upon which the Sufferers applied to Parliament, and a Compensation was allowed them of above five thousand Pounds; and, now, that my Endeavours may not be wanting, to continue the good Humour, which was raised by the worthy Gentleman who spoke last, and, that Gentlemen may have their laugh out, which, my getting up interrupted, I must say, that the Weavers are *my* Brethren too, and that, I am very willing to hope, they are not so culpable as the worthy Gentleman, who seconded the Motion, seems to think them; I am persuaded, that he speaks from the Conviction he has received by the Examination, but, perhaps, he has seen the Examinations only of one Side, and that Story which is good till another is told, is not always so afterwards. As to the Master and Wardens of the Company, I have

I have frequently converfed with them upon the Subject; and, if they are not the greateft Hypocrites, as well as the wickedeft Men in the World, they are wholly Innocent in this Affair; for they have afferted their Innocence with the moſt folemn and repeated Afleverations.

Mr *J— G—*, S. G. in a fhort Reply, gave fome farther Reafons, why he believed the Mafter and Wardens of the Corporation, to have been effentially, and originally, concerned in the Riot: And Mr *C— C—*, made a fhort Speech, with a View to palliate what had been advanced againſt the Mafter Weavers, and to throw the whole Blame upon their Journeymen.

TUESDAY, *Nov.* 2, 1763.

EIGHTH DAY.

The R—t H—ble *F— A—*.

Mr S——,

I Have, in my Hand, a Petition, figned by the Mayor, Corporation, and principal Inhabitants of the City of *Londonderry*; it has always been held, Sir, that the rewarding eminent Merit, in particulars, is a general Benefit, by ftimulating others to Emulation, and exciting them to the fame Defert, by hopes of the fame Advantage. I, therefore, flatter myfelf, that I fhall not be thought unneceffarily to take up your Time, by faying a few Words in favour of your prefent Petitioners. If this Nation had been fo happy as to have its Hiftory written by any Author of Abilities equal to the Work, the Actions of the Citizens of *Derry*, would have furnifhed its moft fhining Paffages; Paffages, which would have embellifhed the moft illuftrious Hifiory, 'and highly honoured the moft heroic Nation. The want of fuch Hiftorians,

torians, is, indeed, the less to be regretted, as we have the most authentic Records of such Loyalty, Magnanimity, and public Spirit, in that antient, protestant, and unconquered City, as would shake the Credit of any Historian, however eminent for Impartiality and Truth, if they depended merely upon his Testimony. The Records I mean, Sir, are the Journals of this House, and of the Commons in *England*; you will there find the Citizens of *Derry*, supporting the Laws, the Religion, and the Liberty of their Country, in defiance of all the Miseries, that the Cruelty of War, aggravated by the sanguinary Rage of Bigotry, and Superstition, could bring upon them; to say, that they gave their Lives a Ransom for the Blessings, which their Posterity enjoy, is to wrong them of more than half their Praise, if we do not consider the Manner, in which it was paid; the Pomp of War, and the Sound of the Trumpet, awake in almost every Mind a sudden and tumultuous Courage, which, rather overlooks Danger, than defies it; and, rather suspends our Attention to Life, than reconciles us to the Loss of it; the Soldier rushes forward with Impetuosity, and, when he hears the Thunder of the Battle, can glory in the Elation of his Mind; but when Death

ap-

approaches, with a flow and filent Pace, when he is feen at leifure, and, contemplated in all his Terrors, the Spirits fhrink back to the Heart, the Love of Fame, and, even the Hope of Heaven is chilled within us, and the Man at once prevails, not over the Hero only, but the Saint. Of the few, that, in this Hour of Horror, have furmounted the Senfe of their own Condition, who is he that has looked with the fame Equanimity upon the Partner of his Fortune, and the Pledges of his Love? When a Wife, or a Child, has been a Hoftage, and the Tyrant's Dagger has been lifted to their Breaft, how has the Hero and the Patriot melted in the Hufband and the Father! By what Name, then, fhall we diftinguifh the Virtue of the Citizens of *Derry*, who did not rufh upon Death for their Country, in the momentary Ardor of fudden Conteft, in the Pomp and Tumult of the Field of Battle, but waited his deliberate, though irrefiftable approach, fhut up within their own Walls, in the gloomy Recefles of Sicknefs and Famine; and who, while they felt the Pangs of Hunger, undermining Life in themfelves, beheld, alfo, its deftructive Influence in thofe whofe Lives were ftill dearer than their own; who heard the faltering Voice of helplefs Infancy

fancy complain, till the Sounds, at laft, died upon the Tongue; and, who faw the languid Eye of fainting Beauty exprefs what no Language could utter, till it was clofed in Death! In this Trial to ftand firm, in this Conflict to be more than Conquerors, was it not, alfo, to be more than Men! To have been the Birth-Place, or the Refidence of one fuch Hero, would have fired a thoufand Cities with Envy, and have rendered the meaneft Hamlet illuftrious for ever; what, then, is *Derry*, whofe whole Inhabitants were animated by this divine Virtue, like a common Soul! Nor is it ftrange, that their Pofterity fhould be ftill diftinguifhed by the fame Spirit; for, how is it poffible they fhould hear the Recital of thefe Wonders, and enjoy the Benefits they procured, without glowing at once with Gratitude and Emulation: Their Virtue, from whatever Caufe, has been long hereditary already. In the Civil Wars of 1641, *Derry* was the impregnable City, which baffled all the Force of the Rebels, to the Encouragement and Support of the whole North of *Ireland*. In the glorious Revolution of 1688, a Crifis, perhaps, the moft important that ever happened in any Age, or any Country, *Derry* ftood forth the Bulwark

of

of the Laws, Religion, and Liberty, of this Nation; to *Derry* we all owe, in a great Measure, the ample and peaceable Possession of them in which we are happy at this Day; and, how *Derry* behaved, during the late Insurrections, we need not be told. A Series of Acknowledgments and Thanks, recorded in the Journals of this House, from its first Institution, to the present Time, are, at once, the most authentic Testimony of the distinguished Merit of this City, and its most glorious and permanent Reward. But, though all private Encomium may be precluded, as an Honour to *Derry*, it may, perhaps, be indulged as a Pleasure to me, and, let me add, to those, also, before whom I speak; for, I am confident, that, among all who hear me, there is not one, who would not, from the same Motive, and, with the same Pleasure, have spoken of her Citizens as I have done, except where my Language has been inadequate to my Ideas, and there, I am confident, they would have supplied the Defect. As to the Allegation, and the Prayer of the Petition, though, as I observed, it is a general Benefit to reward Merit, yet, I must do my Constituents this farther Justice to say, that, if what they solicit, had not, exclusive of this Principle,

ple, been a national Advantage, they would not have made it the Object of their Solicitation; that Modesty and Moderation, which are the inseperable Concomitants of Merit, and that Uprightness, and Generosity of Mind, which would disdain to request the Application of any Part of the public Treasure to a private Use, would have prevented them. The Trade of the City of *Derry*, Sir, is, within these few Years, greatly increased, with Respect to Imports and Exports; the single Article of the Linen Manufacture, amounts to no less than 200,000*l. per Ann.* There are, belonging to this Port, four and twenty Ships, from two hundred to three hundred Tons burthen, and, I believe, there are very few other Ports, in the Kingdom, which employ as many; but the Water is too shallow, even at high Tide, to float these Vessels to the Quay; the River, also, is so narrow, as to render the Navigation very inconvenient, so that the Merchants of *Derry* are obliged to pay eight Pence a Ton for Lighterage of all Goods, both in and out, and are considerable Sufferers by Risque, Damage, and Delay. To render this Part of the River more commodious, and to deepen the Channel, will require about 1,600*l.* by the best Computation

that

that can be made ; the Sum is, comparatively, very fmall, and the Advantage will be great, not only to *Derry*, but to the Nation in general ; for every Encouragement given to Trade, is like an Addition of vital Strength to the Heart, which is immediately diffufed to the remoteft Parts of the Body. I, therefore, pray, that this Petition may be read.

The Petition was read accordingly, to the Purport as fet forth above, and, it was ordered to be referred to a Committee ; upon which a Committee was appointed accordingly.

A Petition of *Margaret Afhworth*, Widow of *Thomas Afhworth*, late of *Dennybrook*, in the County of the City of *Dublin*, Linnen, Cotton, Callico, and Paper Printer, deceafed ; praying Aid to enable her to carry on thofe Manufactures, was prefented, and read.

Mr *T— M—* then moved, that it might be referred to a Committee.

Mr E— S— P—.

Mr S——,

I find that vast Numbers of People have come from every Part of the Kingdom, with Petitions of this Kind, praying parliamentary Aid to carry on different Manufactures; and, as it would be imprudent to detain them from their Business, and cruel to keep them in Suspence, it being impossible to gratify half of them, I think, it is fit we should know the Sense of the House with Respect to Petitions, of this Kind in general: The granting of Money, by Parliament, on these Occasions, is a Practice but of late Years; however, I confess, that I was one of those who thought it for the Benefit of Trade, by improving various Manufactures into greater Degrees of Perfection; but Experience, Sir, from which there can be no Appeal, has, at length, convinced me that I was mistaken, and, that it has produced an Effect directly opposite to that which was intended; in some Instances it has put an End to the very Manufacture it was supposed to encourage, and, in others, it has favoured a Monopoly, and repressed the Industry

Induſtry of many, by giving to a few an undue Superiority over them, which muſt always be the Caſe, when large Sums of Money are poured into the Hands of particular Perſons; I mean large, with Reſpect to the Circumſtances of thoſe who receive them, and ſuch have been the ſmalleſt that Parliament has thought fit to grant. I am very ſenſible, Sir, that Manufacturers ſhould be encouraged by all poſſible Means, and, that no Object can be more worthy either of the Attention, or the Bounty, of Parliament. It is impoſſible that many ſhould live, where few can be employed; it is by Labour, only, that the Inhabitants of a civilized Country can ſubſiſt; and it is, therefore, impoſſible, that any civilized Country ſhould be populous, where there is little to do. As no Country, that is not populous, can be either flouriſhing or ſtrong, and, as it is manifeſtly the Intereſt of every Individual, that the Country, in which he lives, ſhould be both, it follows, that the Encouragement of Manufactures, by which, alone, Multitudes can be employed, is eſſential to the Proſperity, if not to the very Subſiſtence of the State. Upon this Principle, therefore, inſtead of granting large Sums, to particular Perſons, to diſpoſe of

as

as they pleafe, I think we fhould apply them in liberal Premiums, for different Manufactures, as they are brought to Market, in Proportion to their Quantity and Excellence; this would be an univerfal Encouragement, and would diffufe an univerfal Spirit of Diligence and Emulation, as every Man would afpire to gain what was offered, not to this, or the other Individual, but to whomfoever fhould excel. I have, myfelf, within this few Days, had many Petitions of the fame Kind, with that now offered, put into my Hand, all which I refufed to prefent, and, fhall give it as my Opinion, that no more fhould be received, and that one only fhould lie upon the Table, to determine the Fate of the reft.

Mr *T— M—* anfwered, that other Petitions, of the fame Kind, had been introduced, without being objected to; that he thought it very hard his fhould be the firft that was refufed, and, that he did not fee why he fhould not have his JOBB done as well as another.

Mr *E— S— P—*, in reply, declared, upon his Honour, that this was the firft Petition of the Kind that he had heard introduced,

and,

and, that if he had been prefent, when others were introduced, he would have objected to them; that he had the higheſt Reſpect for the honourable Member who introduced this, and, he was ſo far from meaning any Thing like a perſonal Oppoſition, that if he could bring himſelf to ſubmit to do a JOBB at all, he would do his JOBB as ſoon as any Man's.

The Queſtion being put, that the ſaid Petition be referred to a Committee, it was carried in the Affirmative, by 69 againſt 55; and a Committee was appointed accordingly.

Mr E— S— P—.

Mr S——,

As I ſhall always be diſpoſed to ſubmit my private Judgment to that of this Houſe, I conclude, that I had made a wrong Determination, as I ſee the Majority is againſt me, and ſhall, therefore, preſent many Petitions, which have been offered me, and which I ſhould, otherwiſe, have refuſed. But, notwithſtanding the Diviſion for reading this Petition, I am perſuaded that many Gentlemen, who divided for it, muſt be extremely ſorry to ſee the public Money laviſhed away in
JOBBS,

Jobes, which might be otherwise employed to public Advantage: I am very sorry that I happened not to be present when the first Petition of this Kind was introduced, that I might have objected against it; but, I hope, some Method will still be found to signify the Disinclination which, I am sure, the House has to these Applications.

Dr C— L—.

Mr S——,

I do not rise up to oppose the worthy Gentleman, who made the Motion with Respect to the Petition, for, I believe, the utmost that he requires, is, that it should be referred to a Committee, for them to enquire into the Merits, and report to the House; but I am very much against Petitions of this Kind, in general, and so, I hope, every Gentleman will be, who recollects the vast Sums that have been granted upon them, and the Use that has been made of the Money. I remember, a considerable Sum was given last Sessions to the Proprietor of a Glass-House on the *Strand*, who, the Moment he got it, instead of setting himself to blow Bottles, set his House on Fire, blew it up, and then went about his Bufinefs. Large Sums were alfo given to the Cambric Manufactory, and, the next Thing we heard of it, was, that the Proprietors were Bankrupts. One *Delamain* got Money for making *Rhone* Ware, and the Work has been difcontinued from that Time to this. The Parliament has, alfo, difpofed of large Sums, for the like Purpofes, by the *Dublin* Society; and, I think, fome Enquiry fhould be made, whether the Money, with the Difpofal of which they have been entrufted, has turned to a better Account than what we diftributed ourfelves. But an Incident has happened, Sir, in this Debate, much more alarming than the Mifapplication of Money granted to Manufacturers; a Word has been ufed as a Denifon of this Houfe, which is a Difgrace to Language, as it expreffes what cannot exift without difgracing human Nature, by the moft flagitious Sacrifice of public to private Intereft, under a Pretence of Patriotifm, and Attention, to National Advantages. I have heard, Sir, the Word JOBB, and, I have heard it ufed as an avowed Name for a Meafure recommended to Parliament, under Colour of encouraging a Manufacture: Do Gentlemen, then, acknowledge the bringing in, and foliciting JOBBS? and, do the

Mem-

Members of this House, professedly, do JOBBS for one another, instead of fulfilling the Trust reposed in them by their Constituents, and transacting the Business of the Nation! I am now, unfortunately, seated between two Gentlemen who have banded the Word JOBB from one to another in a Sense, and Manner, which makes it justly to be apprehended, that we have lost not only Virtue, but Shame; that we have done Evil till we have mistaken it for Good. One asks, " Why should not I have my JOBB done, as well as another?" he is answered, from the opposite Side of the House, " If you will do my JOBBS, I will do yours." The very Air, Sir, that conveys such Sounds, is contaminated, and it has crossed me till it has made me sick; the Word JOBB is not only an odious, but a pestilential Monosyllable, and, I most sincerely hope, that I shall never again hear it mentioned in this House, without the most opprobrious Epithets that can possibly be invented, as none can sufficiently express its Turpitude and Malignity *.

---

* Though Dr *L—*'s Observations were just, with Respect to Mr *M—*, yet he has mistaken Mr *P—*; for Mr

Mr *R— F—*.

Mr S——,

As I perceive many Gentlemen have taken the Liberty to deviate, confiderably, from the Matter in Debate, I hope I may be indulged in a fmall Digreffion, with Refpect to a certain Monofyllable, which has greatly affected a Gentleman at the other End of the Houfe; and, he himfelf has declared, has even made him fick: This Monofyllable, Sir, is the Name of a certain illegitimate Child, of *Publick Spirit*, whom the World has agreed to call JOBB. He is well known in this Houfe, and, I am forry to fay, has not been ill received in it; permit me, therefore, to give fome farther Account of his Defcent and Family, his Character and Qualifications. I have already obferved, that his Mother is *Publick Spirit*; this Lady, though fhe is defervedly efteemed for many great and good Qualities,

---

Mr *P—* did not fay, if Mr *M—* would do his JOBBS, he would do Mr *M---*'s; but, that if he could fubmit to do a JOBB at all, he would as foon do it for Mr *M---* as for any Man.

is known to have a *Freedom of Principle*, and a *Warmth of Conſtitution*, which, concurring with Opportunity, ſpecious Pretences, and ſolemn Aſſurances, have frequently ſubverted her Chaſtity, and ſeduced her to the Embraces of the meaneſt and the moſt unworthy Wretches in the World: Among theſe was *Self-Intereſt*, by whom *Publick Spirit* has a numerous Iſſue, diſtinguiſhed by the Name of JOBB; how they came to be ſo called I ſhall not at preſent enquire, but, it is certain, that, as to their outward Appearance, they greatly reſemble their Mother, and that, in their Principles and Diſpoſitions, they are altogether like their Father. Their Reſemblance to *Public Spirit* has enabled them to do much Miſchief, by executing the Projects of *Private Intereſt*; they have been diſperſed all over the World, and have acted in every Sphere. They have eſtabliſhed great Empires, and brought them to Deſtruction; they have placed Monarchs upon a Throne, and baniſhed them to a Deſert; they have appeared in the Character of *Alexanders*, *Bourbons*, and *Ravilliacs:* They have been active both in Church and State, from the Miniſter to the Contractor, from the Archbishop to the Curate, from the Judge to the *Newgate* Sollicitor, from the Commander in Chief to the Quarter Master, from the Court Physician to the Itinerant Quack; they have always flourished in Proportion to the Wealth and Generosity of the Country, where they have resided; and, though this Country cannot boast to have been visited by many of the Offspring, which *Public Spirit* has born to a worthy Father, yet many of the *Jobbs*, her Children, by *Self-Interest*, have come over hither from a neighbouring Kingdom, and have, with great Success, played, both upon our Virtues and our Weakness: They have flattered us, by telling us, that we were Rich; and, they have amused us, by pretending to encrease our Riches; they have applauded our Generosity; and, to give us an Opportunity of shewing, that we have deserved the Complement, have been very free in soliciting Favours; this Opportunity we have seldom failed to improve; we have lavished upon them whatever they required; they, in return have gone off with their Booty, exulting in their own Cunning, and despising our Simplicity.

One

One of this hopeful Progeny, who happened to be born on this Side of the Water, about ten Years ago, found a Hoard of Money, which, as is a common Cafe, betrayed him into ftrange Inconfiftencies, fo that fome Perfons did not fcruple to fay, he was befide himfelf; it was his Cuftom, for fome time afterwards, to fally forth, attended by Drummers and Trumpeters, and a licentious, and diforderly Rabble, crying out, in a difmal and frantic Tone, O! my Country! my bleeding Country! The little Boys ran away, crying and frighted, and the Women fell into fits; but, at laft, he fat down with his Affociates about him, treated them with Whifky, and Tobacco, till they could neither fee, fpeak, nor ftir; and, declared, that *Ireland* was the happieft Country in the World, that all Minifters were Patriots, and, attended to nothing but eftablifhing Liberty, and rewarding Merit *.

Some

---

* In the Year 1753, it was difcovered, that there was a very large Sum in the Treafury unapplied, and, for which, there was no call; many Perfons affected great Fears, that it would be unconftitutionally difpofed of.

Some of the Family of the *Jobbs*, are still among us, and endeavour to conceal themselves under borrowed Names, and Characters; but it is most certainly the Duty, and, I most sincerely hope, the Inclination, of every Member, of this august Assembly to detect, and banish them for ever.

That they may be the more easily discovered, I shall mention several particular Characteristics, which, by a penetrating Eye, may be seen through all their Disguises. They very often assume their Mother's Name, and pretend, that their Father was *Integrity*, a Gentleman of very honourable Descent, who, having of late Times, been much neglected, by Persons of Power and Interest, has fallen into Misfortunes, and been obliged to play at Hide and Seek, so that having been long in Obscurity, nobody knows where he is. This Pretence, frequently procures them great Po-

---

of. An Opposition against the Court was made, by a numerous Party, but, some time afterwards, finding themselves mistaken, they accepted of Court Preferment, and tacitly acquiesced in Court Measures.

pularity,

Day VIII.] *Affairs of* IRELAND.   141

pularity, of which they are very fond; but, the Fallacy may eafily be difcovered, by attending to their Conduct, for that will always demonftrate their Relation to *Self Intereft*, from whofe Principles alone it proceeds. They fometimes affect a violent Paffion for cultivating the Arts of Peace, for the Improvement of Trade, Shipping, Manufactures, high Roads, and Bridges; at other Times, they are very bufy in Preparations for War, in erecting and repairing Fortifications, Ramparts, and Barracks; and, of late, they have condefcended to amufe themfelves with great Guns, Haubitzers, and Mortars; with Powder, and Ball, and Fire, and Smoke; with warlike Peace, and peaceful War; but their true Character will always be difcovered, by a Dilatorinefs and Inconfiftency of Conduct, in whatever they undertake. They are always zealous and in hafte to begin a Work; but they do not care how long it is in Hand, and take care, to do all in their Power to prevent its being finifhed. They will alfo be found, frequently, to begin their Undertaking at the wrong End; for they have been feen very bufy in preparing Implements of War, for the Defence of Fortifications, before there were any Fortifications to defend. Their

Paffion

Paſſion for *Land-Works* is not more conſpicuous than for *Water-Works*. Some time ago, they were exerting all their Influence to make Inroads into the Sea; they were building Keys, and projecting Piers; crying to the Ocean " hitherto ſhalt thou come, and here ſhall thy proud Waves be ſtayed;" but, at preſent, they ſeem to take greater delight in the more gentle and innocent Entertainment of tracing the Meandering of Canals, and Rivers, through Meads and Lawns, from one great City to another. But neither is Land nor Water ſufficient to circumſcribe their Projects; they mount the Air, and, pretend to erect Caſtles, for the Accommodation of thoſe that ſhall undertake a Journey to the Moon †.

As to the Places where they are to be found, they love good Company, and aſſociate much with thoſe, in whom you Gentlemen, place great Confidence; they are found at the Treaſury Board, the Linnen Board, the Barrack Board, and, in ſhort, at every other

---

† Alluding to the impractical Schemes, for which, Money has been obtained, by Cabal and Private Intereſt.

Board; nor are they ever to be missed at Grand Juries, or Societies that have the Disposal of Money. It has been said, by some that they have a necromantic Power, which, others suppose to have been long since lost, and, which, some modern Sceptics suppose never to have existed: It is insinuated, that they may, for ought we know to the contrary, be, at this Moment floating in the Air, within this sacred Rotunda; that they may appear to some among us, like the Dagger of *Macbeth*, with the Handle towards us; but, let none of us say to it, as he did, " come, let me clutch thee." Let us suspect the Appearance of every " questionable Shape," and, if any JOBBS approach in their own, whether they attempt to slip in at the back Door, to pop from behind the Arras, or to skulk privately in it; or whether, hoping to pass unsuspected, by appearing to have nothing to fear, they may boldly endeavour to enter in front, let us unite at once, to seize, and to expel them, as Pests of Society, and Traitors, to the State, with all the Ignominy and Contempt that is their due.

The R—t H—ble Mr *B— M—*, moved, that the Committee appointed to consider the

Peti-

Petition, of *Mary Ashworth*, should sit in the House, and, that it should take into Consideration all the Petitions of the same Kind, praying Encouragement, for carrying on Arts and Manufactures.

Some other Member, also moved, that this Committee should always sit in the House, and, not as usual, in the Speaker's Chamber; in Order that the Transactions might be the more publicly known, because, it sometimes happened that three or four Friends of the Party got together, and, agreed to just what they pleased; and, because, the House seldom thought fit to differ from their Committee; it was added, that the more public the Inquiry into the Utility of allotting the publick Money to particular Purposes was made the better.

The H—ble E— S—, represented, that very great Inconveniency, and Danger, frequently rose, to the Subjects of this Kingdom, from the Neglect of the Masters of Ships trading to *England*, who, neither provided a proper Number of Hands, to navigate the Vessel, nor a sufficient Quantity of Necessaries, to serve the Purposes of Life, if the

Ship

Ship happened to be a few Days longer in her Voyage than usual, by bad Weather, which, frequently drove her out of her Course; particularly, Candles and fresh Water; he said, that, he was himself, a Passenger, very lately, on board the *Lively*, and, that the Danger, and Distress, which he, and the rest of the Passengers suffered, by the Want of those Articles was inexpressible; that the Terror they felt from the Danger of the Storm was nothing in comparison of their suffering for want of Water, and their dread of perishing by Thirst; he, therefore, prayed that he might have leave to bring in the Heads of a Bill, to prevent such Evils for the future.

" Ordered, that leave be given, to bring in Heads of a Bill, for the better Regulation of such Ships as Trade between the Kingdom of *Ireland*, and that of *Great Britain*; and, for making it penal, for the Masters and Commanders of such Vessels, to proceed to Sea, without a sufficient Number of able Sea-men, to navigate them, and a competency of Bread, Water, and Candles, for the Number of Passengers and Hands on Board, allowing, even for the Chance of a tedious Passage. W E D-

WEDNESDAY, Nov. 3, 1763.

NINTH DAY.

THERE was a Meeting of the Committee of Accounts, of which Mr *J— B—*, Senior, was Chairman, when there arose the following Debate:

The R—t H—ble Mr *P— T—*, the A. G.

Mr S———,

I think it my Duty to propose, that the Facts, which I shall now lay before you, be made part of your Report to the House: The Facts are these: In the Year 1729, it was found, that the usual Supplies had not been sufficient to answer the Exigencies of Government; to make good the Deficiency, therefore, 200,000 *l.* was raised, by Parliament, in the subsequent Sessions, after the usual Manner: When this Sum came to be accounted for, in the Year 1731, the Publick got Credit for Six-pence in the Pound out of it, such a Deduction being made from all publick Money, when it goes out of the Treasury.

fury. This Deduction of Six-pence in the Pound, from the Hereditary Revenue, is paid as a Fee or Perquifite to the Vice Treafurer; but, the Deduction of Six-pence in the Pound, from the Additional Duties, has always been made an additional Aid to Government, and the Treafury has been made Debtor for it accordingly. The public Accounts were paffed the fame Year, and, this faving of Sixpence in the Pound, upon the 200,000 *l.* additional Duty, was voted and allowed as an Aid to Government, nor did the Vice Treafurer pretend to lay any Claim to it.

The fame Year, it was alfo found Neceffary, to raife the farther additional Duty of 100,000 *l.* and this Sum being accounted for in the Year 1733, the faving of Six-pence a Pound upon it, like that, upon the other 200,000 *l.* was placed as a farther Aid, and, this has been the conftant Practice, and voted as fuch from Seffions to Seffions.

In the Year 1759, the Sum of 150,000 *l.* was raifed, and a Vote of Credit given for 200,000 *l.* more: This 200,000 *l.* was raifed in the fubfequent Year, and the Deputy Vice-Treafurer thought proper to pay the

Deduction of Six-pence in the Pound out of it, to the Vice-Treasurer, instead of retaining it in his Hands, as a farther Aid to Government.

In the Year 1761, the public Accounts were passed, and, by some Mistake, the Payment of the Six-pence in the Pound, upon 200,000 *l.* being the Sum of 5,000 *l.* to the Vice Treasurer, was allowed, and the Deputy Vice Treasurer was not, as usual, made accountable for it as an Aid to Government.

Sometime afterwards, however, I applied to the Deputy-Vice-Treasurer, and told him, that I did not think him safe, in having paid the 5,000 *l.* to the Vice Treasurer, it being my Opinion, that, as the 200,000 *l.* from which it was a Deduction, had been raised upon a Vote of Credit, and was an additional Duty, the Poundage ought to have been made a saving to the Government, as all Poundage upon additional Duties had actually been, in all preceding Times, and, that, though the Accounts had been passed by Parliament, yet they might be over-hauled, and, he might be made Debtor to the Treasury, for the Money,

and

and obliged to pay it. This, I thought it my Duty, as a Servant of the Crown, to do; and the Deputy-Vice-Treasurer was so sensible of the Weight of what I said, that he thought proper to make Stoppages for his own Indemnification of two Thirds of the Sum he had paid, from a Ballance in his Hands, due to two Vice-Treasurers, and he would have stopped the other Third, from a third Vice-Treasurer, but, he being out of Office, the Deputy had no Ballance due to him in his Hands; to this Gentleman, however, who, was then in *England*, he wrote a Letter, stating the Fact, and relating my Opinion; upon this, the Vice Treasurers took an Opinion in that Kingdom, and filed a Bill in Chancery against the Deputy, in order to recover the Money he had stopped; to this Bill they made me, as A— G—, a Party, and I freely confess, that hitherto I have put in no Answer to it, for, as the Question litigated, relates to the Disposal of public Money, I thought the Parliament had the best Right to determine it.

The R—t H—ble F— A—.

Mr S——,

I am very sorry to say, that, I cannot but draw a Conclusion, directly opposite to that of the worthy Gentleman who spoke last, from the very same Premises; for, it appears to me, from the whole of what he has said, that it would be in the highest Degree improper, and unbecoming, for the House, to interfere in the Question, which he would recommend to its determination. The honourable Gentleman, has very freely confessed, that he has obstructed the common Course of Justice, by a wilful and intended delay; but shall we take Advantage of such delay, to preclude the Determination of a Court, to which the Parties have regularly appealed? Does it become us to wrest a Suit out of the Hands of the Court of Chancery, or to forejudge a Cause, that has been properly brought before it? Besides, Sir, the very Pretence for taking this Affair out of the Jurisdiction, into which it is properly brought, is fallacious. The Vice-Treasurer, by Virtue of the Patent, which he holds under the Sanction of the Laws

Laws of this Kingdom, is intitled to a Poundage of Six-pence in twenty Shillings, out of all Monies paid out of the Treasury, if there is not an express Resolution of this House to the contrary; now, it is not pretended, that there was a Resolution of the House against it, with Respect to the Sum in Question, and indeed, the contrary appears by incontestible Evidence, for the Poundage has actually been allowed by the House, and no Man can suppose the House would allow a Deduction, that had been made contrary to its express Resolution. But, as there has been no Resolution against this Deduction, neither is it equitable that there should, for, it is no more than a reasonable Salary to the Vice-Treasurers, and, is made from the Individuals, only, that receive Money from the Exchequer, and, not from the Public, who would be charged with a Salary, for these Officers, if they were not paid by this more equitable, and less burdensome Method. They are intitled to this Money, raised in this Manner, by the Act of Parliament, under which they hold their Patent; and they have received this Money by the Execution of that Act; and can we, by any Resolution, say, that this Act ought not to have been executed? or, that it shall not be executed for the future? An Act, indeed, may be repealed, but the Execution of it can never be fuspended, while it continues in force, without the Exertion of an unconftitutional and rebellious Power, which muft neceffarily throw all Things into Confufion. Neither is it the Province of this Houfe to explain the Laws, otherwife than by new Statutes properly paffed for that End; the Courts of Law are appointed for this Purpofe, and to them the Subject is, by the Inftitution of his Country, to apply: Nor, in the prefent Cafe, is the Object worthy of parliamentary Notice, being only a paltry Sum of about five thoufand Pounds. It was, indeed, the Object of parliamentary Attention, when it came regularly before the Parliament, connected with other Matters of greater Importance; and the Parliament, as I have already obferved, confirmed the Difpofition of it, which is now controverted; if the Refolutions of any former Seffions are to be reviewed, and we are to undo this Seffions what we did laft, I do not fee, why we may not go back twenty Years, or, bring the Authority of our Refolutions into Queftion, from the Time that Refolutions were firft made. If it was lawful to take Cognizance of this Affair,

fair, in wrong of the Court of Chancery, to which the Parties have appealed, yet, I think, we should be bound to establish our Resolution, both for our own Honour, and, in Justice to the Gentlemen it concerns; for it would surely be a piteous and cruel Case, to make Gentlemen refund, what we have allowed them as their Right, and what, in consequence of such Allowance, they have received and spent. Upon the whole, I am clearly of Opinion, that the House should do nothing in the Affair.

Sir R— C—.

Mr S—,

As I always listen, with the greatest Attention, to the Arguments of that learned Gentleman, nothing that he says escapes me, and, I shall, therefore, endeavour to trace him step by step, and offer my Thoughts, upon the very same Points, which he has made the Subject of his own. I shall, however, begin where he has ended, and, as he has thought fit to say it would be a cruel, and pitiable thing, to bring the Vice-Treasurers to an Account, for what they have spent, I think it would be proper to afcertain how far they are Objects of Commifferation, and, therefore, move, that the proper Officer do lay before the Houfe, an Account of the Sums that have been paid to the Vice-Treafurers, as Salaries for feven Years laft paft; we fhall then know, not only how far they are to be pitied, but how far the want of fufficient Salaries will juftify their having 5,000 *l*. of the public Money, which, except in this fingle Inftance, they never had before. The honourable Gentleman, has, indeed, told us, that it is a reafonable Salary, and, he would perfuade us that the Public does not pay it, becaufe, it is raifed by Deductions from Sums received by Individuals out of the Treafury; according to him, granting it to be a reafonable Salary, the Publick actually faves 5,000 *l*. (which it would be otherwife taxed to pay this Salary,) by the ingenious Contrivance of mulcting thofe, who have Claims on the Treafury. Whether this Sum is a reafonable Part of their Salary now, will be beft determined, when the Amount of their Salary fhall be known, but their Salary was certainly thought fufficient without it, both by their Mafters, and themfelves, from the Time of the Eftablifhment of their Office, till the paffing of their

laft

last Accounts. As to the Pretence, that, if they receive this Increase of Wages, by a Poundage from Individuals, the Public will not pay it; a Moment's Consideration will shew it to be a Fallacy. This Poundage must be applied, either as an additional Aid to Government, or an Increase of Salary to the Vice-Treasurer. If it is applied as an additional Aid to Government, the Public necessarily saves a Sum equal to its Amount; for if, instead of being applied as an additional Aid, it is paid as an Increase of Salary, the Public must raise such a Sum, to replace it in the Treasury; so that, as long as this Poundage is paid to Vice-Treasurers, so long the Publick must pay just as much as that amounts to, more than they would pay if the Poundage was applied as an Aid to Government.—— But, we are farther told, that we ought not to bring the Vice-Treasurers to an Account for an unjust Application of public Money, because it is now several Years since the public Money was mis-applied; I confess this is the first Time I ever heard that the Age of a Crime ought to be its Protection. Give me leave to say, that it is the indispensible Duty, as well as the most important Privilege of this House, to enquire into the Distribution

of

of public Money, and to take Cognizance of the Mis-application of it, at any Time past, however remote, if there is a Possibility of recovering the Sum, or punishing the Offender. If Sir *William Robinson*, who was so long ago dismissed from his Office, for corrupt Practices, was in being, and had wherewithall to satisfy the Public, we should be inexcusable, if we did not compell him to do it. I intend to set on foot an Enquiry myself, with Respect to seven thousand Pounds that was not accounted for in the Year 1742; and, if Length of Time should not be allowed to screen Guilt, neither should the Neglect of those, whose Business it is to detect it, deter others from the Attempt. The Neglect of that Sessions, which passed the Accounts, in which the Sum in question was misapplied, gives no Sanction to the Misapplication: Is our having once done wrong, a Reason that we should never do right? On the contrary, it is the Duty of this Parliament to rectify the Mistakes of former Parliaments; and, I think, that he who labours to find Causes why this House should not, to the utmost, fulfill its Trust, with Respect to the Confidence which the Public has reposed in it, by making it the Keeper of its Purse, does not

act

act as the Friend of his Country. The Fact, at prefent before us, is this; the Vice-Treafurers, and their Deputy, who are Servants of the Public, have a Difpute among themfelves about the Difpofal of public Money; of Money which this Houfe has put into their Hands for particular Purpofes, and, inftead of applying to this Houfe, to know what thofe Purpofes were, they carry their Difpute into a Court of Law; and, fhall we acquiefce in a Meafure, in which we are fo contemptuoufly paffed by, and which fo effentially affects us, with Refpect to our higheft Privilege and greateft Truft? Surely Mr A— G— acted with the utmoft Propriety, with the greateft Attention to his Duty, and the higheft Regard to the Honour of this Houfe, by preventing the Determination of this Queftion in Chancery, before we had an Opportunity of taking Cognizance of it ourfelves. The honourable Gentleman, who fpoke laft, has told us, that the Vice-Treafurers are intitled to this Money by the Act of Parliament under which they hold their Patent; and that we cannot condemn, or fufpend, the Execution of an Act otherwife than by repealing it. But, does not this Gentleman know, that, to fay they are intitled to the Money, under an Act of Parliament,

ment, is begging the very Question in dispute? Does he think the Parties are applying to a Court of Chancery, to know whether an Act of Parliament shall be executed or not? If this House has no Power to suspend the Execution of a Law of the Land, does he think any such Power is claimed, or supposed to be claimed, by a Court of Chancery? The Patent of the Vice-Treasurer was made, when no public Money was raised here but the hereditary Revenue, when there was no such Thing as additional Aids, and, therefore, this hereditary Revenue could only be intended by the Spirit of the Law, which then enacted, that the Vice-Treasurer should have Six-pence in the Pound out of all Monies issuing out of the Exchequer. That this was the Spirit of the Law, and always understood to be so, will appear from the uninterrupted, and uniform Practice of Parliament, for no less than sixty Years; for, so long ago as the Year 1703, a Saving was made of Six-pence in the Pound, upon all additional Duties, and this Saving has been regularly continued, till, by the Precipitation, or Connivance, of the last Sessions, it was lost. If the House hitherto has had a Right to determine how the Sixpence in the Pound, on additional Supplies, should

should be disposed of, how comes it that they have not a Right now? and, if it has hitherto been the Sense of the House, that this Deduction should be a Saving, and that it was not a necessary Encrease of the Vice-Treasurer's Salary, what should make it not the Sense of the House now? Is it upon the Principle, that " to them that have it shall be given;" is the great Increase of the Vice-Treasurer's Revenue, in other Respects, a Reason why it should be increased still more, by 5,000*l*. taken out of the public Purse? Is it because the Vice-Treasurers are *Englishmen*, and will spend their Revenue on the other Side of the Water! or is it, because the Employment is so great that it is divided among three, and because the Disposal of it will create a ministerial Dependance, in Proportion to its Revenue and importance? or is there any other Reason why 5,000*l*. of the public Money should be now thrown into the Lap of Servants, who were most amply paid before, and who, till now, never claimed or expected, so unmerited and unnecessary an Addition to their Income; but this Sum, however large, as the Increase of a Servant's Wages, is said to be unworthy the Attention of Parliament: I am, however, equally concerned and

and furprized, to find that any Perverfion of parliamentary Purpofes, any Mifapplication of public Money, any Meafure, injurious to our Privileges, or derogatory from our Honour, fhould be thought unworthy of our Notice: Thefe Things are important from their Nature, not their Degree. The fmalleft Injury offered to the Public, or to this Houfe, is of more Moment than the greateft Injury that one Individual can do to another; as only to imagine the Death of the King, is, by our Laws, confidered to be a greater Crime than the actual Murder of a Subject. Upon the whole, I am clearly and fully of Opinion, that the Facts, ftated by Mr A— G—, fhould be reported to the Houfe.

The R—t H—ble Mr F— A—.

Mr S—,

I am extreamly obliged to the honourable Gentleman, who fpoke laft, for the Attention that he is pleafed to fay, he always pays me, and yet I could wifh it were ftill greater, for, at prefent, it has not been fufficient to take my meaning. I did not fay, that the Age of Crimes fhould protect them from Enquiry and

Pu-

Punishment, nor had I any Ideas in my Mind that could prompt me to say it, for, I never considered the Vice-Treasurers, as being guilty of a Crime, in the Appropriation of the Poundage, on the additional Supplies, and the principal Purport of what I said, was, to shew that I thought it their due. Neither did I say, that they were Objects of Pity, I said, it was a Pity that Justice should be impeded in its legal, regular, and proper Course. I am so far from thinking Vice-Treasurers Objects of Pity, that I think there is the greatest Reason to consider them as Objects of Envy; but, I shall for ever adhere to the Opinion, that, for this House to interfere with the Courts of Justice, is of very dangerous Consequence; with the Courts of Law they should certainly co-operate, and place a Confidence in them, if it was only for Example sake, and, if possible, to encrease their Influence, and the Reverence, that is paid them, as the Administrators of Justice, whose Office it is, by the very Constitution of our Government, to explain the Laws made by this House, and carry them into Execution.

Sir

Sir R— C—.

Mr S——,

I think it a Duty, that I owe to that honourable Gentleman, to suppose his meaning was, what he now explains it to be; but I think it also a Duty due to myself, to observe, that his Words did not express the Meaning, which he has now explained; he said, that he thought the Resolutions of a former Sessions, ought not to be reviewed; and does not this plainly imply, that, if that Resolution justified a Crime, the Crime must remain justified? whether a Crime has been committed or not, is the Matter to be determined, by the very Review that he would prevent; but, he said, he thought, that if we took Cognizance of the same Question again, we ought to determine, as we have determined already, and, what is this but saying, that, having once done Wrong, we ought never to do Right? he said, also, that it would be a piteous and cruel Case, to make Gentlemen refund Money they had been allowed to take, and, which, they had, in consequence of that Allowance, spent already; and, surely, Gentlemen in a
piteous

piteous Cafe, are Objects of Pity; however, if thefe Officers, according to the Opinion now explained, are Objects not of Pity, but of Envy, it is difficult to conceive what can induce the honourable Gentleman to make them ftill more fo, at the Expence of the Public, at the Expence of this poor Country, from which they already draw fo confiderable a Sum to diffipate in another. Upon the whole, I muft declare, that I fee no Reafon from any Thing that Gentleman has faid, to change my Opinion, that this Houfe fhould be zealous, on all Occafions, to maintain its undoubted Right of ordering the Difpofal of publick Money, and that no other Part of the Legiflature, much lefs a Court of Law, fhould intermeddle with it.

The R—t H—ble Mr *N— C—*, D— V— T—, got up, in his Place, and acknowledged that as the 200,000 *l.* raifed on the Vote of Credit, went out of the Treafury, he charged the Fees on it to the Account of the Vice-Treafurers, and, on fettling the Accounts, paid them the Ballance. He obferved, that no Objection was made to this, on paffing the Accounts; but, he faid, that, in a Converfation with the Attorney, and Sollicitortor-General, he found Reafon to doubt whether he was fafe in what he had done, notwithftanding the Accounts had been paffed, and that, therefore, he ftopped, from the next Payment, to two of the Vice-Treafurers, their Proportions of the Poundage they had received, on the Sum in Queftion, and that he would have done fo with Refpect to Mr E— the third, but he being gone out of Office, there was no Money in Hand belonging to him out of which the Stoppage could be made. He faid, alfo, that the two former had taken the Opinion of the Attorney and Sollicitor-General, in *England*, upon the Cafe, and, by their Advice, had filed a Bill in Chancery here againft him, to recover the Money he had ftopped, and that they had made the Attorney-General a Party to the Bill; he added, that Mr E— had written him Word, that, if the Suit in Chancery went againft the Vice-Treafurers, he would refund the Money.

The S— G— gave his Opinion, that the Tranfaction fhould be taken Notice of by the Committee, and reported to the Houfe, and this was agreed to without a Divifion.

Sir

Sir *R— C—* reprefented, that many Inconveniencies might happen, and that, in general, it was fcarce poffible to carry on the Bufinefs of the Seffion with the Exactnefs and Deliberation neceffary to its being carried on effectually, if *Monday* was always kept as a Holiday; and he, therefore, moved that the Houfe fhould meet on the next *Monday*.

The R—t H—ble *F— A—* faid, that he thought it of more Importance to appoint the Houfe to meet earlier, that it might not be obliged to fit fo late, for that the Attendance of that Houfe till feven or eight o'Clock at Night was a very great Fatigue, and, as long as this continued, he thought one Day in a Week little enough for Relaxation: The Bufinefs of the Houfe, he faid, would be better attended to on the other five Days, and that, as to their meeting the next *Monday*, he did not know any particular Bufinefs that made it neceffary.

Sir *R— C—* replied, that, when the Bufinefs of the Nation was to be done, Gentlemen fhould attend to it as diligently fix Days as they would five, notwithftanding the Fatigue,

tigue, for that no private Indulgence ought to preclude public Benefit: That there was not a Gentleman in the Houfe to whom Indulgence was more neceffary than himfelf, as his State of Health was fuch as made extraordinary Application and Fatigue very prejudicial, yet he defired no fuch Relaxation as was now contended for. He faid, the Allowance of the 5,000*l.* upon the additional Supplies, to the Vice-Treafurer, a Miftake which, in every View, was attended with the moft difagreeable Confequences, arofe from the Precipitation of the laft Seffion, owing to the Want of Time, and that he could not but be extremely furprized to hear any Gentleman fay, that he did not know what Bufinefs was to be done, when they were to pafs the national Accounts.

Mr *H— F—* faid, that he did not know any Reafon why *Monday* fhould be a Holiday, except that fome Gentlemen might, perhaps, think themfelves ftill at School, and fo imagine it to be black *Monday*.

Upon a Divifion, it was ordered, that the Houfe, for the future, fhould meet on *Monday*.

Dr

Dr *C— L—.*

Mr S——,

I have obferved a Negative put upon a Motion *, in the Votes lately publifhed, that gives me the greateft Surprize. I was not prefent when it happened, and I am inclined to impute it to a Miftake of the Clerk, or the Printer, becaufe, I think, it is impoffible that this Houfe, the great national Council, whofe Duty it is to make the ftricteft Enquiry into every Thing that affects the Conftitution, could reject any Motion which tended to throw a Light on an Enquiry of the higheft Importance.

Mr *M— P—.*

Mr S——,

I rife up, Sir, to call that Gentleman to Order; for, it is contrary to all the Rules of this Houfe, for any Member to object againft

---

* The Motion to lay the Opinion of the A--- and S--- G--- concerning the Grant of the Offices of Chancellor of the Exchequer, and Mafter of the Rolls, for Life, before the Houfe.

Proceedings which he muſt know, whatever he may pretend to the contrary, were agreed to by a large Majority, and it is a much groſſer Violation of theſe Rules to caſt Reflections of an odious and invidious Nature, upon any ſuch Proceedings, fcr this can be nothing leſs than an Inſult upon the Houſe, whoſe Act all the Acts of a Majority are known to be: His Pretence of a Miſtake in the Clerk, or the Printer, is ridiculous, becauſe it implies an Impoſſibility; for the Votes are always carefully read by the Speaker, before they are ſent to the Preſs, and the Speaker alſo inſpects them, after they are printed, to prevent any Errors of the Preſs from ſtanding upon the Journals of the Houſe; beſides, ſuppoſing the Poſſibility, that the Entry in the Votes aroſe from a Miſtake, he is irregular, for, if he had ſuppoſed that to be the Caſe, he ought to have deſired that the Votes of the Day might be read, and that the Senſe of the Houſe might be taken upon them.

Dr C— L—.

Mr S——,

Nothing could have induced me to make the Suppoſition in Queſtion, but the very extraortraordinary Nature of the Proceeding, to which it relates; a Proceeding which is neither supported by Juſtice, nor countenanced by Precedent; this I imputed rather to Error than Deſign, and, conſidering it in that Light, I have caſt no Reflection on the Houſe, and I apprehend that every Member has a Right to expreſs his Surprize at what ſtrikes him, as extraordinary and unaccountable, and is no more obliged to impute it to a Cauſe which he thinks impoſſible, than other Gentlemen are obliged to impute it to a Cauſe, which they think impoſſible: If I have injured this Houſe, by ſuppoſing its Concurrence in a Meaſure deſtructive of the Conſtitution of the Country, and the Happineſs and the Freedom of the People, to be impoſſible, I am very, very ſorry, and as ſuch an Injury could never proceed from a diſhonourable Opinion of the Houſe, or from any Malignity to it, I hope it may be forgiven. The Conſtitution of the Country, Sir, and the Happineſs and Freedom of the People, depend upon the proper Diſtribution of Juſtice in the Courts of Law, and there is no Court of Law of greater Conſequence, and Dignity, than the Court of Exchequer, which has immenſe Property in its Diſpoſal. It is well known in this Houſe, that the Object of an Enquiry now set on Foot, to which my Supposition relates, is the Legality of a Patent appointing a Judge of that Court, and therefore every Thing that could throw Light upon that Enquiry is of the greatest Importance, and every Attempt to prevent Light from being thrown upon it, is an Attempt tending to subvert the Constitution, and affect the Happiness and Freedom of the People. A Gentleman of the greatest Abilities in the Law, Sir, formerly sate upon the Bench, and the Business of that Court was then carried on with the greatest Expedition, and perfectly to the Satisfaction of every Person who had a Suit depending in it. I am now extremely sorry to say that this Court, great and respectable as it is known to have been, has lost its Dignity, and fallen into Contempt, an Event equally unhappy and unavoidable, when such Persons, as the present, preside upon the Bench.

Mr M—— P——.

Mr S-—,

I am extremely sorry to find myself under a Necessity of calling that Gentleman a second

cond Time to Order; his very Pretence, which he would perfuade us prevents what he has faid, from being a Reflection upon the Houfe, is itfelf an invidious Reflection, for the Proceedings of the Houfe are manifeftly condemned by being imputed to miftake, efpecially by being imputed to a Miftake that was impoffible, and that he knew to be fo. This Infult I cannot hear and be filent; neither can I filently hear it faid, that the moft important of our Courts of Judicature has loft its Dignity, and is fallen into Contempt, or fuffer the Character of our Judges, who prefide in it to be injurioufly treated, without repreffing a Behaviour fo licentious and unparliamentary, fo great a Trefpafs upon the Propriety, and Decency, which fhould always be obferved in this Houfe, and fo grofs a Deviation from the Character of a Gentleman, which ought always to be maintained by its Members. I appeal to the Houfe, whether all this is not contrary to Order.

Dr *C— L—*.

Mr S—,

As to what has been faid, concerning the Court of Exchequer, and its Judges, I can
never

never conceive it to be a Violation of Order, except it is a Violation of Order for this House, to discharge its Duty to the Public, and fulfill the Ends of its Institution. I have always understood, Sir, that it was the peculiar Province of this National Council to enquire into the State of our Courts of Judicature, and the Character and Conduct of its Officers: Have we not a Committee appointed for that very Purpose, and, can the Duty, referred to this Committee, be performed without communicating to the House, what appears to be amiss in the Courts or their Officers? Is it not, Sir, contrary to all Rule and Order, to deprive us of the Liberty of so doing? and is it not asserting the Liberty, and, acting consonant to the Rules of this House, to mention whatever relates to the Courts, or their Officers, without reserve?

Mr *T— H—*.

Mr S——,

I acknowledge, Sir, that this House has a Right to make a strict Enquiry into the Conduct of the Judges of our Courts, and that we have a standing Committee, appointed for that

that Purpofe; but, furely it does by no Means follow that any Member of this Houfe has a Right to cenfure the whole Bench of any Court indifcriminately, or to throw out general Reflections upon the Judges of it, unfupported by any particular Fact, either real or pretended. It is lawful, Sir, to apply for a Commiffion of Bankruptcy, againft a Merchant, founded upon a particular Fact; but it is unlawful to fay in general, that a Merchant cannot pay his Debts. If any particular Act of Mal-adminiftration was alledged againft any Judge of our Courts of Law, the Committee of Juftice would immediately caufe Enquiry to be made, whether the Fact alledged was true, and would pafs Judgement accordingly; but, even in alledging a particular Fact, there fhould be no general Abufe, and fuch Language, as we have juft now heard, would be unbecoming and unparliamentary.

Mr *J— G—*, the S. G.

Mr S——,

I am entirely of Opinion, with the honourable Gentleman who fpoke laft, that it is improper, in the higheft Degree, to vilify and de-

depreciate Gentlemen in a moſt reſpectable Office, without laying any thing particular to their Charge. It is certainly incumbent upon this Houſe, and every Member of it, to ſupport the Dignity and Credit of the Courts of Law, by which alone its Determinations can be effectually, and ultimately, carried into Execution. It is more eſpecially incumbent upon them, at this time, when the ſolemn Acts of the Legiſlature of this Kingdom are oppoſed by factious and unlawful Combinations, in every Corner of it, and the executive Power ſet at Defiance, by treaſonable and outrageous Practices, which are a Diſgrace to our Government and Country; to throw out invidious Reflections againſt this Power, at a Time when we ſo eminently need its Service, is eventually to join the public Enemies of our Laws, and Countenance the Violence which is ſo flagitiouſly offered them. Our Galleries, I ſee, are full, and there is not a Word ſaid in this Houſe, that will not be carried abroad; and, is this a Time to have it reported, that one of the moſt reſpectable of our Courts of Law is fallen from its Dignity, into Contempt, and thus encourage an Oppoſition to its Juriſdiction, and a Diſcontent at its Proceedings! As to myſelf, I think it

my

my indispensable Duty, to support the Credit, and Influence, of that Court to the utmost of my Power, and, I am pleased to have this Opportunity of declaring my Sentiments upon the Subject, and of giving the worthy Gentleman, from whom I have the Misfortune so widely to differ, a proper Time to recollect himself, and to remember, both of whom, and to whom he shall speak, in what he has farther to offer on the Occasion, so that he may neither offend against the Laws of Decency, nor the Respect due to the Dignity of this House.

Mr W— H—.

Mr S———,

Notwithstanding, what has been so justly and so forcibly urged by others, I think it my Duty to make some Reply to what has been thrown out relative to the Court of Exchequer, which, I have the Honour to attend, and some Profit besides. The Gentlemen of the Law, who appear frequently in that Court, are the best Judges, how far it has preserved its Dignity, and, I appeal to all those of the Profession that hear me, whether it has fallen into Contempt. The Gentlemen who

who preside in that Court, and who have been attacked, in a very extraordinary Manner, are not here to defend themselves, and therefore, I think it my Duty to declare thus publickly, and directly, that the Reflections thrown out against them are *not true*, and that the Language used, upon the Occasion, is a Dishonour and Disgrace to this House: It may be proper Language in the Weaver's-Hall, but it is not so in a House of Commons.

Dr C— L—.

Mr S——,

I have the greatest Honour and Esteem for the worthy Gentleman who spoke before the last on the Floor; and shall always pay the highest Regard to his Judgment and Opinion. It is, therefore, with great regret that I differ from him now; however, I must declare, that, I think, if there is any Thing amiss in our Courts of Justice, either with Respect to the Legality of the Patents, by which the Officers are appointed, or the Characters and Abilities of the Officers themselves, it would be the greatest Absurdity in itself, and the greatest Injury to our Constituents, if we were to forbear an Enquiry into it, for fear it should be be known abroad that such an Enquiry was made. If nothing amiss is to be imputed till it is proved, I shall be glad to know how such Proof is to be brought on: If no Felon is to be taken up upon Suspicion, it is plain that no Felon can be punished: The Proof of a Crime must, in the Nature of Things, be subsequent to the Imputation of it, and a publick and judicial Enquiry will, if the Crime has been falsely imputed, be for the Honour of the Party, and, if it is proved, for the Benefit of the Public. With Respect to the present Question, then, it is an Insult, upon common Sense, to pretend that People without Doors ought to think our Courts impeccable, and that we ought, therefore, to suffer them to become useless, or corrupt, with Impunity. As to the Gentleman, upon the Floor, who has thought fit to complain of Indecency, and reproach me for Expressions, unbecoming this House, I am sure I may, at least, recriminate; for I have never observed greater Indecency than in the Expressions he has made Use of: He has, besides, been pleased to misrepresent me; for, though I said the Court had fallen from its Dignity, I did not say it had fallen into Contempt.

Here

Here Dr *L—* was again stopped, and called to Order by Mr *T—*, the A— G—.

Dr *C— L—*.

Mr S——,

I must own I think it is very hard that Gentlemen will not suffer me to explain myself; they catch up half Sentences, without permitting me to continue them till they express my meaning; I have been very roundly treated, and called to Order, for what I have said, and yet, I am confident, that, if I had been permitted to explain myself, the House would have found that I advanced no Opinion, in which all present did not concur. The Court of Exchequer, Sir, consists of the Chancellor, Treasurer, Chief Baron, and two Judges: These Persons, five in Number, act in a judicial Capacity; and, if from these five Judges, two are eventually taken away, by appointing two Persons to fill two of the Places, who do not act, whether from Want of Inclination, or Ability, surely no Gentleman will pretend to say, that, by such diminution, the Court has not fallen from its Dignity: Will not five Judges of Ability give the Court

in

in which they preside more Dignity than three? at least, will not a Court, which, by its Constitution, is to consist of five Judges, lose its Dignity if two of them are Cyphers? When five Judges were appointed to that Court, it was surely intended that five Judges should act, and by what Contrivances the Places of two of them have been made Sine-Cures, I do not know, but this I know, that we pay them very large Salaries for doing a Duty, which they do not do; and, I should be glad to know if the Business of that Court can be effectually done, and its Dignity effectually maintained, by the acting of three Judges, why we are to pay five? As, I believe, no Gentleman present can deny that two of these Judges are Cyphers, nor that a Court loses its Dignity, by having such Judges, I conclude that I might, in this Sense, without Reproach, say, that the Court in question has fallen from its Dignity, and, that every Gentleman here is of the same Opinion. The Fact is, indeed, proved by the very State of the Court, with Respect to the Business of it, at this Time. When the learned Gentleman, who formerly presided, sat there as Judge, there was, at least, twice as much Business done in it as there has been since. What sort of Men are the present Judges? The Lawyers will say excellent, and I shall take it for granted; but of past Judges I may speak my own Opinion: The learned Person I have just mentioned, was succeeded by one ——, was he a proper Man for such an Employment? Did he add Weight, or Dignity, to that Court? There is a Fact that says otherwise, and Facts are generally believed: From the Moment this ———— was appointed, no Business came before that Court, that it was possible to avoid bringing thither.

Here he was interrupted by Mr *W— H—*, who, when he was about to speak, and, at the Beginning of every Period, while he was speaking, gave two Hems, or short Coughs, which were very singular and comical: When Dr *L—* mentioned ——, who is Mr *H—*'s particular Friend, he gave his two Coughs louder, and with greater Vehemence, than usual, and then got up to speak; this caused a general Laugh in the House, upon which Mr *H—* said, he was extremely glad to see the House so merry, upon the Occasion of his rising up to speak, but, that his rising up, was, to himself, tragical, as it was to call a Member to Order, for indecently and injuriously treat-

treating the Character of a Gentleman of great Worth and Honour, who was not prefent to defend himfelf.

Dr *L——*.

Mr S——,

I can never think, Sir, that it is a Breach of Order in this Houfe, to enquire into the Character of thofe who have filled, or who are to fill an Employment of fuch Dignity, and Importance, as that in Queftion, with a View to have it filled as it ought to be. I think, Sir, that all perfonal and private Regard ought to give Way to public Intereft, whenever they come in competition; and, as to the Gentleman I have juft mentioned, he feems, himfelf, to have been confcious of his own Inability to fill the Place for which I have faid he was not qualified: If I have faid nothing more than he has, by his Conduct, tacitly admitted to be true, I apprehend I have done him no wrong; and that, as he would have had no Defence to make, if he had been here, he can lofe no Advantage by being abfent. That he has admitted his Inability for this Office, is clear, from his having thought fit to relinquifh it for a Penfion, and, indeed, he judged very properly, that he might as well take the Nation's Money, without pretending to do any Thing for it, as take it for an Employment, in which he was capable of doing nothing, if he had pretended it. While, he was in that Employment, he was a Load upon the Bench, and, when he quitted it, he became a Load upon the Public; the Burthen is the fame, but, of the two, the Public is beſt able to bear it. There has, indeed, been a very ſhameful Tranſmutation of Employment and Penſion; ſhameful if it had been only an Abuſe of Power legally veſted, but much more ſhameful, as effected without ſuch Power, and as being not only injurious, but illegal. The two Gentlemen who are ſo liberally paid by the Publick, as Judges, without ever acting, or pretending to act in that Capacity, put me in Mind of a Story I have heard of two *Iriſhmen*, who were ſeen, by their Maſter that paid them their Wages, idling on the Top of a Hay-cock; upon which, calling out to one of them, " Sirrah! what are you doing there for my Money?" The Fellow anſwered, *Ugh, by my Shoul now, and I am doing nothing:* "And what, ſays the Maſter, is that other Fellow doing along with you?" *By my Soul,* ſays Teague, *and he is helping me.* If one

one of thefe Gentlemen was afked the fame Queftion, by thofe that pay him, he might make the fame Reply; and, indeed, fo might an hundred others, both Male and Female, who have Places and Penfions at the Expence of this Country. Upon the whole, as I think the ftricteft Enquiry ought to be made into the Legality of the Grant of the Chancellor-fhip of the Exchequer, I humbly move, that the proper Officer may lay before the Houfe the Fiat for making out the Patent for that Place, and alfo the Fiat for making out the Patent of the Mafter of the Rolls.

Ordered accordingly, *Nemine Contradicente*.

Sir R—— D——.

Mr S——,

The greateft Diftinction, and higheft Privilege, of this Houfe, is to be the Purfe-bearer of the Nation: To have the Power of determining what Proportion of national Wealth, confifting of the aggregate Property of Individuals, fhall be applied to public Purpofes: This Power, which is exercifed by laying Taxes upon the People, as it is of the higheft Importance, fhould be delegated to others with the greatest Caution, and only in Cafes of the utmost Neceffity. In Cafes of fuch Neceffity, the Houfe has delegated this Power to Grand-Juries, who have, from their peculiar Knowledge of the feveral Counties, to which they belong, the only Means of knowing the Exigencies of thofe Counties, and the Sums neceffary to anfwer them: In Confequence of this Delagation, Grand-Juries have a Power to tax the Inhabitants with fuch Sums as fhall appear to them, by Affidavits, and proper Vouchers, to be neceffary for public Ufes: But there is too much Reafon to fufpect that this Power is frequently abufed, and, therefore, I beg leave to bring in Heads of a Bill for the better Regulation of the Proceedings of Grand-Juries, in the preparing and forming of Prefentments, for the levying of Money.

Ordered, that leave be given accordingly; and that Sir *R— D—*, Mr *F—*, and Dr *L—*, prepare and bring in the Heads of fuch a Bill.

Ordered, that the Order for the Day be adjourned till *Monday* Morning next.

And

And then the House adjourned until *Monday* Morning next, Ten of the Clock.

MONDAY, *Nov.* 8, 1763.

TENTH DAY.

IN the Committee for examining the national Accounts, Mr *J— B—* Chairman:

Mr *W— H—* got up, and said, that he could not help mentioning his Surprize at a Charge which had been just read of 170 *l.* paid to certain Persons for Pigs, which had been killed by a *Dublin* Mob. He said his Suprize was the greater, as the Demand of the Proprietors of those Pigs was only 70 *l.* how this 70 *l.* during a late Administration, had swelled to 170 *l.* he said he could not imagine. It is true, says he, these Pigs are mentioned under the Denomination of Cattle, but, whatever Honour they may derive from this Appellation, it cannot be supposed to increase their Value. I only mention this, to shew that these Pigs are among the dear Bargains which the Public has lately paid for.

Mr R— F—.

Before this Committee for examining the national Accounts is adjourned, I think it incumbent upon me to take Notice of, what I think, a very important Object of their Attention, as it relates to the public Income and Expences, with Respect to an Article, upon which, in my Opinion, the very being of our Constitution in great Measure depends. In the first Place, Sir, I am extremely sorry to say, that though our Revenue has, of late Years, very considerably increased, yet our Expences very considerably exceed our Revenue: This Circumstance is the more alarming, as no National Advantage is procured by this Increase of Expence, and as it has arisen at a Time, when our publick Affairs were in the same Situation as they were, when our Expences were greatly less than our Income, though our Income was greatly less than it is. This, Sir, seems to indicate, at least, an injudicious Management in the Disposal of public Money, and lays the Foundation of a public Debt, which, by a Continuation of the same Management, must perpetually encrease. I may, perhaps, be told that the

the Sum, annually added to this Debt, will be but ſmall, but, I anſwer, that we could not poſſibly ſupport it, if it were large, and that as large and ſmall are relative Terms, a Debt that would be ſmall to another Nation, will be large to ours. The Country is of conſiderable Extent, and contains many more People than we can properly employ; in theſe Circumſtances, the Neceſſaries of Life will always be procured with difficulty; for, if there is not an extenſive Commerce, and briſk Trade, or, in other Words, if thoſe, that want the Neceſſaries of Life are not enabled to procure them, by the Practice of thoſe Arts, that ſupply the Superfluities of it to others, they will be rather a Burthen than a Benefit to the Public. Now, it is unhappily, but too true, that the Commerce of this Country lies under very great Diſadvantages, and its home Trade, or Manufactories, are very much reſtrained by a miſtaken Policy, that is perpetually operating in Favour of a ſiſter Country. Our People, in general, therefore, muſt neceſſarily be poor, and unable, to ſupport Taxes, like other Countries, to pay Intereſt for a public Debt; on the contrary, it is neceſſary, that we ſhould be able to make ſome Savings from our public Revenue, in order

order to counter-ballance our National Disadvantages, by pecuniary Encouragements, for the Encreafe of our Manufactories, and the Improvement of our Trade: Upon this View of our Situation, and I appeal to all that hear me, whether it is not true; it is manifeft that a National Debt, comparatively very fmall, will to us be total ruin; and, give me leave to fay, it would be fo, if our Trade and Manufactures were in a much better State than they are; becaufe our Money, what we have of it, does not circulate among us, but is drained off by Abfentees, and fquandered on the other Side of the Water: I might here enlarge upon the very mortifying Topics I have mentioned, I might fhew in what particulars our Trade and Commerce are reftrained, I might fhew that the Poverty of our People renders our Home Confumption fmall, and that we import no Article, upon which we have a Profit, to export again, and I might draw a Parallel between our Situation and that of others, with Refpect to Trade, in a great Variety of Particulars, and fhew our Difadvantage in each; but, as it is not neceffary for the Proof of what I have advanced in general, I fhall fpare myfelf, and the other Members of this Affembly, the Pain that a minute

minute Examination of our Disadvantages, and Distresses, must inevitably produce. I shall only say, that I have, with some Pains and Trouble, made a very exact Calculation of our Income, and our Expence, for some Years back, and that I find there was, in the Year 1757, a Saving to this Country, after the Demands of Government were satisfied, of 86,095 *l.* to be laid out in Improvements; there was also, in the Year 1759, a Saving of 96,184*l.* but in the Year 1761, though the Revenue was then considerably encreased, the Demands of Government exceeded it no less than 79,181 *l.* and, in the Year 1763, though the Revenue still continued to encrease, yet the Exceedings amounted to 66,680 *l.* I must observe, also, that, in this Computation, I have taken no Account of the Duties appropriated to the Payment of Interest, for the Loan, because they have very little more than answered that purpose. This Increase, in our Expences, being so great, notwithstanding an increased Revenue, as, instead of leaving us a Surplus of 96,184*l.* to bring us in debt 79,181*l.* in one Year, requires a particular Examination. One Article is obvious, the Pensions; Sums, large Sums, annually paid to Persons for performing no public Service;

Per-

Persons who have never contributed to the Honour, or the Advantage, of this Country, to the Value of a Mite, from whom it cannot receive the least Degree of either, and from whom it is not even pretended that it will; but besides this, there is a much larger Sum than formerly allowed for the Concordatum: The Allowance, during the late Reign, was 5,000*l*. but in the present it increased to 10,000*l*. which is one half, and to that there has since been an additional Increase of no less than 16,000*l*. more; so that the whole Increase, in this one Article, is no less than 26,000*l*. But there is an Increase, in another Article, that seems more extraordinary still, and, I cannot mention it without some Degree both of Shame and Indignation—Secret Service—Of what Nature, Sir, is this secret Service? We have no Treaties to carry on with other Nations, no secret Intelligence to procure from abroad; nor do I know of any Intelligence at Home, which it is necessary secretly to procure, and secretly to communicate to Government. I should, therefore, think a very small Sum would suffice for this Article. 2,991 *l*. was found sufficient in the Height of the War, for two Years, the Years 1759 and 1760, and yet, for the two last Years, when the Exigencies of State must

cer-

certainly have required less, we are charged 2,209 *l.* more, the whole Charge for those Years being 5,200*l.* This, Sir, appears extremely mysterious to me, and, I dare say, does so to every Gentleman that hears me. The Increase in the Pensions is immense, for, at present, they amount to no less than 42,627*l.* 19 *s.* 2 *d.* more than the Civil List. I, therefore, humbly move, that this Fact may be recognized by this Committee, and that it be the Resolution of this Committee, that the Pensions do exceed the Civil List 42,627 *l.* 19 *s.* 2 *d.*

Mr *P— T—*, the A— G—.

As the Computation, by which the Pensions appear to exceed the Civil List, is entirely an arithmetical Operation, I think it is proper that every Gentleman should have Time to satisfy himself of the Result of it, before he concurs in a Resolution by which that Result is declared: The honourable Gentleman, who spoke last, says, it has cost him some Pains and Trouble, to make this Computation, and, therefore, it is reasonable to suppose, that other Gentlemen cannot make it without; so that, if they are not to take it implicitly from him

him, some Time must be allowed them, and, I think, the Time of this Committee may be better employed, as I do not see what End the Resolution proposed will answer, when it is made.

Mr R⸺ F⸺.

Though the Computation cost me some Time, and Trouble, as it was necessary for me to state the Articles, both of our Income and our Expence, and then to compare the Amount, it may now be done with the greatest Facility, because the Accounts, ready drawn up, and stated, lie upon the Table, so that nothing more is necessary than to write down two short Lines of Figures, and, by the most simple and easy Operation in Arithmetic, to deduct one from the other. I, therefore, desire that the Chairman may make it on behalf of us all, and report it, which, I apprehend, will, at once, put an End to doubt, and carry universal Conviction with it: The mere Conviction of the Truth of the Fact, is not, however, the Intent of my Motion, which I think it now the more necessary to explain, as the honourable Gentleman, who spoke last seems wholly at a Loss to guess

guess what it may be. My View, Sir, in the Resolution, for which I moved, is, with all possible Duty and Respect, to lay before his Majesty the Sense of this House, with Respect to the great Increase of the public Expence, in an Article from which we can derive no Advantage, and to a Degree, which, by gradually burthening us with a Debt, that we are wholly unable to bear, will terminate in our Ruin; this, I think, we owe, as an Act of Duty, to his Majesty; and, as our Votes are printed for the Information of the Public, I think this Fact, in which the Public is so nearly interested, should appear in them. I would not, however, have it supposed that I am an Enemy to all Pensions indiscriminately, for I think that Gentlemen, who have distinguished themselves in the Service of their Country, have a Right to a Gratification, and I think it is the Interest of their Country that they should have it; to reward Merit is to produce it; the Public, therefore, will purchase greater Advantage by thus stimulating Individuals to signalize themselves in its Service, than by expending the same Sum in any other Manner: All that I mean, is, to shew that this Article is swelled beyond its due Bounds, and that the Disadvantage of contracttracting Debts, the Interest of which can only be paid by the Imposition of Taxes, which cannot be born, is greater than even the Reward of Merit itself can counter-ballance; and, I am confident, that if his Majesty was apprized of the Weight of our Burthen, he would not suffer us to bear it.

Mr M— P—.

I shall not enquire whether what is proposed, would, or would not, take up more Time than can now be allotted for it, but, as the honourable Gentleman who spoke last, said, that the Resolution, for which he moved, was intended to be laid before his Majesty, as a solemn Act of the House, I am for that Reason, against his Motion, for, making it on a sudden; such a Resolution would come with infinitely more Weight and Dignity, after the Members have taken Time for Consideration; there are many Objects of Consideration that will offer themselves on this Question, besides the mere Truth of the Fact: Deliberation always gives Weight and Force; Precipitancy always has a contrary Effect; the advantage of Deliberation we may secure by adjourning the Question till to-

to-morrow, and, as I do not fee that the fmalleft Inconvenience can refult from the Delay I think this fhould be done.

Mr *P— T—*, the A. G. then made the Motion for Adjournment.

Mr *E— S— P—.*

As there can be no previous Queftion moved for in a Committee, the Motion, for Adjournment, is always confidered as a previous Queftion, I muft, therefore, declare I am fo far from thinking the Refolution in Queftion will gain Weight and Force, by delay, that I think it will greatly lofe, with Refpect to both; as the Fact itfelf is manifeft at fight, we can deliberate only whether we will declare it, and furely this can fhew nothing, but an Irrefolution, and Lukewarmnefs, which can neither do us Credit, nor our Country Service; is not the Excefs of Expences, above our Revenue, a Grievance that calls for inftant Redrefs? Is not the Confequence of it equally manifeft and fatal? Ought we not to feize the firft Opportunity of making it known to him, from whom alone Redrefs is to be expected? And can delay have any other

other Tendency, than to convince him, either that our Danger is problematical, or, that we have not a proper Sense of it; will it not, therefore, tend directly to counteract the very Resolution we are urged to delay, when at last it shall be made? If a Man was to see his Friend drowning, would he deliberate about throwing out a Rope to save him? Would this Action lose any of its Weight, or Force, or Use, by that haste which the honest Impatience of Affection would naturally give it? And would not Deliberation, on the contrary, be a Proof, either that no Danger was apprehended, or no Deliverance designed? I confess, Sir, that I cannot but see Deliberation, in this Case, and in ours, exactly in the same Light, and, therefore, I oppose the Motion, for Adjournment, on this Occasion.

Mr C— C—.

I am sorry to say, that the very Reason, which has been most plausibly urged for our coming to this Resolution, is with me a Reason against it. It is said to be intended for the Information of his Majesty, but, in that View, I must declare, it appears to me, not only unnecessary, but officious. I have the greatest

Day X.] *Affairs of* Ireland.

greateſt Reaſon to believe that his Majeſty is already well acquainted with the State of the Finances of this Country, and, with the Purpoſes to which its Revenue is appropriated; and, I have very good Authority to ſay, that our amiable and benevolent Prince will, from his truly parental Tenderneſs for us, his loyal and affectionate People, take every Method to redreſs whatever ſhall appear to be really a Grievance: I will venture to ſay farther, that the Lord Lieutenant, who has the good of this Country equally at Heart, has already received ſuch Inſtructions from his Majeſty, relative to the Penſions, as, if known, would effectually preclude the Motion, which the honourable Gentleman, at the lower End of the Houſe, propoſed. I thought it my Duty on the preſent Occaſion, to mention this to the Committee.

Mr *E— S— P—.*

As I am fully perſuaded of the Veracity of the honourable Member that ſpoke laſt, and make no doubt of his having very good Intelligence, I ſhall readily admit what he has been pleaſed to advance; but, as he has not any Appointment under his Majeſty, which

which can give him Authority to communicate this Intelligence, I think, it ought not, in any Degree, to influence our Determinations.

Mr C— C—.

I do not prefume to fay, that I had any Authority to communicate what I have juft now mentioned to the Committee, nor fhould I have taken the Liberty to have done it, had it not been publicly faid this Day, by a Number of Gentlemen at the Caftle. The Gratitude that I owe to his Majefty, for the gracious Declaration he has made, and the high Senfe I have of the Obligations we are under to his Excellency the Lord Lieutenant, for the kind Part he has been pleafed to take, in this Affair, animated me fo far to trefpafs againft the ftrict Rules of Propriety, as to be the firft to communicate what I thought would be very acceptable to the Committee, though there are many Perfons in it, whofe Employment, Confequence, and Experience, give them a better Right to have done it.

Mr P— T—, the A. G.

Though I did not intend to mention this Affair

Affair, at this Time, yet, I now think, I am called upon to declare what I know about it. I am informed, that his Excellency the Lord Lieutenant, upon his firſt coming to the Adminiſtration here, repreſented the State of this Country, with Reſpect to Penſions, in ſuch a Light, to his Majeſty, as induced him to take them into Conſideration, and, I am informed, that his Majeſty's Secretary of State has ſince written a Letter to the Lord Lieutenant, which came to his Hand laſt Night, impowering him to communicate to this Houſe, his Majeſty's Intention, not to grant Penſions upon this Eſtabliſhment hereafter, except, upon very extraordinary Occaſions, either for Life, or Years.

Mr J— Fitz G—.

I beg leave to obſerve, that, in my Opinion, the Intelligence communicated by the honourable Gentleman, who ſpoke laſt, is premature, and contrary to Order. It is premature, becauſe when it is known that a parliamentary Enquiry is immediately to be made, concerning the Legality of granting away a very great Part of the Sum, annually paid in Penſions, it is improper to anticipate, in this Committe, a Debate, which is to come on at a Meeting of the Houfe; and, it is contrary to Order, to mention any Intelligence of this Kind in a Committee at all. Befides, it is at all Times improper, as well in the Houfe, as in a Committee, to mention the King, or his Minifters, in a manner that may, in the leaft Degree, influence the Determination of this Part of the Legiflature, in a Queftion, upon which the Public Intereft fo effentially depends. When his Majefty intends us the Honour of a Meffage, and it is brought to us by the proper Officers, at his command, it is our Duty to receive and confider it; but, when we are deliberating upon a Queftion, that comes properly before us as Reprefentatives of the People, we are not to be told that his Majefty has faid this, or his Minifter has faid that, much lefs are we to regard the Whifpers of a Levy, or any thing that a Minifter thinks fit to drop in a felect Junto, with a View to have it reach this Houfe, in the Courfe of its Circulation *. I exprefs myfelf with

---

* The Lord Lieutenant, upon the firft Intelligence of his Majefty's Intention, with Refpect to Penfions, thought

with the greatest Zeal, on this Occasion, as it certainly behoves us not only to avoid, with the utmost Care, all Royal or Ministerial Influence, but even the Appearances of it.

Mr P— T—, A. G.

Not to controvert what has been offered to shew that the Intelligence just communicated to the Committee, is premature, or contrary to Order, it is sufficient, for my own Justification, to repeat what I said before, that I did not intend to communicate it, and that I had not received any Authority so to do; but, as some Hints had been thrown out, I thought it better to explain the whole Matter, than to let Gentlemen go away with uncertain Surmises, and conceive Prejudices, which it might afterwards be difficult to remove.

---

thought fit to communicate it to a *few* of the principal Gentlemen; but, not thinking he had sufficient Authority to make it Publick, he wrote to his Majesty for permission so to do; this Permission he received, in the Letter mentioned in this Debate, to have come to his Hand the Night before; and he then communicated it to a Number of Gentlemen *at the Castle.*

Mr *R— F—*.

Admitting what that honourable Gentleman has said, with Respect to his Majesty's Intention, and that his Intelligence was properly conveyed, I think it should by no means preclude the Resolution it is supposed to render unnecessary; for, I observe, that the Royal Intention, as it has been reported to us, relates only to Pensions for Lives, or Years; whereas, the great Burthen upon this Establishment is Pensions *during Pleasure*, which we seldom see revoked, because they are generally effectual for the Purpose intended. It is manifest, from the uniform Conduct of those to whom they are granted, that their Influence is more certain, and, therefore, more dangerous, than that of others, and for this Reason, as to their immediate Tendency, more worthy to be the Subject of an Address.

Mr *J— D—* made use of some Arguments, in Favour of the Adjournment, upon which, Mr *B——* got up, and spoke to the following Effect:

Mr

I should certainly oppose the Adjournment, if I had no other Objection against it, than the ill Use which may possibly be made of it; I am sorry to say, that, upon these Occasions, I have frequently known six or seven Gentlemen meet, who have an Influence in this House, which is too often more prevalent than Conviction itself. In the present Case, I should be very sorry to have such a Meeting, and, therefore, I am against the Adjournment.

The Question for the Adjournment was then put, and carried in the Negative 80 against 71.

The Question was then put for the Motion, and passed in the Affirmative *Nem. Con.*

It is remarkable, that the very same Question, on the very same Occasion, was determined by the first Division last Sessions, when it passed against the Adjournment 82 against 80.

The Speaker then resumed the Chair.

Mr *E— S— P—* said, that he should be glad to know what Day it would be agreeable

ble for him to bring into that House a Complaint of a Breach of Privilege, with Respect to Letters coming free to Members of that House; this Privilege, he said, he thought should be supported, and, he alledged, that an *English* Letter, directed to him at his Mother's House in *Limerick*, was charged at the Post-Office there, because, when it came thither, he happened to be at *Dublin*; this, he said, he thought a Breach of Privilege.

The R——t H——ble *W— H— F—*, P. M. G. got up, and said, that he was of a different Opinion: The Post-Office in *Ireland*, he said, was a Branch of the Post-Office in *England*, and he apprehended that the Privilege of Members of Parliament here, with Respect to their Letters passing free, was not more extensive than that of the Members in *England*, where it was an established Rule, that, if the Letter was not directed to the dwelling House of the Member, or to a Place where he was actually resident at the Time, it should be charged. He said, that a Member of Parliament, in *England*, had made a Complaint of exactly the same Kind as this of Mr *P—*, with Respect to the charging two Letters, which he could produce, and, that being in

the

the Course of the Debate, convinced of the Impropriety of Letters directed to Members of Parliament going free to Places, where the Member was not, and of the ill Purposes to which it might be abused, he acquiesced in the Charge, and dropped his Complaint: Mr F——, however, added, that he would not anticipate the Debate, which would arise on the Day that should be fixed for Complaints of Breach of Privilege being heard, and examined, and that he was willing it should be fixed as soon as was thought proper.

Mr P— replied, that he agreed, with the Post-Master, in allowing that the Post-Office in *Ireland* was a Branch of the Post-Office in *England*, but insisted that the Privilege of the Members in *Ireland* had no dependance upon that Country.

Mr F— interrupting him, answered, he did not say that it had.

Mr P— then proceeded, and said, he was fired at a Breach of Privilege of this Kind, as many Arts had been practised to prevent the Members from enjoying the Advantages of it. He added, that it once happened that the Resolufolutions of the Houfe, relative to this Queftion, and in Favour of the Privilege, had been fecreted and not printed.

TUESDAY, *Nov.* 8, 1763.

ELEVENTH DAY.

Mr J— Fitz-G—.

Mr S——,

THE Penfions that are now charged upon the civil Eftablifhment of this Kingdom, amount to no lefs than *feventy-two Thoufand Pounds per Annum*, befides the *French* and military Penfions, and befides the Sums paid as Salaries for old, and new unneceffary Employments, and thofe paid in unneceffary Additions to the Salaries of others; the Penfions, therefore, on the Civil Eftablifhment alone, exceed the Civil Lift above *forty-two Thoufand Pounds*. It appears to have been the unanimous Refolution of this Houfe, in the Year 1757, that the Increafe of Penfions was then very alarming, and, as the Increafe of of Penſions, ſince that Time, has been very conſiderable, it muſt be now alarming, in a much greater Degree. Penſions have gradually increaſed every Year, from the Time that their Increaſe was declared to be alarming, by a ſolemn Reſolution of this Houſe. I ſpeak it with equal Aſtoniſhment and Concern, and, I think, it muſt aſtoniſh and concern all that hear me. There are many other Circumſtances that aggravate this Evil. Penſions were not only increaſed by the Miniſters, immediately after the ſolemn Declaration of this Houſe, that they were already ſo great as to be of the moſt fatal Conſequence, had been communicated, in a moſt ſubmiſſive Manner, by an Addreſs, to the Crown; but at a Time when an expenſive War increaſed the real Exigencies of the State, and when a large Supply, large, with Reſpect to the pecuniary Abilities of this poor Country, was required, and granted, and a very conſiderable national Debt willingly, and chearfully, contracted: At a Time, too, when many new Regiments were raiſed, which, as they would neceſſarily increaſe the Influence of a Miniſter, by creating new Appointments, might well have excuſed us from paying penſionary Gratifications: It might, reaſonably, have been hoped,

that

that our general Inability, our neceffary Increafe of Expence, our contracting Debts, and our Increafe of the Minifter's Power, by raifing new Troops, the Command of which would be in his Difpofal, would, without any Remonftrance from the Commons, have been fufficient to deter him from laying upon us the additional and odious Burthen of new Penfions; yet, unhappily for us, Penfions have been increafed, in Proportion to the very Caufes why they fhould not encreafe; and, while our Ability has been growing lefs, and the Influence of the Minifter more, we have not only had our Money given away, in new Penfions, but in Augmentations of the Salaries that we have too long paid for doing nothing. It is always, with Regret, that I difcover the Nakednefs of my Country, but, upon this Occafion, I ought not to hide it: Upon this Occafion, I muft remind you, that *Ireland* is not more than one third peopled; that our Trade lies under fuch Difadvantages, that two-thirds of the People we have are unemployed, and are, confequently, condemned to the moft deplorable Indigence; a State which cannot fail to render them wretched, in Proportion as the Luxury of a few has multiplied artificial Wants, to which they are

no

no Strangers, but of which they have no farther Knowledge than juft ferves to excite Envy and Difcontent. We have neither foreign Trade, nor home Confumption, fufficient to diftribute the Conveniencies of Life among us, with a reafonable Equality; or to enable us to pay any Tax, proportioned to our Number. This Ifland is fuppofed to contain three Millions; and, of thefe, two Millions live like the Beafts of the Field, upon a Root picked out of the Earth; almoft without Hovels for Shelter, or Cloaths for covering. What muft become of a Nation, in this Situation, which, at the fame Time, is contracting a Debt that muft every Year increafe, by a very confiderable Excefs of its Expences above its Income? What muft become of a Nation whofe idle Hands, inftead of being employed, by the Introduction of Trade, and the Eftablifhment of Manufactures, are formed into Corps of mercenary Soldiers, whom the unhappy Community to which they belong, and to the Profperity of which their Labour ought to contribute, is taxed to pay; with this Aggravation, that the Expence they can fo ill bear, is unneceffarily increafed, upon the Penfion Principles, by the Number of Regiments, and Officers, being greatly more

than

than in Proportion to the Number of Men; by the Money paid to thefe Officers being fpent in another Country, almoft all the Staff, which is very weighty, being Abfentees, and feveral of the Regiments themfelves being ordered out of the Kingdom? What Method can be found to prevent the Ruin of a State, in which thefe Evils not only continue, but increafe? What new Mode of Taxation can be devifed? Shall we tax Leather where no Shoes are worn, or Tallow, where no Candles are burnt? What Tax can be raifed upon the Neceffaries of Life, where they confift wholly of Roots and Water? and, where Conveniencies can but juft be procured? What Tax can be laid upon them that will not operate as a Prohibition, and, confequently, can never be raifed? If we cannot increafe our Revenue, we have but one Alternative, we muft either leffen our Expences, or be undone: Surely, it is not neceffary to confider how Ruin may be aggravated, to determine our Choice; and yet there are many Circumftances that will aggravate our Ruin, if we fuffer it to take Place; thofe who have fuffered in a good Caufe, who have facrificed a private to a public Intereft, who have fuftained fuffering Virtue, or, afferted the Claim of

ne-

neglected Merit, have derived Confolation from a noble Source, and have not only triumphed, but rejoiced in Misfortune. Will this be our Cafe? If we ourfelves, our Wives, and Children, and all that are near and dear to us, are ftript of our whole Birthright; if our Conftitution is fubverted, our Freedom deftroyed, and the wretched Inhabitants of this loyal and magnanimous Country left to perifh, for Want, in the Streets, what Comfort fhall we have in this dreadful Day of our Vifitation? Can we then reflect, with the Patriot's Elation of Mind, that we fuffer for the general Good of Mankind? Can we footh ourfelves with the confcious Generofity of having procured any important Benefit to our Sifter Country? Can we flatter Ourfelves with a Loyalty that has facrificed all to the Gratification of our Prince? or with a romantic, but noble Liberality, that has lavifhed our whole Poffeffions, in rewarding thofe who have opened new Mines of Knowledge, or unlocked new Springs of Felicity?—No; mortifying Confideration! we are facrificing Ourfelves to increafe the Folly and Extravagance of thofe, whom Opulence has already made extravagant and foolifh; or to enrich the Servile and the Corrupt, whom it is the

Interest of every State to keep poor. Some private Service done to the King's Advisers, is the Claim, the only Claim, of both Classes, to the Vitals of our Country; and, what is our consenting to pay Pensions to such Wretches as these, but leaving our Property to those who have stabbed us to the Heart! It is written, *That the Wages of Sin is Death*; but whoever will look into our List of Pensions, will have Reason to say, "That the Wages of Sin is *Ireland*." There are, indeed, on that List, two Persons who have an indubitable Claim to our Gratitude; one in this Kingdom, and the other in *England*; but many of the rest, on the List, are Names that are no where else to be found, that blot the Paper, and dishonour the two worthy Persons, who are mentioned in the same Margin: It is not, indeed, pretended that they have Merit, even in the Preamble of the very Patent that gives them our Wealth; it is there confessed that they are selected to good Fortune by *special* Grace, and *mere Motion*: If we enquire what it was that qualified them for this Distinction, we shall find, that the Qualification of some, was, their having had Pensions before, that were too small to gratify their Vices; the Qualification of others, their contributing

buting to the Vices of their Superiors, and of some, their Dexterity at procuring for a Minister, a parliamentary Influence: They are of both Sexes, of all Countries, and of all Classes: The Foreigner, by having a Pension for Life, or Years, may employ our own Money against us; for, though the Grant, in that Case, might be resumed, yet it might, before that Time, be transferred for an equivalent Sum, which would be thus out of our reach: The Native being worthless and corrupt, and his very Demerit being his Recommendation, is already actually employed against us, by secretly undermining our Independence, and Liberty, and both concur in draining us of Money to an Amount that must load us with an unsupportable Debt, and terminate in our inevitable Ruin. Our Case, however, is not desperate; our Hope is in the Best of Princes, the Friend of Virtue, the Father of his People: To redress this enormous Grievance, nothing more can be necessary than to acquaint him with it: To expose the delusive Arts of his Advisers, and convince him, by the Representation I have now made, that they are sacrificing the Happiness, almost the Existence, of three Million of his loyal and dutiful Subjects, to a few Wretches, of whom

he

he is totally ignorant, and whom, if he knew, he would defpife and deteſt. It can never be fuppofed, that our moſt gracious Sovereign would concur in fuch Meafures, if he might do it without an exprefs Violation of the Law, much lefs can it be fuppofed, that he would fuffer the Law to be violated, which he has publickly and folemnly engaged to defend. That the Grant of the Penfions, in Queſtion, is contrary to Law, I ſhall now prove, by inconteſtible Evidence, and, whatever Doubt fome Gentlemen may have, or pretend to have, about the fatal Confequences of our Penfions, I prefume that there are none who doubt, or pretend to doubt, whether a Practice ſhould be fuffered, by which Laws, that immediately affect, not Individuals only, but the very Conſtitution are trampled under Foot.

The Crown, Sir, has a public and a private Revenue; the public Revenue it receives as a Truſtee for the Public; and the private Revenue it receives in its own Right. The public Revenue arifes from the hereditary and temporary Duties, and thefe are exprefly appropriated to particular Purpofes; fo that the Crown is not a Truſtee with a difcretionary Power,

Power, but a Trustee, limited and prescribed; receiving the Money, merely to apply it for the Purposes to which it is appropriated. The private Revenue arises from the ancient Demesne Lands, from Forfeitures for Treason, and Felony, Prisage of Wines, Light-House Duties, and a small Part of the casual Revenue, not granted by Parliament, and, in this, the Crown has the same unlimitted Property that a Subject has in his own Freehold. Now, Sir, the private Revenue of the Crown, probably, does not amount to 7,000 *l.* a Year, so that the Pensions, amounting to 72,000 *l.* a Year, include an illegal Appropriation of 65,000 *l.* a Year, of an unalienable Revenue, limitted to public Uses.

That the public Revenue is thus limitted, appears incontestible, by the very Statutes on which the several Duties that constitute it are raised.

The Grant of the Excise is said, in the Preamble, to be for " Pay of the Army, and " defraying other public Charges, in Defence " and Preservation of this Kingdom;" the Grant of Tonnage and additional Poundage, " for protecting the Trade of this Kingdom

" at Sea, and augmenting the public Reve-
" nue;" and the Grant of Hearth-Money, as
" a public Revenue for public Charges and
" Expences."

This Grant of Hearth-Money was made *in lieu of the Irish Court of Wards*, in which the Crown had private Property; and on which Pensions had been charged; and, therefore, the Legislature, apprehending that those to whom these Pensions had been paid, might endeavour to obtain them out of this new Revenue, was not content that they should only be *voidable* by the general Appropriation of the Grant in the Preamble, but added a Clause, expresly enacting, that all such Pensions should be *void*; enabling the Court of Exchequer, in a summary Way, to compell the Grantee to re-pay all the Pension that should be received, on Pretence of such Grant, and inflicting a Forfeiture of double the Value, on every Person, who should accept of such Pension; it must also be remarked, that the Clause annulling Pensions contains no Exception in Favour of Pensions granted as Rewards for public Services; it is, therefore, manifest, that the Legislature did not consider such Pensions as Part of the *public Charges*;

if

if they did, this Act would be inconsistent with itself.

The Act for granting the Revenue of Ale-Licenses, not mentioning the Uses for which it was granted, in the Preamble, has restrained the Crown from charging it with Pensions, by an express Clause.

The Act granting the Revenue of strong Water, and Wine-Licences, was principally intended to regulate the Retail of those Liquors, and not for the Income, which was supposed to be inconsiderable; therefore no Preamble was thought of, to declare the Uses of it, nor any express Clause to guard it against Pensions; yet, as there is nothing in it that shews an Intention of private Property, the Construction of this Act must be governed by the usual Intention of such Grants, for this is the universal Practice, with Respect to Constructions in Law, as might be shewn from a hundred Instances.

The Grant of Poundage is manifestly intended for public Uses: It was originally granted in the 14th of *Henry* the IVth, to the military Fraternity of St *George,* for *maintain-*

taining a military Force, in Defence of the *Englifh* Pale *againft Rebels*: An Act of the 10th of of *Henry* the VIIth, recites, that the Tax had been converted by the Fraternity to *private Ufes*, and, THEREFORE, grants it to the Crown for five Years; at the Expiration of this Term it was made perpetual by the Act now in Force.

The *Irifh* Quit-rents, and Crown-rents, were referved on Grants of Lands, in which the Crown had a private Property, and, therefore, thefe Rents were originally the private Property of the Crown, but, by the *Englifh* Act of the 11th and 12th of King *William* the IIId. it is enacted "that thefe "Rents fhall *for ever* be for the Maintainance " of the Government of *Ireland*, and that all " Penfions fince the 13th of *February* 1688, " charged or to be charged thereon, fhould " be void." Now, it cannot be argued, that the exprefs Exclufion of Penfions proves them not to be excluded by the general Appropriation of the Duty; becaufe, though the exprefs Appropriation of the Duty, does exclude them, an exprefs Claufe, was, notwithftanding, neceffary for two Purpofes; one was, that Penfions which would otherwife have

have been only *voidable*, might be *void*; and the other, that Penfions, granted between the 13th of *February* 1688, and the Time of making the Act might be null, which might otherwife have been deemed valid. It muft alfo be obferved here, that this Act, like that annulling Penfions on the Hearth-money, makes no Exception in favour of thofe fuppofed to be granted for public Service; fo that fuch Penfions cannot be pretended to be for the Maintenance of Government. It alfo appears that the Legiflatures, both of *England* and *Ireland*, wifely forefaw, that an Exception, in Favour of Penfions, grounded on public Merit, would be abufed, by Servants of the Crown, and Mifleaders of the People; and it is manifeft, that charging the Revenue of *Ireland* with Penfions, is contrary to the Intention of both Legiflatures, in other Words *is contrary to Law.*

This Fact, once eftablifhed, totally precludes all that might be offered on the other Side, yet, I cannot help obferving, that one Argument, in particular, in Favour of Penfions is *felo-de-fe*; it is faid, that Penfions are ufeful for maintaining the Dignity of the Crown; if fo, no Penfion fhould be granted ed for Lives, or Years, either in Poffeffion, or Reverfion, becaufe fuch Grant tends to leffen the Dignity of the Crown in fucceeding Reigns; fome new Kind of Sophiftry, muft, therefore, be invented to frame a plaufible Apology for the Advifers of fuch Penfions.

I think, Sir, it would now be unneceffary to take Notice of a Letter, faid to have been written by one of the Secretaries of State, concerning his Majefty's Intention, with Refpect to Penfions, even if it had come legally before us; I fhall, therefore, only obferve, that it promifes nothing; it fays, as we have been informed, by thofe who affect to believe that it ought to preclude our prefent Enquiry, that Penfions *for Lives or Years*, fhall not be granted for the future, *except on extraordinary Occafions*: Penfions, during Pleafure, therefore, are out of the Queftion; and who but the Minifter is to judge of the Occafion, upon which Penfions are to be granted for Lives, or Years? If the Minifter, Sir, fhall think fit to advife the granting fuch Penfion, for the future, he has nothing to do, but to pretend that the Occafion is extraordinary, to evade the Promife, in which we are now exhorted impliplicitly to trust. Upon the whole, as the present Load of Pensions is ruinous in itself, as it is laid on, in Violation of the constitutional Laws of the Kingdom, as the Acquiescence, in such Violation, is a Breach of the Trust reposed in us, and totally repugnant to our highest Interest, and, as we have at present no effectual Promise of Redress, I humbly beg leave to move

"That an humble Address be presented to to his Majesty, to represent, in the most dutiful Terms, that the Debt of this Kingdom is become very great. That the Pensions, now in being, that have been placed on the Establishments of this Kingdom, are one of the Causes of the Increase of the public Debt. That those Pensions have been paid, and continue to be paid, out of all the Revenues of this Kingdom without Distinction. That it appears to this House to be worthy of his Majesty's Royal Consideration, whether the Grants that have been made of those Pensions, are agreeable to, or warranted by the Laws of Kingdom, and whether the Revenues of the Crown that have been given for public Uses, ought, or can by Law, be applied to Pensions: And, therefore, most
hum-

humbly to beseech his Majesty, to order it to be made known, as his Majesty's Royal Will and Command, to the Officers of the Treasury of this Kingdom, that no Part of the Revenues of Excise, Customs, Poundage, Hearth-Money, Quit-Rents, Ale Licences, Wine, or Strong Water Licences, or of the additional Duties, granted or to be granted in this Kingdom, for any limited Term, be paid or applied to any Pension, or Annuity, granted, or to be granted, out of, or which may any ways charge, or affect the said Revenues of Excise, Customs, Poundage, Hearth Money, Quit Rents, Ale Licences, Wine, and Strong Water Licences, and additional Duties, or any of the said Revenues, till it shall first be determined by a Court of Justice, of competent Jurisdiction, that the Crown may grant Annuities, or Pensions, out of the said Revenues; and that his Majesty may be graciously pleased to give his Royal Orders to the Officers of the Treasury, that no Pensions be paid out of the said Revenues, in any other Manner, than the Judgment, or Decree, of a Court of competent Jurisdiction, shall determine to be just, and agreeable to the Laws of this Kingdom; and that his Majesty may be graciously pleased to order his Majesty's

Ser-

Servants of the Law in this Kingdom, to make that Defence, that the Laws of the Kingdom shall warrant, to every Suit that shall be commenced or carried on by any Penfioner or Annuitant, claiming any Part of the said Revenues, till it shall be judiciously determined, in the most solemn Manner, and by the dernier resort, that the Crown may grant Pensions, or Annuities, out of the said Revenues. That his Majesty's faithful Commons, nevertheless, do by no Means intend, that the Crown shall be deprived of the Means of rewarding Merit, or of conferring those Bounties, on proper Occasions, that the Honour and Dignity of the Crown may require: But that his Majesty's faithful Commons, on the contrary, will be ready to provide a Revenue, such as the Condition and Circumstances of this Kingdom shall admit of, to enable the Crown to reward Merit, and, on proper Occasions, to confer those Bounties that may be suitable to the Honour and Dignity of the Crown, if it shall be determined, that the present Revenues of the Crown, that have been given for Public Uses, ought not to be applied to Pensions. Provided these Revenues be reserved and applied to the Support of his Majesty's Government in this Kingdom only."

Mr

Mr J— M— said, that he did not pretend to go into the nice Disquisitions of the Law, or enter the Lists with the worthy Member, who spoke last, so justly pre-eminent in the Profession; but that he thought it his Duty, when he intended to oppose a Measure of so great and upright a Man, to disclose his own Sentiments as the Motives of his Conduct, however firmly he might be persuaded they would have but little Influence upon others. Let us suppose, says he, that the House should come into the Motion; that the King, in consequence of it, should give Orders to his Servants, to support a Suit intended to invalidate his own Grants, and distress the deserving, for some such I think the honourable Gentleman has allowed to be in the Pensioners List; let us suppose, that after long litigation, at a vast Expence to the Crown, and to the total Ruin of the Pensioners, the Grant should be declared illegal, and invalidated accordingly; I apprehend that the Evil, resulting from such a Determination, would be greater than the Good; it would immediately injure the Prerogative of the Crown, and, consequently, would be hurtful to the Constitution, of which the Crown is an essential

tial and confiderable Part. It is neceffary, in all Conftitutions, that the Regal Dignity fhould be fupported by a Power to reward as well as to punifh: It is furely, contrary to all Rules, as well as all Senfe of Right, and Wrong, that our amiable and beloved Sovereign, who holds the Sword of Juftice in one Hand, fhould hold a barren Sceptre in the other. The two great Springs of all Action are Hope and Fear, and, where Fear only operates, Love can have no place; a People ftimulated only by Fear, however free, and, whatever Advantages of Government they may boaft, are in a worfe State than the Subjects of a Defpotic Prince; Rewards and Punifhments are allowed to be properly in the Hands of the Divine Being, whom Kings fhould be taught to imitate, and, in every State, it is as neceffary to ftimulate to fuch Actions as are beneficial to a State, as to deter from thofe which are hurtful: If Perfons of great Merit become grey in the Service of their Country, muft they be difmiffed to ftarve when they are capable of this Service no longer? Or muft the Public fuffer by having them continued in Places of which they are unable to difcharge the Duty? To continue them would be furely the moft

ex-

expenfive Way of rewarding them; and to difmifs them, unrewarded, would be little better than adopting the horrid Cuftom of the *Indian* Savages, who deftroy their Parents when they grow old; upon the whole, confidering the prefent, juft, and gracious Difpofition of his Majefty, and the amiable Conduct of the Lord Lieutenant, with Refpect to the Penfions on this Eftablifhment, I really think Reftrictions are unneceffary; and, as I fhould be forry to render his Majefty's divine Characteriftic of delighting to do Good ineffectual, I muft declare myfelf againft the Motion.

Mr *R— L—*.

Mr S——,

I am fo aftonifhed, Sir, at what I have heard from the honourable Gentleman, who fpoke laft, that I know not where to begin my Reply; becaufe it has been admitted, that two Perfons, who receive Penfions from this Eftablifhment are worthy, he fets out upon a Suppofition, that Penfions, in general, are the Reward of Merit, though they have been exprefly faid to be given for the Services firft, of Vice, to Vice, to be a Superfluity added to Wealth, or, the Means of Luxury and Intemperance, to Ignorance and Sloth. If, upon the Principle, that it is better for ten guilty to escape, than for one innocent to suffer, he would infinuate, that all the Penfions fhould be continued, for the Sake of the few who deferve them, he muft, firft, fhew, that the Fund propofed to be eftablifhed for enabling the Crown to reward Merit, will be inadequate to the Deferts of thofe few; for, otherwife, there is no Neceffity for continuing Penfions to the unworthy, upon pretence, that they muft otherwife be taken from the deferving: Befides, Sir, if that was the Cafe, his Principle concludes directly againft him; for many more innocent Perfons will fuffer, by the Continuation of Penfions, as they ftand at prefent, than by the total Annihilation of them all; by their Continuance, Sir, the whole Nation muft fuffer, as the honourable Gentleman, who made the Motion, has fhewn by his mafterly Addrefs, not to the Paffions only, but the Underftanding. What then can the Gentleman mean, by fuppofing, that, an Enquiry into the Legality of thefe Grants, will reftrain the King's Power of doing Good? Is the Gratification of a certain Number of

fervile

servile, obscure, vicious, idle, and voluptuous Wretches, at the Expence of a Nation, doing Good? Will not his Majesty rejoice to be undeceived, and to have his Benevolence directed to its proper Object? Would he not also be glad to have his Bounty kept within its proper Channel, rather than suffered to overflow its Banks, and ruin the Country? This Country, Sir, might easily be made a bright Jewel in the *British* Crown, and, it is now able to contribute something to the general Stock; it may be said, Sir, like the Bird in the Fable, to produce one golden Egg in a Day, but, if those who receive the gradual Tribute are impatient to seize the whole Treasure at its Source, they will fare, as the Peasant did, who ripped up his Bird, and suffer by the same Folly and Rapacity that destroyed their Benefactor. But, I am really, Sir, almost afraid to follow the honourable Gentleman farther; he has told us, Sir, that, if the Grant of Pensions is illegal, it ought to be, notwithstanding, permitted, for fear of hurting the Prerogative.——Is it the Prerogative of the Crown, Sir, to act contrary to Law! And have we lived to hear this Principle advanced in an *Irish* House of Commons! Upon this Occasion, my Humanity

restrains

restrains me from making any Remark, and, I am sure, the Sense of the House must excuse me from a Reply. But, Sir, we have also been told, by a most extraordinary Deduction of Argument, that if we do not suffer ourselves to sink under the present exorbitant Load of Pensions, we shall be in a worse State than the Slaves of a Tyrant in *Barbary*; dreadful Dilemma, and astonishing Paradox! but how is it made out? Why, if we limit the Pensions, we shall totally annihilate the King's Power to reward Merit; if we annihilate his Power to reward Merit, he can never excite Hope; if he excites no Hope, he can act only upon our Fear, and those, that are stimulated only by Fear, are worse off than Slaves in *Barbary*. If it is possible to recollect myself, among all these Wonders, and see my Way through this Confusion, let me ask, has the King of *Great Britain* no Source for the Reward of Merit, but *Irish* Pensions? Let us look round, and take a View of the Servants of the Crown, and their Servants, and the Servants of their Servants, in every Department; and, let us count their Numbers, and the Value of their Employments; we shall soon be convinced, that the Service of the State is most abundantly its own reward; of how many

many does the firſt and principal Claſs conſiſt, who, in general, are paid for doing nothing? And how much more numerous are the ſubordinate Claſſes that are paid for doing, what the others leave undone? While all theſe lucrative Employments are in the Gift of the Crown, is Merit to go wholly unrewarded, if we reduce our Penſions within the Limits of our Ability? Is Merit to be wholly unrewarded, if our Vitals are not drained away for thoſe who have no Merit at all? Amazing Abſurdity! But if our Penſions are reduced, and our Laws kept ſacred, worſe Conſequences ſtill follow; we are then to act from no Motive but Fear, and, if ſo, we are in a worſe State than Slaves in *Barbary*. It is ſomewhat difficult to conceive, what makes the State of the Subjects of *Morocco* deplorable, if it is not a ſlaviſh Subjection from a principal of Fear; and, if it is, there cannot be leſs Difficulty in conceiving how our State can become worſe, ſuppoſing the ſame Effect to be produced among us, from the ſame Cauſe; but is that honourable Gentleman now to learn, that, in *Barbary*, the Innocent are not exempted from that Fear, which in *Britain* can only operate upon the Guilty? Will any Man in *Britain* fear that his

his Property should be arbitrarily seized by a Creature of Power, that his Person should be ill treated, or his Family turned into the Street, by the brutal and capricious Displeasure of some Delegate of Despotism, of whom he does not dare to complain? Will honest Industry be brought under the Fear of these Evils, by a Limitation of *Irish* Pensions, or a Defence of our Constitution, against illegal Demands? Of what, Sir, are we to live in fear? In *Britain* we can fear nothing, but Punishment for breaking the Law; if we do not suffer that Law, which is equally the Safeguard of the Innocent, and the Scourge of the Guilty, to be rendered ineffectual, and broken with Impunity. While we act in a steady Conformity to our public and private Duties, we may set Power at defiance, and live sacred from the Fear that makes Slaves, in *Barbary*, wretched, though not one Farthing should be paid, in Pensions, from this Time for ever. But this Gentleman has asked, whether those who have grown grey, in the public Service, are to be left to starve, when they can serve the Public no longer? Let me ask, in my turn, has this Gentleman never heard of Employments being executed by Deputies; if a Deputy is admitted when the Incumbent is able, can he suppose a Deputy will not be permitted, when the Incumbent has survived his Ability? He asks, must the Public be injured, by continuing Persons in Office, whom Age has rendered unable to perform their Duty? And, I ask, is the Public injured by putting those into Office who were never able to perform their Duty at all; when the Service is constantly exacted from those whom the Public pays for performing it, and when none are appointed to receive this Pay of the Public, but those who are able to perform the Service effectually, for which it is allotted, it will then be time enough to consider of Expedients, for rewarding the past Services of those who are disabled from future. I should be sorry to impute the very extraordinary Things, which, that honourable Gentleman has thought fit to drop in this Assembly, to the least favourable Cause; but I solemnly declare, they appear to me to be of such a Nature, that I do not know whether it is more to his Disadvantage, to suppose, that he does or does not believe what he has advanced; however, as he has thought fit to declare, that he would not oppose the Motion, without Reason, I hope he will now see no Reason to oppose it, at least, no Reason against

gainſt providing ſome Remedy for the Evil which it was intended to remove.

Mr *J— D—* ſpoke next, againſt the Motion, but his Speech conſiſted chiefly of ſome nice Diſtinctions between the Statute and Common Law, which he ſtated with great Force and Perſpicuity.

Mr *J— G—*, the S. G.

Mr S——,

However prejudicial I may think the encreaſe of Penſions to this Kingdom, I muſt confeſs, that the Method propoſed by the honourable and learned Gentleman, as a Remedy, is ſuch as I ſhall oppoſe, with as ſtrong a Conviction of its Impropriety, as of any Meaſure that has hitherto come to my Knowledge. In the firſt Place, Sir, I ſhould be very ſorry to admit, that the Conſtitutional Power of this Houſe was ſo inconſiderable, as to require Aſſiſtance from a Court of Law, to remedy a ſuppoſed Grievance, with Reſpect to the Diſpoſal of public Money; ſuch Aſſiſtance is wholly unprecedented, and totally inconſiſtent with an Opinion of great Importance, hitherto uncontroverted, that the Houſe

House has a Power within itself, adequate to the Purpose.

I must also observe, that, among the many Prerogatives with which the Crown is constitutionally invested, that of disposing of the public Money, when deposited as an aggregate Fund, in the Treasury, is one: The Crown is restrained, in the Disposal of public Money, only with Respect to such Duties as are, by Act of Parliament, expresly appropriated to some separate and particular Use, without being brought to such aggregate Fund. There must be, in some Part of the Legislature, an executive and directing Power, and, in our Constitution, this Power is well known to be lodged in the King: It is also well known, that, to prevent the Abuse of this Power, it is made liable to the immediate inspection, and controul, of the other Parts of the Legislature, particularly of this House: If the Crown is intrusted with the Power of making Peace and War, raising and disbanding Armies, building Fortifications, and Ships, for the Defence of the State, creating such new Employments as may be thought necessary for its Service, and rewarding public Merit, to stimulate others to deserve Reward; surely

surely the Power of doing these Things would be nugatory, and insignificant, if the Means of exerting it were not in the same Hands; it would, indeed, be a mere nominal, not an actual Power; in other Words, it would be no Power at all; for, in what Sense can the King be said to have a Power of raising an Army, or creating an Employment, if he has not the Power of appointing the Sums, necessary for those Purposes, to be paid out of the Treasury? This Power is discretionary, but it is under controul, as I have before observed, so that the Crown must be considered as a Trustee for the Public, with Respect to the public Money, and, though intrusted with the Application, yet accountable for it: But, I desire it may be understood, that, when I mention the Crown, I mean the Servants of the Crown, for, it is an inviolable Maxim, that the King can do no Wrong. Now Pensions, Sir, I think, must be considered as Expences necessary for carrying on Government, and there are two Ways by which they may be issued, one is by Patent, under the great Seal, for Lives, or Years; the other, by the King's Letters, under the Privy Seal: Both these Acts are carried into Execution by the King's Servants, who are all accountable to

this

this House, whenever it shall think proper to make an Enquiry into their Conduct, with Respect to the Application of public Money; and, without the Forms, by which the Officers, who act in such Application, are ascertained, no Money can be legally issued: It happened, in King *William*'s Time, that there was a small Overplus, in the Hands of Lord *Falkland*, first Lord of the Admiralty, and, that the King wrote to him for it, upon which it was sent. But the Parliament thought him so blameable for paying the Money, without the Warrant for its having gone through the proper Offices, that they were very near expelling him. It appears, therefore, I think, with the strongest Evidence, that this House has, in itself, a sufficient Power to prevent the Mis-application of public Money, and to call the great Officers of the Crown to account for it, if it has been mis-applied. It can effectually prevent the Mis-application of it, by stopping the Supplies; and this was actually done in the Year 1703, for, though but few Pensions were then granted, yet two of them were so improper, that the House discontinued them. As this House, therefore, is able to prevent the Abuse of the Power of rewarding past Services, and Sufferings, which the Crown

Crown has ever claimed, and exercifed, and which appears to be effentially neceffary to Government, it feems to me wholly unaccountable, and unreafonable, to bring this Power into Queftion, merely upon Pretence, that it has been abufed. If the King, Sir, fhould pardon every Felon, that is capitally convicted, can it be concluded, that he has, therefore, no Power to pardon Felony? The long Practice of the Crown to grant Penfions, is, alone, a ftrong Prefumption of its Legality: Penfions were granted fo long ago as the Reign of *Henry* the VIIIth, and, from that Hour to this, the Power of granting them has never been called in Queftion, though the Abufe of it has been frequently the Subject of Complaint, and, at a Time, when there has been the ftrongeft Difpofition to catch at every Thing that might reftrain the Prerogative. But, Sir, the Conduct of this Houfe furnifhes more than negative Proof, that the Grant of Penfions is legal. Penfions, Sir, have been made fubject to a Tax of Six-pence in the Pound, but, if they were confidered by this Houfe as illegal, they could not be legally taxed. Befides, Sir, I do not fee by what Rules of Conftruction, Penfions, in Reward of paft Services, can be fhewn not to be in-

clud-

cluded in the Words *public Charges,* or the *necessary Support of Government*; if they cannot, the granting them is authorized by the very Acts of Supply. The Preamble of the Acts of Excise, and the additional Tonnage, and Poundage, express that those Duties are granted for certain Purposes of public Utility, and *defraying other public Charges.* In the Preamble to the Act, by which Hearth-Money was instituted, on the abolishing of the *Irish* Court of Wards, and, in that, for Ale-Licences, those Duties, being said to be for *public Charges and Expences,* are secured from being liable to Pensions, by an express Clause: Now, Sir, if the Words, which submitted them to public Charges, and Expences, did not make them liable to Pensions, why were Pensions expresly excepted? I know we have been told, that this Exception was made expresſly, because it was apprehended that those who had Pensions, on the Court of Wards, and lost them on its Abolition, would apply for Redress out of these new Duties? but, does the Application make any Difference in the Thing applied for? If the Crown had not a Power to grant these Pensioners Redress by the Act, did their Desire to be redressed, make it necessary to fortify the Act with

with new Power againſt them? The Crown either had, or had not, a legal Power, to grant them Penſions out of theſe new Duties; if it had, the Words *public Charges* includes Penſions; if it had not, the Exception was redundant and abſurd: It is ſaid, indeed, that it was added to render ſuch Penſions not only *voidable*, but *void*; but who can imagine, Sir, that the Legiſlature was then ſo ſhort ſighted as to ſee only a ſingle Spot of the Object before them? Who can imagine, that, for the ſake of rendering *void*, what was already *voidable*, they would eſtabliſh the Conſtruction of all Acts in which Penſions were not expreſsly guarded againſt, in ſuch a Senſe as to include the Power of granting Penſions? The Legiſlature knew that all Acts had always been ſo conſtrued, whether right or wrong, and, if they had intended effectually to prevent Penſions in general, they would not have excepted them, by a particular Clauſe, in a particular Act, which would, by the ſtrongeſt Implication, render the Duties granted by all other Acts liable to them. I need not tell the honourable Gentleman, who made the Motion, that the common Law conſiſts of Cuſtoms and Uſages, of long Preſcription, and that no Right, claimed by common Law,

can

can cease, except it is expresly taken away by Statute. Now, Sir, I have proved, that the Crown has a Right, by common Law, to grant Pensions out of the aggregate Sum, paid, by Duties, into the Treasury, because the Crown has done it prescriptively for Time immemorial; and it is incumbent, upon the honourable Gentleman, to prove, that this Right is taken away expresly, except by the particular Clauses of the particular Acts just mentioned; there is no need to prove that the Words *for public Charges,* give this Power, but only, that neither they, nor any other Words in those Acts, where Pensions are not excepted, take it away. Why Pensions were expresly prohibited, in particular Statutes, it is not my Business to enquire; for the Duties, granted by those Acts, are out of the Question; but it may reasonably be supposed, that the Court of Wards was entirely given in Pensions, and that the Money was paid away to the Claimants, before it came into the Exchequer, with other Particulars of Abuse, and Mismanagement, which made the Exception more expedient in that Statute than in others.

But let us admit, that the Measure, proposed by the Motion, was not incongruous, nor im-

improper in itself, it is still certain that the Execution of it would be attended with insuperable Difficulty, and produce the most aggravated Distress. It has been admitted, that there are some Persons of Merit on the Pensioner's List; and, it cannot be denied, that there are also some Noblemen, who have no other Support, and that, as the Peerage constitutes one third of the Legislature, it ought to be supported. Many Persons, too, who have obtained Pensions by their Merit, have, by the Necessity of their Affairs, been obliged to sell them, for a valuable Consideration, to others; the Possessors of Pensions have all formed Habits of Life, proportioned to their Incomes, which they had the greatest Reason to think permanent and secure, for the Life, or the Term, on which they were granted. Now, Sir, if such a Suit is commenced as the Motion proposes, the immediate Consequence will be, that the Payment of all these Pensions must be stopped, till its Determination, which, as the Suit would be of a very nice and complicated Nature, would probably be a great Number of Years, especially, as the Crown will be under no difficulty in carrying it on, whatever may be the Expence, and will certainly carry it through all

the

the Courts by appeal; let us now confider, a Moment, the Diftrefs that will inftantly and inevitably follow our agreeing to this Motion; what Numbers will, at one fudden Stroke, be reduced from a State of Comfort, and Convenience, to a Want even of Bread. Perfons, who have no Means of fupplying themfelves, with the Neceffaries of Life, having been taught no manual Art, and having neither the Knowledge, nor the Money, neceffary to Trade; Perfons who have not been ufed to ftruggle with Adverfity; Women that muft perifh with Penury and Anguifh; Children that muft be left to the Storms of Life, without Shelter or Protection. What muft become of the hoary Veteran, after a long Life fpent in the public Service? What muft become of the honeft Affignee, who, perhaps, has laid out the whole Product of long Labour, Diligence, and Induftry, in the Purchafe of a Penfion? And what muft become of thofe to whom thefe Perfons are indebted, whofe only Security was the Penfion, and many of whofe Subfiftence depends upon the Sum that they are to receive at Quarter-Day? I expect an Anfwer to thefe Queftions, not from the Underftanding only, but the Humanity of thofe that hear me, and, as I think, I have proved,

firft,

firſt, that the Crown has a Right to grant Penſions out of the aggregate Fund, paid into the Treaſury; ſecondly, that this Houſe has a Right, and a Power, inherent in itſelf, to reſtrain them when exorbitant; and, thirdly, that it would be cruel, and injurious, inſtantly to ſuſpend the Payment of thoſe already granted. I hope no Gentleman preſent will think it expedient to call this Power of the Crown into Queſtion; to have Recourſe to a Court of Law for Redreſs, which is in their own Power; or to ſuſpend the Payment of all the Penſions, now granted, till ſuch Suit is determined; and, if not, they muſt give their Voices, with me, againſt the Motion, as a moſt extraordinary, unprecedented, and unconſtitutional Meaſure.

Mr *T— B—* then got up, and ſaid, that he could not help adding one Obſervation to the many that had been juſt made, by the learned Gentleman, againſt the Motion: He ſaid, that the commencing a Suit, and obliging the Crown to defend the Validity of its own Grants, in a Court of Law, might raiſe very dangerous Suſpicions, and Doubts, in the Minds of the lower Claſs of People, who might, too probably, infer, that the Proceedings of Government were unwarrantable and unstable, at a Time when they seemed almost universally disposed to doubt the Validity of the Laws, and dispute their Execution; he added, that he understood that the Suit, proposed by the Motion, would be of Disadvantage, to every Class of People, except the Gentlemen of the Law.

Mr *J— Fitz-G—* replied, that no Apprehension of any Irregularity, which might be committed by an unthinking and misguided Populace, ought to intimidate that House from doing its Duty, or prevent an Enquiry into any Practice, concerning the Legality of which there was the least Doubt: He added, also, that, in his Opinion, the most effectual Way of preventing such Irregularities, and quieting the Minds of the People, was, to shew a proper Zeal and Activity in redressing Grievances of every Kind. That, as to the Hint, with Respect to the Gentlemen of the Law, it did not, in the least, touch him, for he declared, he should never be Counsel for a Pensioner, and, he was very well persuaded, he should not be employed on the other Side of the Question.

Mr

Mr H— F—.

Mr S—,

I have attended very diligently, Sir, to the Arguments of the learned and honourable Gentleman, who firſt ſpoke againſt the Motion, and, I think, his Objections may be reduced to three Heads ; firſt, that the King has a Power over the public Money, paid as an aggregate Sum into the Treaſury, by common Law ; or, if he has not ſuch Right, by common Law, he derives it from general Words, in the Preambles of the Statutes, for laying certain Duties reſpectively, except where Penſions are expreſsly excluded : Secondly, that this Power is under the Controul of Parliament, and, therefore, we have no need to have recourſe to a Court of Law : And, thirdly, that the Suit propoſed will greatly diſtreſs many Individuals, ſome of whom have deſerved their Emoluments. Now, Sir, notwithſtanding what that Gentleman has ſaid, the Right of the Crown to grant Penſions indiſcriminately, out of all Branches of the Revenue, not expreſsly excepted, whether by common Law, or by general Terms, in the Preambles of the Statutes themselves, is a Question about which Gentlemen, of equal Learning and Ability, have formed Judgments diametrically opposite to each other: Some have decided in the Affirmative, some in the Negative: It follows, therefore, that whether these Grants of the Crown are, or are not legal, is uncertain; and, I think, it is an uncertainty under which we should not sit down, in a supine Indifference, and negligent Content. Does it become that Part of the Legislature, which was constituted as a Barrier to the Liberties of the People, against Encroachments of the Prerogative, to suffer a Practice, of so much Moment to the Public, to continue, while it remains doubtful, whether, besides its pernicious Consequences, it is not, radically, a Breach of our Constitution? But how, Sir, is this great Question to be authoritatively decided? Surely in the Manner which the Constitution has prescribed; and, what is this Manner, Sir, but a regular Process in our Courts of Law, where all Questions of Right, from the least to the greatest, are, and can only, be decided: It is true, Sir, that this House can controul the Power in Question, supposing it to be legal, and we do not apply to a Court of Law to do

this

this for us, as has been infinuated under the fecond Head; no, Sir, we apply to a Court of Law, not to controul this Power, but conftitutionally, and finally, to determine whether it exifts; this Determination, Sir, we are not qualified to make, and, upon this, the whole Matter fundamentally depends. Our checking this Power, only when it produces fecondary and collateral Evils, does not take the Grievance at its Root. Are we, Sir, to fuffer a Practice, that is thought to infringe our Conftitution, becaufe we have a Power of preventing fuch Mifchiefs as it might do, fuppofing it to be Conftitutional? Let the Law, which alone can, determine whether the Practice in Queftion is legal; if this Determination is in the Affirmative, let us exert the Power, inherent in us, to regulate and reftrain it: Far be it from me to think of applying to a Court of Law for this Purpofe; but, if the Determination is in the Negative, we fhall fall by our own Hand, with all the Guilt and Folly of Suicide, by fuffering this Practice at all. Under the third Head, Sir, the honourable Gentleman has expatiated, with great Eloquence, on the Diftrefs, which will be brought upon particular Perfons, by the Suit propofed. As I fhould be very forry to reprefs

the

the Emotions of Pity in any Breast, or be thought not to feel them in my own, I must declare, that I think, on this Occasion, they ought to be indulged, and that we ought to act wholly in Conformity to them, but then let our Pity be directed to its proper Object: The Affairs of Mankind, in this imperfect and mixed State of Things, are so circumstanced, that our best Wisdom, and most extensive Benevolence, can only chuse the least of two Evils; in the Case before us, we have the Pensioners on one Side, and the Nation on the other. Can it be seriously asked, which should be preferred? Can it be pretended that we ought to incur a public Debt that we can never pay? that the Faces of the Poor ought to be ground by new Taxes? that our Constitution is to be infringed, and the Privileges, which our Fore-fathers purchased, not only with their Treasure, but with their Blood, are to be given away, rather than a handfull of People shall be deprived of Pensions, to which the greatest Number of them have no equitable Right, and which, therefore, they ought never to have had? Our Ancestors, Sir, voluntarily suffered Distresses, at least equal to what these Persons will suffer, to secure to us what we now seem so ready

ready to give up with a Cruelty to the many, difguifed under the Mafk of Pity to a few, merely to make our own Court, and pay a Complement to minifterial Power. We have been afked, what is to become of the hoary Veteran, of the penfioned Lord, and the honeft Affignee? I might reply, by another Queftion, what is to become of the blamelefs, but laborious Peafant, of the honeft induftrious Trader, and the ingenious Artificer, whofe Welfare is the Welfare of the State? But I am under no Neceffity of reducing the Debate to a Dilemma, for, though the Evils of the Public, incurred in Favour of the Penfions, would be irremediable, yet the Evils incurred by the Penfioners (I mean thofe who ought to continue fo) in Favour of the Public, are not without Remedy: Gentlemen feem to forget, that the very Motion which propofes the Suit that is complained of with fuch Pathos of Compaffion, and oppofed with fuch Ardour of Refentment, propofes alfo, to eftablifh a fufficient Fund upon conftitutional Principles, for the Difplay of Royal Bounty, and the Reward of indigent Merit. I would not reply, too minutely, to all that the the worthy Member has thrown out, in the Torrent of his Eloquence; I fhall not, therefore,

fore, obferve, that the Folly of thofe who lay out all the Fruit of long and laborious Induftry, in the Purchafe of a Penfion, for the Life of another, or for a Term that they may poffibly furvive, cannot but leffen our Pity for their Diftrefs; nor is this, fimply, Folly, if fuch Purchafers have a Family which depends upon what they have been able to lay up for their future Support; it is then a criminal Inattention to thofe who have the ftrongeft and tendereft Claim to their Regard, and he that neglects to provide for his own Houfe, by ftaking his whole Subftance on the Life of another, or the Expiration of a Term, is furely, as the Scriptures have expreffed it, *worfe than an Infidel.* Upon the whole, Sir, I declare myfelf a Friend both to Juftice and to Mercy, and, in both Characters, I fhall give my Voice in Favour of the Motion.

Mr *P— T—* the A. G.

Mr S———,

I ftand up, Sir, to declare myfelf of the fame Opinion with the honourable Gentleman, who fpoke laft againft the Motion, with Refpect to the Power of the Crown, to charge

charge the Money brought into the Treasury with Pensions arising from the Words of the Preambles of the Statutes, by which, the several Duties were laid; but I am farther of Opinion, that the Crown has this Power, with Respect to Duties raised by the very Statutes, that declare them expresly not chargeable with Pensions; for I am of Opinion, that the barring Clauses, with Respect to the Hearth Money, and Ale Licences, can affect them only before they are brought into the Treasury, and that the Moment they become Part of the Aggregate Fund, they are, indiscriminately, a Supply for the Exigencies of Government, and its support: I believe, Sir, it was never known, that Orders were issued on one particular Duty, rather than another; or, that any Distinction between the several Duties was ever kept up; receiving Money by Exchequer Tallies in Transience, as it is called, that is, before it comes into the Treasury, may, indeed, be of very bad Consequence, by preventing the Affairs of the Treasury from being properly conducted, and a Sum sufficient for an Emergency, from being kept always in it; and for this Reason, and this alone, I apprehend the Clause was added, in some particular Statutes, to bar the

Charge of Penfions, for when once the Duties were paid in, they had relation to a particular Act no longer. The executive Power muft be lodged fomewhere, and, if it is taken out of the King's Hand, I do not know with what other Part of the Legiflature, confiftent with Law, and the Conftitution, it can be trufted. The Difficulties and Difadvantages, attending the Scheme propofed, have been fo juftly enumerated, and fo forcibly urged, by the learned Gentleman, who fpoke laft, a-gainft the Motion, that I fhall fay nothing of them; but I cannot help taking fome Notice of what has been faid in Reply: Gentlemen feem to think, that a very important Article, in Favour of the Motion, has been unfairly overlooked, and have infifted much on the Conftitutional Fund, that has been offered for the Payment of Penfions, in lieu of fuch Revenues as are to be refcued from the harpy Claws of minifterial Power: Now, Sir, I really think that the Appropriation of that very Fund, exclufively to fuch a Purpofe, is one of the many Evils of which this Motion would be productive. It has been juftly obferved, Sir, that as the Affair ftands at prefent, this Houfe has a Power of reftraining Penfions, not only, when they are exceffive,

but

but when they are improperly applied, and, an Inftance has been given of the Exertion of this Power, with Refpect to two Penfions in the Year 1703. But if this boafted Fund is eftablifhed, it muft be upon the Ruins of this conftitutional and important Power; this Fund will be abfolutely a Privy Purfe, and the Crown, or rather the Minifter, may difpofe of it as fhall beft fuit with the moft corrupt and pernicious Views, without being liable to be called to an Account by this Houfe, which will no longer be a Check upon this dangerous Part of his Power. It will be a total Diminution of the Public Stock, and an irrecoverable Alienation of public Property. I muft alfo confirm what my honourable Friend has faid, about the Difficulties and Delays of a Suit, carried on againft the Crown; it might eafily be proved, by many Facts; but, I remember, one in particular, which I fhall beg leave to relate. A Perfon had a Demand upon the Government for a very confiderable Sum of Money, which it not being convenient immediately to pay, he got a Grant of five and twenty thoufand Pounds a Year, till his Debt fhould be difcharged; but a Suit was commenced againft him

him in Lord Chancellor *Somers*'s Time, to prove that the Grant was invalid; this Suit was determined in his Favour, and the Grant confirmed, but an Appeal being lodged to the Exchequer Chamber, the Decree was reverfed, and it never went further.

Here Mr *Fitz-G——* got up, and faid, that he muft beg his Pardon for that, the firft Decree was confirmed in the Houfe of Lords.

Mr *P— T—* the A. G. replied, he was fure it muft be fo, if that learned Gentleman affirmed it, but that he had never heard it before, and he concluded his Speech by giving fome other Inftances of Expence and Delay attending Suits againft the Crown.

Mr *J— H— H—*, the P. S.

Mr S——,

It is always with the greateft Reluctance that I differ from the honourable and very learned Gentleman who made the Motion, and whom I have always confidered as a fhining Ornament of his Profeffion, and yet I muft freely confefs, that the Motion is fo extraordinary, that it furprizes me in the great-

greateſt Degree. I confeſs, that I am not convinced by any Thing that has been ſaid by him, or any other Gentleman on the ſame Side of the Queſtion, of the Expediency of our having recourſe to a Court, to determine whether the Sums that we have granted are legally applied; I think, by this Meaſure, we ſhall be both injured and degraded; we ſhall be degraded by ſubmitting to an inferiour Deciſion, and we ſhall be injured, by loſing our undoubted Right of determining Queſtions of the ſame Kind for Ourſelves. It has been ſaid, Sir, that the Court of Law can only determine, whether the Crown can legally grant Penſions out of our Revenue, and that we do not apply to a Court of Law to know what Penſions the Crown ſhall grant, if it can legally grant them. But, I am clearly of Opinion, that this Houſe, whoſe peculiar Province it is to grant Supplies, and afterwards to ſee that they are properly laid out, has a Right to determine what is and what is not lawful, with Reſpect to thoſe Supplies. If we think the Crown acts illegally, in appropriating the Supplies to the Payment of Penſions, have we not a Power of cutting off thoſe Supplies at the Root? and can we not inſiſt on Reformation, with Reſpect to

what

what has been done, as well as Conditions for the future? are we ignorant that there are such Things as Acts of Resumption? or that such Acts were passed, even in the Time of our great Deliverer King *William*? We have been told of our Constitutional Power, we seem to know it, and we are shewing a Spirit that ought to act by the Exertion of it, and yet, by some strange Infatuation, we are driven to take a most unaccountable and unprecedented Measure, by which this Spirit will be misled, and this Power eventually denied and renounced. But if the Measure proposed was not pernicious in itself, surely it is ill-timed; the Attention, and good Inclination of our amiable, humane, and noble-minded Lord Lieutenant, have brought about for this Country, what all our Resolutions, expressed in the strongest Terms, could not do, I mean the Attention of his Majesty, to this Grievance, as appears by his Letter; and have we not the greatest Reason to expect some Fruit from so promising a Bud? If his Excellency has been so humane as to inform his Majesty of our Complaint, while he is yet among us, with so happy a Dawn of Success, what may we not expect from so kind, so zealous, so able an Advocate, when he returns

turns into the Royal Presence? And what may we not expect from so amiable, so gracious, and so illustrious a Prince, whose principal Object is the Happiness of his People? At this Time, surely, we have sufficient Cause rather to Hope than to Fear; rather to repose in the pleasing Prospect before us, than to stimulate each other to a Measure in the highest Degree rash, violent, and injurious; every Thing, surely, is better than a Law-suit, the Inconvenience, Confusion, and Distress of which must be great, in proportion to the greatness of the Grievance complained of, which we have Reason to hope will be redressed in another Way. The greater the Number of Pensioners, and the greater the Sums they receive, the more extensive the Distress, and the more complicated the Suit. The Suit, indeed, will be a Jumble of all Interests, Classes, and Characters; King, Parliament, Pensioners, Judges, and Lawyers, will all be in contest together; the Pensioners alone will include all Countries, and Classes; and all their Families, Dependants, and Creditors, with all the Families of such Creditors, and Dependants, will be involved; and, at last, what is all this Bustle, and Confusion, and Distress to do? Why, it is to weaken

the

the Hands of the Crown, at a Time, when they moſt need to be ſtrengthened; when the Regal Authority, and all Commiſſions under it, are defpiſed, and trampled upon; when the Law is ſet at nought, and a Spirit of Contumacy and Rebellion univerſally prevails; when all Subordination and Reſtraint is caſt off, even in our Capital, where the public Peace is perpetually diſturbed by Licenciouſneſs and Riot, and Murder is ſtaining the Streets with Blood. At this Time, furely, the Legiſlative Powers ſhould unite againſt the common Enemy, whom our Diſcontents and Diviſions muſt encourage and countenance, and for all theſe Reaſons, and many others that have been urged, and ſupported by the honourable Gentlemen, who have ſpoken on the ſame Side, I declare myſelf ſtrongly againſt the Motion.

Mr E— S— P—.

Mr S———,

I am forry to ſay, Sir, that I have been more mortified and aſtoniſhed at what I have heard, during this Debate, than I ever was in my Life, particularly from the honourable
Gen-

Gentleman who fpoke laft. We have, in the fame Breath, been admonifhed againft rafh and violent Meafures, and urged to cut off the whole Supply granted to the Crown, becaufe we think Part of it mifapplied; we have heard a pompous Encomium on our Dignity, and, at the fame Time, have been reprefented, as feeble and needy, as relying on the *Humanity* of a Lord Lieutenant, and being under the greateft Obligations to his *Pity*, for obtaining of his Majefty, by the Power of his Interceffion, what we could not by all our Efforts obtain for Ourfelves. Whether this would be proper Language if we were foliciting a Favour may well be queftioned, but it is fuch as I cannot hear without Indignation, when we are pleading our Right. If we have not effected that for ourfelves, which we are now told we are likely to obtain by the Compaffion of an Interceffor, and the Partiality of our Sovereign, who has liftened to him, though he difregarded us, to what is it owing? Surely, to that Conduct, which we are now urged to continue; to a tame Acquiefcence in minifterial Promifes, and an implicit Concurrence with minifterial Meafures; we have undoubtedly the Power of doing ourfelves Right, and, our only juft reproach is, that we have not exerted it to Effect; if we have not, it is certainly Time we should. Gentlemen who have recommended Gentleness, Patience, and Repose in good Prospects, a placid Expectation of Fruit from Blossoms that have already appeared, have been very lavish in their Encomiums on his Majesty; and, no Man, Sir, can think more highly of his Majesty than I do, but, surely, they might justly be suspected of concealing the bitterest Satire, under the Appearance of Panegyric; when they tell us, that the Voice of an injured People has been heard in vain; that all our Resolutions, as Representatives of the Commons of this Kingdom, made in the most solemn Manner, have not been able to attract that Regard which has at once been paid to an Instrument of his own Power, in the Person of our Lord Lieutenant; far be it from me, Sir, to think thus of his Majesty; if our Resolutions have not been effectual, it is because they have not come properly before him; there is, therefore, greater Necessity for an Address, and his Attention to the Representations of our worthy Lord Lieutenant give us the most reasonable Ground to hope that it will succeed; what Reason can there be, Sir, not to act in Person, on an Occasion

casion so urgent and important, and what ground is there to fear that the gracious Sovereign, who has heard another on our behalf, will not hear us for Ourselves? But the Objections that have been urged against the Subject of our Addrefs are not more extraodinary than those against the Addrefs itself. Is it not a most extraordinary Maxim, Sir, " that every thing is better than a Law-suit?" Could the greatest Enemy of our Country give it a worse Character, than that every Thing is better than a regular Appeal for the Decision of her Laws? That it is better to suffer every Evil that can be suffered, than seek redrefs from the Remedy that our Legiflators have provided? Where is the Difference, Sir, of being totally without Law, and having Laws to which we cannot appeal, without incurring a greater Evil than we can suffer by the Breach of them? It is, indeed, too true, that in Law-suits, there is Chicanery, Delay, and Expence; and, with these Evils, the Gentleman must necessarily be well acquainted; but, God forbid, that these, or any other Evils, arising from the Abuse of the Law, should be so enormous as to render the Law of no Effect. But Chicane, and Delay, and Expence, are not the only Mischiefs, we are alarmed

alarmed with; we have been told, that a judicial Procefs is, not only fruitlefs, but criminal; we have been told, Sir, that it is a rafh and violent Meafure to determine a doubtful Queftion by Law; nay, ftranger ftill, we have been told, that it is rafh and violent, not to commence Judges in our own Caufe; that it is rafh and violent, not to cut off all Supplies, becaufe we believe fome to have been mifapplied ! Surely, Sir, thefe Affertions and Infinuations are aftonifhing in the higheft Degree, efpecially if we confider from whom they come. Thefe feem intended to fright us from our Duty, to fpread a general Pannick, by difcovering a Glimpfe of fome dreadful Evils, and then hiding them in tremendous Obfcurity. *Chaos* is reprefented as coming again, and we are alarmed with a Confufion not lefs than that among the Elements of Nature before Creation; all Interefts, Claffes, and Characters, are to be jumbled together; King, Parliament, Penfioners, Judges, and Lawyers, with Families upon Families, are to be involved in Doubt, Darknefs, and Diftrefs; this, indeed, is very dreadful; but let us fee if with a very little Light, and a very little Reafon, we cannot palliate the Diftrefs, and diffipate both the Darknefs and

the

the Doubt. To drop all Metaphor, and Figure, Sir, the Law-fuit propofed will not be complicated in Proportion to the Number of Penfioners, or the Diverfity of their Circumftances, and Situation, as has been infinuated; for the Queftion to be determined does not refpect the Claims of thefe Penfioners, but the Right of the Crown to difpofe, in a particular Manner, of public Money; the Suit, Sir, would have a fingle Object, if the Penfioners were ever fo much more numerous and diverfified than they are; and may be commenced by any Individual, with the fame Advantage to the whole as if all were Parties. But ftill other Bugbears have been held up before us; we have been told of Faction, and Riot, of Contumacy, and of Murder; and to be fure fuch Monfters there are among us, but how are they to be deftroyed? The honourable Gentleman feems to fuppofe, that an Infringement of the Law above, will contribute to the keeping it facred below; he fuppofes, that if thofe who are intrufted with the Rights of the People fit quiet and filent, and fee them taken away, that the People will be lefs likely to attempt the righting of themfelves, than if they faw the Struggle made in their behalf, by that Power which was moft likely to succeed; he supposes, that the readiest Way to quiet the Populace, is to strip and starve them, for the sake of Pampering an idle and voluptuous Set of Miscreants, on the other Side of the Water, with *French* Cookery, and *French* Cloaths. The only way, Sir, to quell the Spirit of Discontent, that is risen among us, is to see the Laws kept inviolate, and to enforce them upon those of the highest Rank, and the most ample Power; to shew to our Country, and to the World, that the Money raised for public Purposes is used for the public Benefit; and that every Penny that is paid in Taxes is laid out to procure such National Advantages, of which all participate, as are more than equivalent to any Advantage that would accrue to the Individual, by witholding his Contribution. Subordination, Sir, is always best preserved by the apparent Attention of the Superior to the Interest of those below him; Contumacy and rebellious Opposition to those in Power are produced only by Oppression, or the Appearance of it; and, when all real Oppression is at an end, the Appearance will soon vanish; upon the whole, Sir, as the Pensions at present are an Evil not less oppressive than odious, I am an Advocate for the Motion, upon

the

the very Principles on which that honourable Gentleman has oppofed it, at leaft, till fome other Meafure is fuggefted, that appears more likely to produce the fame Effect, or to produce it in a more elegible Way.

The Queftion was then put, that the Houfe do agree in the faid moved Addrefs.

It paffed in the Negative by a fmall Majority.

WEDNESDAY, Nov. 9, 1763.

TWELFTH DAY.

Mr *M— C—* moved, in the Committee of Accounts, that the proper Officer might lay before the House, the Papers relative to the Military Contingencies, which, he thought in many Particulars, a very extraordinary Charge.

On the Speaker's resuming the Chair:

Mr *E— S— P—* said, that it was allowed, by every Person, who spoke in the Debate of Yesterday, that the extraordinary Encrease of Pensions, had laid a Burden upon the Nation which it could not possibly bear; and, as the Continuation of them must, therefore, tend to subvert the Constitution, he thought it his Duty to mention this to the House, that some Method might be thought of to represent the Sense of the House, in the humblest Manner to his Majesty, in hopes of redress; and, though the Mode that was proposed Yesterday for making that Representation, was

was not generally approved, he made no doubt but that another might be found that would be fo; and was confident that every Member would concur in the Attempt; he, therefore, propofed to move that a Committee might be appointed to enquire what Method of Reprefentation would be moft proper, and to draw up fuch Reprefentation accordingly.

Mr *P— T—*, the A. G. faid, that he thought an Enquiry into the Penfions very proper, but that he could not agree with the worthy Member who fpoke laft, with Refpect to the Form of his Motion; becaufe he was of Opinion, that a Committee fhould not be named to draw up a Reprefentation to his Majefty for Relief from Penfions as a Grievance, till the Senfe of the Committee was reported, whether they were a Grievance or not; he faid, when the Committee had enquired into the State of the Penfions, and how far the Eftablifhment was able to bear them, if they found that the Eftablifhment was not able to bear them, and reported accordingly, it would then, and then only be proper to addrefs his Majefty againft encreafing them. He added, that for his Part he
could

could not see so great a Difference between the State of the Revenue, and the Pensions, as had been represented.

Mr *P—* replied, that he believed that the honourable Member, who spoke last, was the only Gentleman in that House, who had the least Doubt, whether the exorbitant Encrease of Pensions was a Grievance; and, as it seemed to be the unanimous Opinion, even of those that spoke, and divided against the Question Yesterday, that they were a Grievance, he begged leave to have his Motion put, as he first proposed it.

In this Mr *T—* acquiesced, and

Mr *P—* accordingly moved, That a Committee of the whole House might take into Consideration, the State of the Pensions upon the Civil Establishment of this Kingdom, and how the Increase of them might be prevented.

Resolved, *Nem. Con.* That this House will, on *Tuesday* next, resolve itself into a Committee of the whole House for that Purpose.

Major

Major *W— B—* recommended an Encouragement for the manufacturing of Blubber in the Barony of *Inishoen*, in the County of *Donnegal*, where, he said, several Whales had been taken the last Year, as the Nation had suffered great Loss for want of knowing how to extract what is called Train-Oil from the Blubber, being obliged to send the Blubber, unmanufactured, to *England*.

He also presented a Petition of Mess. *Thomas* and *Andrew Nesbit*, *Paul* and *James Benson*, Merchants, and *Acheson Irwine*, Esq; praying Aid to enable them to carry on a Whale Fishery, on the North-West Coast of the Kingdom.

Upon Mr *J— A—* jun. presenting a Petition in favour of a Bounty for erecting Corn-Mills, it was proposed, that that Petition should be referred to the same Committee to which the Petition of *Mary Ashworth* was referred; but Mr *M—*, who was Chairman of that Committee, opposed it, and said, it would be very hard upon him, if he should be obliged to sit as Chairman upon all the Petitions that should be brought into the House, notwithstanding that they would lead to Enquiries wholly different from each other. He added, that, having made up his Report, as Chairman of *Ashworth*'s Committee, he apprehended he was discharged from any other Duty, with Respect to that Committee.

Sir *R— C—* got up, and said, that, in his Opinion, that Committees, to which Petitions of this Kind were referred, ought to consist of Gentlemen, properly selected, who had made the Manufacture, to which the Petition related, the particular Object of their Attention: He said, that the honourable Gentleman, who spoke last, might, perhaps, have turned his Mind to the Operation of stamping Linnen, of which he might, therefore, be a very able Judge; but that he could see no Analogy between stamping of Linnen, and Mills and Mill-Stones, though others might, and, therefore, because a Gentleman's Study, or Inclination, inclined him to consider the Implements used in a particular Manufacture of Cloth, he could see no Reason why he should be obliged to sit, as Chairman, in a Committee, for the Examination of Mills and Mill-Stones. Sir *R——* also proposed, that a standing Committee might be fixed for
Stamp-

Stampers of Linnen, and all under that Clafs; and another for Mills, and all under that Clafs; and fo of other Articles of Trade and Manufacture.

Dr *C— L—* then faid, that he much approved of public and large Committees to fit in the Houfe, becaufe when Committees were held in the Speaker's Chamber, he could not help thinking that Jobbs were fometimes carried on, and Premiums given, in a Way that made them little better than occafional Penfions.

The H—ble Mr *B— M—* alfo fpoke much in Favour of public Committees, to fit always in the Houfe, each of which fhould take under Confideration all the Petitions that came under one Clafs; for, as to the Committees that fat in the Speaker's Chamber, he faid he fcarce ever knew an Inftance in which they did not report the Allegations of the Petition to be true, and the Petitioner worthy of Encouragement.

Mr *J— G—*, the R— of *D—*, objected to thefe ftanding Committees, becaufe, he faid, they would greatly retard the Bufinefs of the Houfe, and could not, at laft, give Time and
At-

Attention enough to the Variety of Petitions that muſt neceſſarily come before them, to conſider the Merits, with a Preciſion and minuteneſs ſufficient to determine how far they would, or would not, be of Utility to the Public: He added, that, though he was far from thinking that Mode of encouraging uſeful Undertakings, a good one, yet, till a better was found, and eſtabliſhed, he thought it ſhould be followed.

The R—t H—ble *H— L— R—*, ſaid, that he was equally ſurprized, and ſorry, to find that any Reflections were caſt on Committees of Gentlemen of that Houſe, intruſted to enquire into any Matter that came before them; that they were all Perſons of Honour and Worth, and, he was perſuaded, would not, for any private Gratification, laviſh away the public Money: That, in a ſeparate Committee, appointed for each Petition that ſhould be received, the Subject of it would be examined and diſcuſſed by Gentlemen intereſted in the Encouragement, in a more minute and particular Manner than could be done in ſuch general Committees as were propoſed, and that, upon their Report, the Houſe was the ultimate Judge, whether ſuch an Encouragement was proper or not.

THURSDAY, *Nov.* 10, 1763.

THIRTEENTH DAY.

Mr R— L— made the following Motion: That an humble Addrefs be prefented to his Excellency, the Lord Lieutenant, that he will be pleafed to reprefent to his Majefty the Prayer of his moft faithful Commons, in Parliament affembled, that he will be gracioufly pleafed to give Orders to his Attorney-General of this Kingdom, to bring a Writ of *Scire facias*, to enquire into the Legality of the Patent, by which the Office of Chancellor of the Exchequer is now held.

Mr *R— Fitz-G—*.

Mr S—,

I do not think it neceffary, Sir, to enter into the Arguments that might be deduced from the Act of the 10th of *Henry* the VIIth, to prove, that the Grant of the Office of Chancellor of the Exchequer, for Life, by Patent, is illegal; not only becaufe I take for grant-

granted, that a very nice Difquifition into the Meaning of that Act will be made by others, but becaufe, fuppofing this Employment to be judicial, and, as fuch, prohibited from being granted for Life, by that Act, I fhall, neverthelefs, be forry to difpute the Grant, becaufe I have always underftood, that granting judicial Employments for Life, or during good Behaviour, is, in every Conftitution, a moft defirable Thing. An Independance of the Judges upon the Crown, is certainly the moft likely to fecure an unbiaffed and unreftrained Determination, according to the Laws of the Country; and, if we look into Hiftory, we fhall find, that this Principle is not only fpecious in Theory, but eftablifhed by Fact: The Opinions of Judges who held their Employments during the King's Pleafure, have, in Cafes where the King has had an Intereft, been given in Favour of that Intereft to fecure their own; but where they have been independant, their Determinations have been in Favour of Right, without Regard to the Views or Wifhes of regal, or rather of minifterial Power; befides, if thefe Employments are held during Pleafure, and a Minifter has any Point to carry, in which he only doubts of Succefs, he has nothing to do but

Day XIII.] *Affairs of* Ireland.   275

but to remove the Judge, and put a Creature of his own in his Place, and the Bufinefs is done. The Employments of Chancellor of the Exchequer, and Mafter of the Rolls, are, at prefent, conferred upon Gentlemen of the greateft Ability, and fuch as have deferved well of their Country. As to the Right Honourable Gentleman, who is Chancellor of the Exchequer, I muft be excufed from mentioning, particularly, his many amiable Qualities, and great Endowments, becaufe he is prefent; but, as to the other Gentleman, the Mafter of the Rolls, I cannot fay too much in his Favour. As a Statefman, his Abilities, Penetration, and Steadinefs of Conduct, deferve the higheft Recompence; and, in private Life, the warm, fincere, and perfevering Friend, the free, open-hearted, and, I may even fay, the jolly Companion, are univerfally efteemed and beloved. Upon his late Arrival here, every Body ftrove who fhould fhew him the greateft Regard and Affection; and a Gentleman, of the firft Confequence, not being prefent to receive him in Perfon, expreffed his Efteem and Kindnefs for him, in the ftrongeft Terms, by Letter. Upon the whole, I muft declare, freely, that, for my own Part, I cannot fee any one good Purpofe that an Enquiry into the Legality of thefe Patents can anfwer, and, therefore, I declare myfelf ftrongly againft the Motion.

Mr *J— M—* faid, that the Motion was the moft extraordinary Meafure he had ever known in his Life, and wholly new and unprecedented. It was very ftrange, he faid, to addrefs the King to order his Servants to fupport the Extenfion of his own Prerogative, by invalidating his own Act; and ftill ftranger, that it fhould be propofed by Gentlemen of that Houfe, in direct Oppofition to their own Intereft: He added, that it was very indifferent to him how the Act of the 10th of *Henry* VII. fhould be conftrued, becaufe he never could approve of the Acts procured to be paffed by that Prince, or of his Minifter *Poining*'s Law, which he confidered, in every Circumftance, as a Defect in the Conftitution. He therefore moved, that the Motion fhould be put off till the firft of next *Auguft*.

Mr *L— O—*.

Mr S——,

I fhall always be well pleafed to have an Enquiry made into any Act of the Crown, which

which appears to be contrary to Law; but, as the Illegality of the Act in Question is doubtful, and as the Statute has been construed in the Sense in which his Majesty has taken it, I think there is no Occasion for setting on Foot an Enquiry, which, if carried against the Grant, will defeat his Majesty's Intention, not to avail himself of his Prerogative, in Cases in which it is doubtful. I shall very readily allow, that Violations of Law, like Violations of Truth, may have the worst Effects, in a general and extensive View, though upon particular Occasions they may be attended with Advantage; but, in the present Case, I think it is better to suppose that the Act in Question, is lawful, and, upon that Supposition, to establish it, than to commence an Enquiry, which may terminate in its being declared unlawful; because, if that should be the Case, it must be set aside, which would certainly be a Disadvantage to the Constitution, for, though we are not to suppose that any bad Use will be made, during his Majesty's Reign, of a Power to dismiss Judicial Officers, in Consequence of their being appointed only during Pleasure, yet the Appointment of a Chancellor of the Exchequer, for Life, will, as a Precedent, have a very good Effect.

As to the Act of the 10th of *Henry* VII. I have always considered it, as well as every other Transaction of that Reign, to be extremely detrimental to the constitutional Interest of this Kingdom, even in those Particulars in which its Construction can admit of no Doubt, and, therefore, we are, I think, *felo-de-se*, by every Attempt to extend it, where its Construction is uncertain. Before the Reign of *Henry* the VIIth, the *English* Statutes were accepted and executed in *Ireland*, by the Consent of its Parliaments, and Government was conducted in a proper and constitutional Manner; but, upon certain Disturbances which rose in this Country, *Henry* sent over Sir *John Poinings*, who was much more the turbulent and violent Soldier, than the judicious and steady Politician, and he found Affairs in such a Situation as induced him to make Use of every Artifice, and exert every Effort, to extend the Prerogative of the King, at the Expence of the Rights of the People: He convened Parliaments wherever he thought proper, sometimes in the most obscure Part of the Kingdom; and these Parliaments consisted of Persons chosen entirely by himself; what Wonder, then is it that they enacted whatever he directed, and, in a great Degree,
de-

destroyed their own constitutional Power. We had a recent Instance of the bad Effects of *Poining*'s Administration, in the Dispute between the Privy Council here, and the Ministry on the other Side of the Water, last Year. It has, indeed, been said, in this House, that *Poining*'s Law is the Palladium of the Constitution, but, I wish to God, that an *Ulysses* could be found to steal it away; and, whenever the Crown shall think fit to abridge its own Prerogative, by adopting a Construction of that Law, favourable to the Rights of the People, I shall most joyfully acquiesce in it, as I am fully persuaded the Constitution is much more likely to suffer, by extending the Prerogative, than by contracting it, and that much worse Consequences may attend the Grant of judicial Employments, during Pleasure, than for Life; I shall, therefore, give my Voice for postponing the Question till the first of next *August*.

Mr E— M— went into the Enquiry, whether the Grant of the Chancellorship of the Exchequer for Life, was, or was not, illegal, by the Statute of the 10th of *Henry* the VIIth, Ch. II. The Clause of the Statute is this:

" No Perfon that fhall have *Miniftration*
" *of Juftice* ; that is for to fay, the Chancel-
" lor, the Treafurer, Judges of the King's-
" Bench, and Common-Pleas ; the chief and
" fecondary Baron of the Exchequer, the
" Clerk, or Mafter of the Rolls, nor any
" Officer Accomptants, fhall have any Au-
" thority by Patent in their fuch Offices, but
" only at the King's Pleafure ; and if any
" Grant be made of any of the faid Offices,
" unto any Perfons, contrary to the Premifes,
" they fhall be deemed void ; and all Acts
" before made to the contrary hereof, to be
" revoked and void."

Mr *E— M—*,

Mr S——,

I think it manifeft, from all the Circumftances of this Statute, that the Chancellor of
the Exchequer is precluded, according to the
Spirit of it, from holding his Employment
by Patent, for Life. It is known to have
been a judicial Employment, of great Importance, from the Time of King *John*, down to
that of *Henry* the VIIth, and the Situation of
that Prince was fuch, when he fent *Poinings*
over,

over, as made it necessary for him to have the Judges of all the Courts in his Power; and, indeed, the chief Officers of State; it is, therefore, impossible to suppose, that an Officer, so considerable as the Chancellor of the Exchequer, should not be intentionally included in the Law in Question, though not expresly named. Suppose the Chancellor mentioned in the Statute, to mean the Lord Chancellor, yet the Chancellor of the Exchequer must certainly be included in the Words " No Person " that shall have the Ministration of Justice," for, that he has the Ministration of Justice, cannot be doubted: There are but two of the Barons of the Exchequer mentioned, " the " chief and secondary Baron," yet it has never been pretended that the third Baron is not included. It appears, indeed, by the common Usage of the Crown, that this Officer has been supposed to be included, for there is not one Instance of this Employment's having been granted for Life, since *Poining*'s Law, except by *Harry* the VIIIth, and *Charles* the Ist. whose Conduct, in this Respect, will, by no Means, furnish a presumptive Proof that they thought the Grant lawful, for they were known not to make the Law the Rule of their Conduct, when it opposed their Inclinations,

tions, or clashed with their Notions of Prerogative: Besides, Sir, in my Opinion, the Law itself is a good one, and, therefore, no Occasion should be sought of eluding it; because, if judicial Employments are granted for Life, they must frequently be held by Persons whom Age and Infirmities have rendered incapable of the Duty; in which Case, the Proceedings in the Court may be totally stopped, and the Rights of the Subject precluded; I admit, however, that the Grant of such Employments, during good Behaviour, is a good Medium between during Life, and during Pleasure, and more eligible than either. Upon the whole, I conclude, that the Grant, as it now stands, is illegal, but I desire that I may not be misunderstood to have been induced, in any Degree, to form this Opinion, by a Disapprobation of the Gentleman who fills the Office, whose great Abilities I am ever ready to acknowledge, of which the Place and Assembly where I stand, has been often Witnesses; I am only sorry that this Gentleman is not to continue among us, and should heartily rejoice to see the Trust properly attended to and executed by so able an Officer. I declare, also, that I have no Objection to the Adjournment of the Question till the first of

August,

August; and, I think, the Commencement of such a Suit as is proposed by the Motion to be unnecessary, because, if the Grant is considered as a Grievance, there is an easier Way of redressing it. Every Suitor that comes to the Exchequer is obliged to pay Fees to the Chancellor, from which Fees his Revenue rises, and every Suitor, therefore, has a Right to commence a Suit against him for these Fees, if he supposes he has not a legal Right to them, which he has not, if the Grant of his Patent is illegal; in the Course of such a Suit the Legality of the Patent must be judicially determined. If there were but one *Hampden* in this Country, he would commence such a Suit for the Value of a Shilling; I therefore give my Vote for postponing the Question.

Sir *R— C—,*

Mr S——,

As I apprehend that the principal Argument against the Legality of the Chancellor of the Exchequer's Patent for Life is drawn from the Meaning, either expressed or implied, of a Clause in the Act of the 10th of *Henry* VII. I think it proper to give my
Opi-

Opinion of the Senfe of that Claufe. Hiftory informs us, that, in the Reign of that Prince, there were great civil Contefts for the regal Power, between the Houfes of *Lancafter* and *York*, which extended to this Kingdom. The two Parties were headed by Chiefs of this Country; the *Yorkifts* by the Earl of *Kildare*, and the *Lancaftrians* by the Duke of *Ormond*: Matters were carried fo far againft *Henry*, who was of the Houfe of *Lancafter*, that his Rival was brought to this Capital, and crowned at *Chrift-Church*; at this Coronation all the great Officers of State attended, among which were the Lord High Chancellor, the Treafurer, and the Judges. *Henry*, to put a Stop to thefe rebellious Proceedings, and fecure his undoubted Right to the Throne, fent over that very wife and brave Man, Sir *John Poinings*, who would never have ventured hither to oppofe the tumultuous and formidable Infurrections againft his Sovereign, if he had not had Courage from the Sole of his Foot to the Crown of his Head ; and, in this Situation, it was very natural for *Poinings* to exert his Spirit, by every Method which his Policy fuggefted, to ftrengthen the Hands of his Royal Mafter; and, by his Diligence and Perfeverance, the Act of the 10th of that Prince

Prince was brought about, and the King obtained a Power, effentially neceffary at that Time, of difplacing his great Officers, and Judges at pleafure. Now, confidering the State of the Exchequer at that Time, I cannot think that the Chancellor was a Perfon of fufficient Importance, to come within the Intention of the Act, or the View with which it was made. The Chancellor, mentioned in it, is undoubtedly the Lord High Chancellor, for he was the primary and chief Object of it; for Hiftory fays, that he affifted at the Coronation of the Pretender of that Time, and he is alfo mentioned in the Act, before the Lord high Treafurer, which the Chancellor of the Exchequer could not have been; I, therefore, conclude, that, as this Statute has not altered the Law with Refpect to this Office, the King has an undoubted Right to grant it for Life, a Conclufion which is juftified by Precedents, which, I think, do not appear to have been ever called in Queftion, either by a parliamentary or judicial Enquiry.

Sir *W— O—*.

Mr S——,

In the prefent Situation of this Country,
Sir,

Sir, I think, our Time might be better employed than in the Discussion of Questions, doubtful in themselves, and trifling in their Consequences, except, that they tend to divide those whom it is our highest Interest to unite, and to produce Enmity where it is of the greatest Importance to conciliate Affection. We exert all the Pathos of our Rhetoric, to display and deplore our Grievances, and at the same Time we irritate those who have both the Power, and the Inclination to redress them; every Thing appears specious and alluring, under the Colour of Patriotism, and Public Spirit, but there are many Measures which, if not viewed in the false Light, which gives them this flattering Appearance, would be found deeply tinged with the sullen Hues of factious Discontent, disappointed Ambition, and sordid Self-Interest; and the bold rhetorical Flourishes that seem to be made only in Defence of our Rights and Liberties, will be often found to be nothing more than the Effusions of personal Enmity, or Party-Rage: The learned Member * who sits beneath me, knows, that upon the Banks

---

* Dr *L*—.

of some Rivers, in the Eastern Parts of the World, there are Fruits which have a most beautiful and alluring Appearance to the Eye, but when brought to the Taste are both putrid and poisonous. It is at this Time the universal Cry that the titular Power which presides over this Country, is LIBERTY; but upon a nearer Approach, and more attentive View, this supposed Goddess will appear to be a shameless Strumpet, abandoned to every Species of Licentiousness, and contaminated with every corrupt Disposition; who wanders about in borrowed Robes, disturbing the Peace, and debauching the Morals of Mankind, by studied Artifice, and deceitful Blandishments; and, is this a Time for us to foment Division and Animosity by unnecessary Disputes? shall we countenance Dis-union, and Discontent by our Example? and, shall we neglect our known Duty, and the real Service of the State, to join in the popular Cry, and promote Contumacy and Faction, by concealing private Views, and selfish Passions, under the specious Pretence of maintaining our Rights, and preserving our Liberties? Let us rather act as one Body, animated by one Soul, for an honester and nobler Purpose; let us exert our whole united Strength, to remove

move real Evils, and produce permanent Good; to restore our Finances which are falling into ruin; to check the fatal Encrease of Pensions; to suppress popular Licentiousness; and to encrease the Trade and Commerce of the interior Parts of the Kingdom. These are Objects worthy the Attention of this House, and, in an active and steady Pursuit of these, we can alone discharge our Trust, and secure the Interest and Honour both of Ourselves and Country; we shall, however, in this laudable Pursuit stand in need of the Assistance of superior Powers, whom we should incline to afford us this Assistance, by every becoming Compliance in trivial and doubtful Matters, instead of giving them Offence, and alienating their Kindness by querulous Opposition, and unprovoked Malignity; from what laudable Motive can Gentlemen oppose the Independance of judicial Officers upon the Crown? How can casual Inability be made a Pretence for not granting an Office for Life, when we know that the Incumbent, during Pleasure, scarce ever resides? It would be endless to trace the Folly and Danger of this Conduct through every particular, and I am willing to flatter myself that it is unnecessary;

for

for my own Part, I shall most heartily give my Vote for putting off the Question to a long Day, if it was only to employ the intermediate Time in Matters of real Importance.

Dr *C— L—* then got up, and dwelt much upon the Importance of the Chancellor of the Exchequer's residing, and paid many Compliments to a Right Honourable Gentleman then in the House, who had formerly filled that Office *; this Gentleman, in a very genteel Manner, begged the Doctor to spare him as he was present; the Doctor, however, still continued his Compliments, and, at the same Time, took occasion to throw out some oblique Hints not very favourable to some of the late Chief Governors.

A right honourable Member† then got up, and said somewhat in Disapprobation of such Hints, and, in the Course of his Speech, happened to mention the Weaver's Hall, by which Company, as well as by most others

---

* The right honourable Mr *A— M—*.

† The Right Honourable *W— H— F---*, Post-Master General.

in the City of *Dublin*, Dr *L—* had been singularly diſtinguiſhed. The Doctor, conſidering the Mention of Weaver's Hall to be intended as a Sneer, and not a Compliment, got up, and ſpoke to the following Effect:

Mr S——,

Sir, I ſhall always remember, with the greateſt Gratitude, the ſingular Honours I have received from the honourable Society, which that Right Honourable Member has juſt now mentioned. The Weavers are a Company diſtinguiſhed by their Induſtry, and, by their ſingular Utility to their Country; the Commodity which they manufacture is the Staple of this Nation, and, to put us in mind of its Importance, and of thoſe that work it up, it has the Honour to be the Seat of our Judges in the Houſe of Lords. As, I think thus honourably of the Weavers, I may, without juſt Cauſe of Offence, ſay, that I believe it would have been well for the Right Honourable Gentleman, if he had been bred a Weaver himſelf; he would then have enjoyed that chearful and agreeable Diſpoſition ſo natural to him, with, perhaps, a greater Guſto than he does at preſent; he would not then have been incumbered with the Cares of of State, but would conftantly have enjoyed that Tranquillity and Flow of Spirits, which are always the Confequence of little Thought, and chearful Induftry. In the great Employment, which he fills at prefent, he has the weighty Affairs of the Nation to think of, and when he has thought of them, and given his Concurrence to what may be neceffary to difpatch them, he has the farther Trouble of difperfing an Account of thefe public Concerns, as well as the private Concerns of the Nation over the whole World; but had he been happily a Weaver, he would have had none of this Trouble, but have been a merry Fellow, and, in the Stile of Sir *John Falftaff*, "a Teller of all Manner of Tales, and a Singer of all Manner of Songs."

The Motion was then made, and the Queftion put, that the further Confideration of this Matter be adjourned to the firft Day of *Auguft* next.

It was carried in the Affirmative.

FRIDAY, *Nov.* 11, 1763.

FOURTEENTH DAY.

Mr *L— O—*.

Mr S——,

THE first and great Object of all Legislatures is the impartial Administration of Justice; Mankind were induced to make a Surrender of their Power to injure others, upon condition, that the Power of others to injure them should be restrained; for, it was very soon discovered, that every Man is liable to suffer more by the unrestrained Power of another exerted against him, than he can enjoy by exerting his own Power, without restraint, against another; this was the Origin of Civil Government, and, when, from this Motive, this common Deposit of Power, was made in the Hands of a Magistrate, it could be with no other View than that he should exert it impartially for the common Benefit, and, therefore, as far as a Magistrate is under any Influence with Respect to his Decisions,

or

or has any Thing to hope, or to fear, in Confequence of any Act performed in his judicial Capacity, fo far, the very End of his Inftitution is defeated, and fo far the Power intrufted with him, that it might operate only to good Purpofes, may be perverted to Evil. The Independance of Judges, therefore, is one of the original and fundamental Rights of Mankind, but, it is impoffible in the Nature of Things, that a Judge fhould be Independant, who holds his Office only during the Pleafure of another; he will then certainly have fomething to hope and fomething to fear, and his Duty may fometimes be incompatible with his Intereft; when this happens, it would be abfurd to fuppofe, that the Senfe of Duty will always predominate; to fuppofe the contrary, is only to fuppofe, that he who becomes a Judge does not then ceafe to be a Man, but, that he is ftill fubject to the fame Paffions, and Infirmities, that he was before, in common with all human Beings. I will readily acknowledge, that there never was a Time when the Dependancy of Judges was lefs likely to produce ill Effects, not, becaufe Judges have any new Powers to refift Temptation, but, becaufe they are lefs likely to be tempted: Our moft amiable and gracious

cious Sovereign feems to found his Happinefs upon the true Principles of Virtue and Juftice, and the Vice-Roy whom he has fent over hither, feems, in every Refpect, difpofed to follow his Example, and to be truly his Reprefentative; but from the Viciffitude natural to every Thing fublunary, and from the Example of our fifter Country, *Great Britain*, I think it now proper to make a Motion, that leave be given to bring in Heads of a Bill for making the Commiffions of Judges, *quam diu fe bene gefferint*.

Mr *E— M—* got up, and faid, that he feconded the Motion, with very great Pleafure, as it would be a Confidence of Security to the Nation, not with Refpect to the prefent Time but the future; he added, that the Support of Dignity, in the Judges, was alfo a Matter of great Confequence, as it gave Weight to their Decrees, and Satisfaction to the Suitors; but more efpecially as it gave Encouragement to Men of the firft Abilities, to fill the Bench, who might otherwife find greater Advantages in continuing at the Bar; he fhould, therefore, he faid, be very well pleafed to have a Claufe tacked to the Bill for the Encreafe of the Judges Salaries; this he
ob-

Day XIV.] *Affairs of* Ireland. 295

obferved, became neceffary upon a mere Suppofition, that the Salary fixed, during the Reign of King *William*, in the Year 1699, was only a reafonable Salary, and, that the Judges now ought not to be worfe provided for, than they were then; becaufe, the Difference between the Value of Money, and the Expences of Life at that Time, and this, were very great, as would appear by *Fleetwood*'s *Chronicum Pretiofum*, and, therefore, though the Appointment at that Time might be fufficient, it would at prefent fall very fhort; for which Reafon, he propofed, that the Increafe of the Judges Salaries might be a *Tack* to the Bill.

Mr *L— O—* faid, in reply, that he fhould be much pleafed to have the Salaries of the Judges increafed, and that he thought it a very proper Meafure, but begged to be excufed from making it a Tack to his Bill, for though there was the greateft Reafon to believe it would be univerfally adopted, yet he was unwilling to load his Bill with any Tack, whatever were the Chances in its Favour, becaufe he confidered it as of very great Moment to the Conftitution of his Country.

The Queſtion being put, it was carried in the Affirmative.

Ordered, That leave be given, to bring in Heads of a Bill, for making the Commiſſions of Judges, *quam diu ſe bene geſſerint*, and that Mr *L— O—*; Mr *M—*; Mr *P—*; Mr Serjeant *M—*; and, Dr *L—*, do prepare and bring in the ſame.

SATURDAY, *Nov.* 12, 1763.

FIFTEENTH DAY.

MR E— S— P— got up, and said, that *Tuesday* next, was fixed for enquiring into the Grievance universally felt, and complained of, the Increase of Pensions; but, that, he apprehended, it would not be a proper Day, as he had been informed, that many Gentlemen would not be ready to attend, and, as the Report of the Committee of Accounts was that Day to be made, which would take up some Time; he added, that he did not blush to say, that he had received a Message, which induced him to put off the Enquiry concerning Pensions; and, therefore, he moved, that it might be put off till *Wednesday*.

The Right Honourable A— M— said, that he considered the Enquiry, concerning Pensions, as a Matter of the highest Importance, that required much Time and Deliberation, and a full Attendance of the Members, and, therefore, he thought it should be put off, even for a longer Day, as well upon that

that Account, as, becaufe, the National Accounts, and the Supply interfered, which fhould not fuffer Delay, as the Money Bills for the Supply fhould be fent off about the four or five and twentieth of the Month, the ufual Time, when the Duty would ceafe; he faid, that, upon the Report of the Committee of Accounts, Debates might arife, and the paffing them might, therefore, take up more Time than was expected; he faid, alfo, that the fixing the Supplies, and fending over the Money Bills might be attended with Delay, and, as it was of the greateft Importance to have whatever related to that Bufinefs, fettled with proper Deliberation, it ought not to be interrupted by any Thing of lefs Confequence; he, therefore, wifhed that the Confideration of the Penfions was deferred till the Money Bills fhould be fent over.

Mr *P*— replied, that he was forry to differ from the Right Honourable Gentleman, who fpoke laft, but that the very Arguments he had ufed for deferring the Confideration of the Penfions to a longer Day, appeared to him to prove that it fhould not be longer deferred. How is it poffible, fays he, that an Eftablifhment fhould be fixed, till we know of what

what it ought to confift? The Eftablifhment of Penfions is already enormous, and if we fhould now fix it, without any Enquiry, or Refolution, the Meafure would be premature; for certainly an Enquiry into fo effential a Part of the Eftablifhment, ought to take Place before the Eftablifhment is fixed; befides, fays he, the very Inconvenience, which the Right Honourable Gentleman wifhes to remedy, would be encreafed by the Remedy he propofes; for if fomething is not determined, concerning Penfions, it will be a Subject of high Debate, throughout the whole Committee of Supplies; he, therefore, hoped that he fhould be excufed, in wifhing to have *Wednefday* fixed for the Penfions, and faid, that as the Duties would not end till the Twenty-eighth of the next Month, there would be Time enough to tranfact the Bufinefs relative to them without Precipitation, or Hurry.

The Order for the next *Tuefday*, being then read, it was refolved.

" That this Houfe will, next *Wednefday*,
" refolve itfelf into a Committee of the whole
" Houfe, to take into Confideration, the
" State of the Penfions upon the Civil Efta-
" blifh-

" blifhment of this Kingdom, and how the
" Encreafe of them may be prevented."

Ordered, That the Agent to the Penfioners do attend this Houfe next *Wednefday*.

Ordered, That the proper Officer do lay before this Houfe, a Lift of the Names of fuch Penfioners as do not refide in this Kingdom, and have Licenfes of Abfence from his Majefty, or from the Lord Lieutenant, or other Chief Governors, with the Dates of fuch Licenfes.

Ordered, That the proper Officer do lay before this Houfe, a Lift of the Names of the Penfioners who do not refide in this Kingdom.

Mr *R— F—* then got up, and faid, that confidering the diftreffed Situation of *Ireland*, at that Time, it was a Matter of the higheft Importance, to enquire into the extraordinary Increafe of the Military Eftablifhment, before the Supplies were granted; he faid, that the Remark made by the honourable Gentleman, who fpoke laft, two Days before, had made a deep Impreffion upon his Mind;

inftead

instead of thirty Regiments upon the Establishment, says he, there is now no less than forty-two, with the same Number of Men, twelve Thousand; this is extreamly dangerous to the Constitution two Ways, first, by encreasing Dependants; and, secondly, by encreasing Expence; the Expence has encreased no less than 150,000 *l.* a Year, since the Year 1757, which this Country is by no Means able to bear; and this Establishment, at present, amounts to 100,000 *l.* a Year more than in the Height of the War, besides Military Contingencies, and Barracks, which amount to a very considerable Sum. He observed, that the Military and Civil Establishment, with the Pensions, would leave only 30,000 *l.* out of the whole Revenue of the Country, and that this Sum and more would be swallowed up by the Artillery, and Laboratory, which are not included in the Military Establishment, though certainly belonging to it, and Articles of very great Expence. The Word Laboratory, he said, was quite new in the House, and scarce a Man in it knew either its Meaning, or its Use; in his Opinion, it was a Place where all Sorts of Combustibles were prepared for Fire-ships, Bombs, Grenadoes, and other Impleplements of Offence, for the Sea Service, and might, probably, run to an Expence of forty, fifty, sixty, or even one hundred thousand Pounds a Year, and, why we should, in a Situation so distressed as we were known to be in, set about making such expensive Preparations for others, he said, he could not tell, especially in a Time of profound Peace, and just after the Conclusion of a War, which it was to be hoped rendered another War highly improbable, at least for some Time. He said, the Ordnance already cost near 30,000 *l.* a Year, and, that he was persuaded, that if this Institution, and the Laboratory went on, without controul, they would be much more injurious to Ourselves than to our Enemies. He added, that the Staff of General Officers, in *Ireland*, amounted to two and twenty thousand Pounds a Year, though in *England* it amounted to no more than Eleven, so that the Expence in that Article was just double, which, he said, was surely surprizing, as in this Town there was seldom General Officers enough to make a Board. He concluded, that if some Regulation, with Respect to the public Expences, in almost every Branch, was not made, there would not be the least Supply left for any Emergency, or for any Improve-

DAY XV.] *Affairs of* IRELAND. 303

provement, of which the Country stood in so much need.

Dr *C— L—* got up, and said, that he was extreamly sorry to find himself under a Necessity of making a Complaint against a very respectable Body, the *Dublin* Society, which had been intrusted by the House with no less a Sum than 10,000 *l.* to be distributed in Premiums: He said they had set out in a very proper Manner, and, after a strict Enquiry into the Merits of several Claimants, they had allotted to each such a Proportion of this Bounty as they appeared to deserve; that they had, in Consequence of such an Enquiry, allotted to a Family of the Name of *Smith*, the Sum of 500 *l.* but that they, soon after, received a Message from a certain great Person, acquainting them, that, in that Person's Opinion, 2,000 *l.* was little enough for that Family, upon which they did, contrary to their Judgment, and, in Breach of their Trust, grant to that Family the full Sum of 2,000 *l.* no less than four Times as much as they had determined to be equal to their Merit; and they took the 1,500*l.* which they had added to the 500 *l.* originally allotted to the *Smiths* of *Waterford*, Manufacturers of Tape, from the

Sums

Sums allotted to other Perfons, whom they had before judged to merit them, in equal Proportions. He faid, alfo, that there were two Glafs-Houfes in *Dublin,* one of *Irifh,* and one of *Englifh* Eftablifhment; that Part of the *Irifh* one had, by Accident, been burnt down, and the Materials for making Glafs fo damaged, that, not being fit for fine Ware, it had been made into Bottles, which were of a good Fabrick, and fold for 18 *s.* a Grofs; but becaufe it was an *Irifh* Glafs-Houfe, no Encouragement was given it by the Society, who, at the fame Time, gave a large Premium to an *Englifh* Glafs-Houfe, which caufed a Monopoly, and raifed Bottles to 20 *s.* a Grofs.

The H—ble *B— M—* faid, that he was prefent when the Meffage was brought to the Society, requiring them to grant 1,500 *l.* more than they had, after a ftrict and fair Examination, allotted to the *Smiths,* and that he propofed the Meffage fhould be entered on their Books, as the Caufe of their granting fuch an Addition.

Mr *J— M—* confirmed what Dr *L—* had faid concerning the Glafs-Houfes.

Upon

Upon which it was ordered, that a Committee be appointed to enquire into the Disposal of 10,000 *l.* granted to the *Dublin* Society, to be, by them, distributed among the several Artificers, and others, who petitioned the House for parliamentary Encouragement, the last Sessions of Parliament; and a Committee was appointed accordingly.

Mr *E— S— P—* said, That he had made a Motion, a few Days ago, that the Sums which the House should think proper to grant for the Encouragement of Manufactories, should be given in Premiums for the superior Quantity, or Quality, of the Manufacture, when it should be brought to Market, and not to particular Manufacturers: That he was persuaded, from the general Disposition of the House, that the Method he proposed was more agreeable to it, than that against which he had excepted, notwithstanding it was rejected, and that it was rejected merely to avoid giving umbrage to the worthy Member who had presented the Petition, that gave Occasion to his Proposal, which, he declared, he made solely with a View to the publick Good, and not from any Disrespect, or ill Will,

Will, to the worthy Gentleman, whom he highly honoured. He now added, that the Petitions which were every Day pouring into the Houfe, were fo numerous, as greatly to obftruct its Bufinefs, and that the mere receiving them, though no Money fhould be granted upon them, would have a difadvantageous Appearance to thofe on the other Side of the Water, as being inconfiftent with the Poverty of which they complained, and the Burthenfomenefs of various Demands, which they laboured to evade.

He therefore prayed, that the Houfe would come to a Refolution, that no Money fhould be granted by the Houfe, this Seffion, for the Encouragement, or Support, of any particular Trade or Manufacture whatfoever.

To this no Oppofition was made, except that one Gentleman faid, he hoped it would not be extended to injure any beneficial Undertaking that had been begun fince the laft Seffions, under the Sanction, and by the Aid of Parliament; for, if it appeared that the Money already received had been honeftly and judicioufly laid out, it would be great Pity that the Undertaking fhould ftop for want of farther Aid.   Some

Some Gentleman, upon this, proposed, that the Motion might be amended; however, it passed in the very Manner that Mr *P—* proposed it, *Nemine Contradicente.*

MONDAY, *Nov.* 14, 1763.

SIXTEENTH DAY.

SIR *W— O—* represented, that, as all Grants to Petitioners, for the Encouragement of Manufactories, had been precluded by the Resolution of *Saturday*, it was the Duty of the House to encourage Manufacturers in general, by every other Way that could be devised; that the Paper Manufacture, in particular, ought to be encouraged, as of great Importance to the Kingdom, and, therefore, as particular Persons concerned in it could receive no pecuniary Encouragement, he begged leave to move, that, for the Encouragement of the Manufacturer, the House should come into a Resolution, that all the Journals, Votes, and other Transactions of that House, should be printed upon Paper manufactured in this Kingdom.

Sir R— C— seconded this Motion, and said, that the Paper Manufacture, being in its Infant State, and of great Importance to the Kingdom, it ought to receive every possible Encouragement.

Mr *A— M—*.

Mr S——,

There is no Man in this House, Sir, more ready to encourage the Manufactures of this Country than myself, as no Man can have a fuller Conviction, that the Riches and Happiness of the Country depend principally upon them. Yet I should be sorry to have this House come so suddenly to a Resolution, which would, in some Degree, operate with the Force of a Law, and which may also give Jealousy and Umbrage to Nations with whom we have Connections, and whose Good-will and Friendship we should do every Thing in our Power to secure; there are also other ill Consequences to be apprehended from the Measure proposed, which, at least, make it adviseable, not to take it precipitately: If we may Credit the Memorial that

that lies upon the Table, we ought rather to encourage than difcourage the Importation of Paper, becaufe we confume more than our Manufacturers can fupply, and do not yet import enough to make good the Deficiency, which it is of great Moment for us to do. Printing is a Manufacture, the Encreafe of which neceffarily depends upon having Paper of a good Kind, and at a reafonable Rate, and there are confiderable Works of Printing now carrying on; if, therefore, we produce a Scarcity of Paper, by prohibiting its Importation, we fhall raife its Price, and we fhall alfo debafe its Quality; for our Paper Makers will have a Monopoly, and impofe upon the Stationer, Printer, and Confumer, what Commodity they think fit, and at what Price; however, as I am wholly ignorant of the State of our Paper Manufactory, and fpeak only upon Conjecture, and the Credit of the Memorial, I have mentioned to be lying before us, I wifh a Committee might be appointed to enquire, how far our own Manufactory of Paper can fupply the Confumption; if it cannot fupply the Confumption, I do not fee that this Motion is neceffary for its Encouragement. It will not encourage the making it by making a Market, for it has a fufficient

Market already; it will not encourage the making it better, for when it is confumed in confequence of an Order, and not by Preference, the Manufacturer, will, be lefs folicitous to recommend it by its Quality, and gain it the Preference, than when the Sale depends upon fuch Preference. I hope, therefore, that the Gentleman will withdraw his Motion, and that a Motion will be made for the Appointment of a Committee, to make fuch Enquiries as may be previoufly neceffary to direct our Determinations.

Sir *W— O—*.

Mr S——,

Whatever Deference I pay to the Judgment of the learned Gentleman, who fpoke laft, I muft be excufed from withdrawing my Motion; as Committees have been frequently appointed, fince the Year 1749, for the very Enquiry he mentions, concerning the State of our Paper Manufactory, and frequent Reports made, and Premiums given for its Encouragement, I think its Progrefs and prefent State muft be fufficiently known; however,
I am

DAY XVI.] *Affairs of* IRELAND. 311

I am commiffioned to affure the Houfe, that the Manufactory of *Cork* alone would furnifh this City with forty thoufand Rheams a Year, and, that there are, at leaft, twenty other Manufactories, which, if they had proper Encouragement, would be able to fupply the whole home Confumption, and, where fo many Mills are conftantly at Work, I fee no danger of a Monopoly; there will be a fufficient Rivalry among them to keep Paper at a reafonable Price, and to furnifh a good Commodity. Befides, I do not fee how the Meafure, propofed by the Motion, can leffen the Importation of foreign Paper any otherwife than by tending to gain the Preference for our own Paper, both with Refpect to Quality and Price, by encouraging the Makers to perfevere in the Exertion of their Diligence, and their Skill. Is a pretended Regard to Foreigners, or a Fear of giving them Umbrage, to prevent our endeavouring to eftablifh Manufactures of our own upon fuch Principles, and by fuch Means as thefe? If the Price of our own Paper is unreafonably raifed, and the Quality rendered worfe by this Motion, it will rather encourage than prevent the Importation of the Commodity; for what fhould hinder the Stationer, Printer,

and

and Confumer, from ufing fuch Paper as deferves the Preference, whether with Refpect to Quality, or Price, fuppofing the Meafure propofed by the Motion to take Place? And how, Sir, can this Meafure tend to make Paper fcarce? Will more Paper be ufed by this Houfe than was ufed before? If we propofed to make an Order, that for every Sheet we ufed we fhould burn another, under a Notion of encouraging the Manufacture, by encreafing the Confumption, then it might be objected, that we fhould make Paper fcarce; but, we propofe no fuch Thing, we only propofe that the Quantity of Paper we have been ufed to confume, fhall, for the future, be fupplied by our own Manufactures; and, furely, there is nothing in this that can hurt any other Manufacture of our own, or juftly give Offence to any other Country, as an Injury to theirs. What Encouragement the Paper Manufacture may receive from the Motion it is not neceffary to enquire, for it is not oppofed, upon Pretence that it will give no Encouragement, but the contrary, that it will give too much. I have already fhewn that this Pretence is groundlefs, and, I fhall now fhew, that fuch Encouragement as it can give to that Manufactory, the Manufactory

tory ought to have: It is a Manufacture of great Importance in itself, and it is also of great Importance as a Branch, though a remote one, of the Linnen Manufacture; Paper is a Commodity fabricated from Materials, which would otherwise be of no value, and it employs a great Number of Persons, who, from their Situation, and Circumstances, could be employed in no other Way than the collecting such Materials together. That the Measure proposed would operate with the Force of a Law, prohibiting the Importation of Paper, I have shewn already to be a mere groundless Pretence: You, Sir, (addressing himself to the Speaker) and this House have a Power of ordering the public Proceedings of Parliament to be printed in what Manner, and upon what Materials you think fit, but your Order cannot extend further, and, therefore, for any Thing yet offered, I must humbly beg leave to be excused from withdrawing my Motion.

Lord *B—* got up, and said, that he had no Objection to any Motion that could produce so salutary a Purpose as the Encouragement of a useful and considerable Manufactory; but that to prevent all Appearance of

Rivalſhip, and render the Meaſure agreeable to every Body, he propoſed to make an Amendment, and that Paper of *Britiſh* Manufacture ſhould be included in the Motion.

Sir R— C—.

Mr S——,

I hope, Sir, I ſhall be excuſed, for making a ſlight Obſervation, on what has been ſaid, by the honourable and learned Gentleman who ſits on the oppoſite Bench; it has been inſinuated by that Gentleman, that the Diſcouragement of Foreign Manufactures, by the Encouragement of our own, may give Umbrage to Countries, with which we are connected; but, if the pleaſing our Allies is to interfere with the Execution of a Meaſure, which, we think for our own interior Advantage, we ſhall be in a State moſt deplorably dependant and confined, and become the Servant of Servants, in the moſt mortifying Senſe of the Words. As to the Amendment in favour of *Britiſh* Paper, I am afraid it would be attended with very great Inconveniencies, and, in a great Meaſure, defeat the Intention of the Motion, for it would be very eaſy

easy for the *English* Factors, in league with the Factors here, to pour in, by the Way of *England*, a vast Quantity of Paper made by the *Dutch*; is there not every Day a vast Quantity of *French* Silk obtruded upon us, as the Manufacture of *England*? Is this Grievance so soon forgotten? Every body knows that the Factors make up the Cockett, and, that the Land-waiter very frequently knows nothing of the Matter, though he is obliged to the contrary by his Duty, and, as we have no Duplicate for Paper, there being no Act of Parliament for that Purpose, and it being made of Rags, that are picked up in the Streets, it will be impossible for the Printer to swear whether the Paper he uses is *British* Manufacture, or Foreign, as there is no possibility for him to ascertain it. Indeed, I am averse to the Encrease of Oaths, for, as far as I have been able to observe, they do little more than increase Perjury. Let me add, that the *British* Manufactory of Paper is not sufficient to supply the Consumption of that Country, and that *Ireland* gets scarce any from thence, for, upon inspecting the Custom-House Books, I find, large Importations of Paper from *Holland*, but little or none from *Great Britain*; I, therefore, chuse

to

to have the Question put, without the Amendment.

It was, however, agreed, that the Question should be put with the Amendment, and then Mr *H—S—* said, That though he should have objected against it, as first proposed, yet he was now ready to give his Vote for it.

Mr *P—T—*, the A. G. said, that he could never vote for any Motion so precipitately put, so late in the Day, and so unexpected by the House; he said, too, that a Resolution of the House would influence many, though it would not bind them; that the House was but one Part of the Legislature, and had no right to do what would bind even a single Person; that Gentlemen who had considered the Motion maturely in their Closets, might be Masters of it, and that other Gentlemen had an undoubted Right to a competent Time for considering it, that they might be upon equal Terms with those who had considered it already, and that he thought no Method so fit for this Purpose as the Appointment of a Committee; but, that as it was insisted, that the Question should be put, he must beg leave to put the previous

previous Question, whether it should be put or not.

The Motion was as follows: "That from and after the first Day of *December* next, all the Votes and Journals of this House, Public Accounts, Acts of Parliament, and other Matters to be printed by Order of this House, or for the Public Use, shall be printed on the best Sort of Paper manufactured in *Great-Britain*, or in this Kingdom; and that no Charge for Paper to be made use of, after the said first Day of *December*, shall be allowed in the National Accounts, or paid by the Public, without an Affidavit made before a Magistrate, by the Person claiming Payment, that the Paper so charged is the Manufacture of *Great-Britain*, or of this Kingdom, or was bought from a Manufacturer of Paper as the Manufacture of *Great-Britain*, or *Ireland*, excepting the Statues now printing under the Direction of the Judges."

And the previous Question being put, that that Question be now put,

It passed in the Negative.

TUESDAY, Nov. 15, 1763.

SEVENTEENTH DAY.

MAJOR *W— B—* made a favourable Report from the Committee appointed to take the Whale Fishery into Confideration, and it was ordered to be referred to the Committee of Supplies.

A Report was made from a Committee, appointed to confider of Repairs, that were wanting to St *Catherine*'s Church, and a Motion was made that this Report fhould be referred to the Committee of Supplies. This Motion was oppofed, and it was urged, that the Parifhoners were able to repair their Church at their own Expence.

Mr *R— F—*.

Mr S——,

I have great Reafon to think, Sir, that the Parifhioners are not able to repair their Church at their own Expence, and, I think, that

that nothing can be more worthy the Attention of Parliament, than the keeping the Places of Worship in the Metropolis in decent Repair. External Appearances have a great Effect upon the Mind, which cannot without the utmost Difficulty be abstracted from sensible Objects, or consider the worship of God as wholly distinct from the Circumstances in which it is performed; we should, therefore, avail ourselves of Associations of Ideas, which we cannot break, and contrive that the Worship of God should be performed in such Circumstances as will most concur to put the Mind in a proper Frame for it, and, consequently, give it a more effectual Influence. A serious Sense of Religion, and a conscientious Performance of its Duties, will dispose the common People to be good Neighbours, and good Subjects, and greatly tend to quell a contumacious and turbulent Spirit, which has of late so much interrupted the Public quiet, and, in some Degree defeated the Purposes of Civil Government.

The Question being then put, whether the Report should be referred, it was carried in the Affirmative 76 against 60.

The

The Committee appointed to confider the Petition of the Minifter and Church-wardens of St *Andrews* reported, that it was neceffary to enlarge the Burial Ground of that Parifh; this Refolution of the Committee was ftrongly oppofed by Dr *L—*, who demonftrated, that the Effluvia of corrupting Bodies, thrown together in great Numbers, but juft below the Surface of the Earth, in populous Cities, could not but produce very pernicious Confequences. He obferved, that the Practice of thus burying the Dead was contrary to that of all Antiquity, and of moft of the great Cities in Europe, to none of which it could be more pernicious than to *Dublin,* as the Streets were very clofely built.

The Refolution was, upon Motion, recommitted.

WEDNESDAY, Nov. 16, 1763.

EIGHTEENTH DAY.

THIS being the Day appointed for considering the State of the Pensions, and how the Encrease of them might be prevented.

Mr *E— S— P—* moved, that the House should proceed upon the Business of the Day.

Mr *J— D—*.

Mr S——,

No Man in this House, Sir, is more sensible of the many Disadvantages that arise from the Encrease of Pensions, as they are now granted, than myself; and an Enquiry into the State of this Grievance, and the Means of redressing it, is certainly a very fit Object of the Attention of this House; but I cannot think, Sir, that such an Enquiry is necessary at this Time, because we have the greatest Reason to believe that all the Advantages which could be expected from it will be obtained without it. I must again mention the Assurance by which his Majesty has been graciously pleased to anticipate our Wishes. He has assured us, that no Pension for Life, or Years, shall be granted for the future, except on extraordinary Occasions; and these are the Pensions, Sir, at which we have most Reason to be alarmed; they are permanent; they are transferrable; and they are not subject to disqualifying Laws: Gentlemen, indeed, have said, that every Occasion, which a Minister shall pretend to be extraordinary, will be sufficient to evade the Promise; and that he will have nothing more to do, when he is inclined to grant a new Pension for Life, or Years, than to say, that there is an extraordinary Occasion for it. But, Ministers, Sir, however corrupt, very seldom venture upon a bad Measure, which they cannot veil, with a Pretence that is at least specious, and will at the first Glance give it the Appearance of Good; that very Attention to their own Interest, which frequently leads them to betray the Interest to the Publick must necessarily restrain them from open and flagitious Insults upon the Reason as well as the Rights

of

of Mankind, and can any Gentleman present believe, that a Minister who has a desire to reward his Pander, or his Borough Jobber, with a Pension for Life, or Years, will have the Effrontery, or the Rashness, to pretend that a Grant of such Pension is upon an extraordinary Occasion, and, therefore, excepted in his Sovereign's Promise to his People? Let us, at least, Sir, give the Assurance we have received a temporary Credit, and suspend our Proceedings till the next Sessions, when, if we see sufficient Reason to distrust it, we may take the very Measure that is now proposed, with more Justice, and a better Grace. At present, it is manifestly premature, and wholly repugnant to the Confidence that we ought to place in his Majesty's Declaration. I, therefore, humbly move, that this Question may be post-poned till the first Day of next *July*.

Mr *E— S— P—*.

Mr *S——,*

I remember, Sir, and so I am sure does every Gentleman present, that when the Motion for determining the Right of granting Pensions by a Trial at Law was rejected, it was the unanimous Opinion of this House, that Pensions were such a Grievance, as a Committee ought to be appointed to enquire into, and consider how to redress; and that the House did, accordingly, come to an unanimous Resolution, to resolve itself into a Committee for that Purpose on the next *Tuesday*: But, as other indispensible Business took up great Part of that Day, it was made another unanimous Resolution of the House, that the Consideration of the State of the Pensions, and how to prevent their Encrease, should be undertaken this Day. But, I am sorry to say, that, notwithstanding these Resolutions, I have but too much Reason to believe the Sitting of such a Committee was never intended; and I think it my Duty to communicate such Reason of my Belief to the House. As I was coming last *Monday* from the four Courts, in my Chair, I was stopped by a particular Friend, a Gentleman of great Worth and Consequence, who asked me, whether I intended to go that Day to the House. I answered, that I did not, as I knew of nothing that made my attendance necessary, and that, as I had been much-fatigued by the Business of the House, and of the Courts, I intended to make that a Day of Rest:

Rest: He replied, " You may not only take your Rest this Day, but every other Day of the Sessions, for Things are now fixed so as to admit of no Alteration; no Enquiry will be made into the State of the Pensions, nor any Thing else done but what has been agreed upon with those who are to take the lead." To this I answered, with great surprize, that I could scarce think what he told me was possible. That the House had been unanimous for an Examination, and had actually appointed a Committee for that Purpose, but a few Days ago; that the Public expected it, and that to disappoint them in an Expectation so reasonable, and on an Occasion so important, would be wholly inconsistent with the Dignity, as well as with the Duty of the House, as the Members would then appear to be nothing more than State Puppets, with Wires in their Noses, by which they were turned first one Way, and then another, just as those who had the Management of them thought fit.

Mr *P*— was here interrupted, by Mr *P*— *T*—, the A. G.

Mr T——.

Mr S——,

Whatever private Converſation, Sir, the Gentleman, who ſpoke laſt, might have with his Friend, it is ſurely improper to introduce it into this Houſe; and it is ſtill more improper that Inſinuations, ſo injurious to its Members, ſhould be ſuppoſed to have any Weight in it. I hope every Gentleman in this Houſe feels a proper Diſdain at being repreſented as a Puppet, moved by the Dictates of another's Will, and ſufficient Spirit to ſhew, by his Conduct, that he acts upon Principles of Freedom, and Independance, in conſequence of his own Principles, and by the Determination of his own Judgment: As to the Enquiry, in Queſtion, I ſhall, for my own Part, oppoſe it, from a full Conviction, that it is unneceſſary; what could we hope more from this very Enquiry than an Aſſurance from his Majeſty, that he has conſidered the Grievance, and will redreſs it? and this Aſſurance he has been gracriouſly pleaſed to give us already. It is, indeed, true that this Aſſurance has not come before the Houſe, with the Solemnity of a formal Meſſage,

sage, but Gentlemen seem to forget that his Majesty could not communicate it in that Manner, consistent with his Character, and Dignity. The Intimation to the Lord Lieutenant is a Favour, and, if his Majesty is graciously pleased to wave his Prerogative in our behalf, are we to expect that he should do it in a Way that would imply a Consciousness of his having abused it. His Majesty has, in this Instance, treated us with a Condescension and Kindness, of which, I may venture to say, we have no Precedent; and shall we return it with Remonstrance, and Complaint? Shall we refuse a Favour from our gracious Prince, merely because it is not offered in a Manner that would degrade himself? I remember, indeed, some Gentlemen asked, with a contemptuous Sneer, what this House had to do with a private Conversation, at the Castle; but, surely, I may now recriminate, and ask, what has this House to do with a private Conversation in the Street. I had, certainly, a better Right to relate what I had heard, from the Lord Lieutenant, with a View to calm Animosities, and conciliate Affection, than the honourable Member, on the Bench near me, had to retail the Impertinencies of a busy Pratler, who took upon him to foretell the Conduct of this House, and impute it to dishonourable Motives, which could tend only to excite Discontent, and Disaffection, at a Time when Peace and Unanimity were essentially necessary, not only to our Prosperity, but our Existence. Upon the whole, Sir, I shall, from the clearest Conviction, and with the most public and disinterested Intention, give my Voice for postponing the Enquiry till the first of *July*.

Mr E— S— P—.

Mr S———,

I am sorry to say, Sir, that the honourable Gentlemen, who is just set down, would not have borne so hard upon me, whatever he might have done upon my Friend, if he had not mistaken my meaning; he has, in the Precipitancy of his Zeal, supposed that I represented the Members of this House as Puppets, actuated by a concealed Power; but, Sir, he will be convinced that I said just contrary: I said, I could not believe what my Friend told me to be a Fact, and my Reason was, that if it had been a Fact, the Members of the House would appear to be Puppets; but, as I did not believe the Fact, neither did I believe

lieve the Members of the House to be Puppets, or to appear to be such; now, Sir, whether the Fact related, by my Friend, was or was not true, I shall leave the honourable Gentleman to determine, and, if it was true, I shall also leave him to reconcile it to the Wisdom, Steadiness, and Consistency, that ought to distinguish so considerable a Branch of the Legislature, as he can.

Mr *W— B—*.

Mr S——,

Give me leave to say, Sir, that at present this House is as free from any Imputation of Dishonour, arising from what the Gentleman who spoke last, let drop to his Friend, as a new-born Child would be from a Declaration, that if he should ever invade the Property of another, he would be a Thief; we have as yet been guilty of no Inconsistency, and, like my honourable Friend, I cannot believe, that we shall: But, in what light shall we stand, if the following Facts should be alledged against us.

" On *Wednesday*, the Ninth of *November*, we agreed that the Pensions, charged on the Civil

Civil Eſtabliſhment, were an intolerable Grievance. On the ſame Day, we paſſed an unanimous Reſolution, That on the *Tueſday* following, we ſhould take that Grievance into Conſideration. On that *Tueſday*, we paſſed another unanimous Reſolution, that we would conſider the Grievance on the next Day, and on that very next Day reſolved, that we ſhould not conſider the Grievance at all!"

I ſay, Sir, if this ſhould be the Caſe, how can ſuch Fluctuation be accounted for? by what ſtrange, by what miraculous Illumination can we ſuppoſe Gentlemen to diſcover inſtantaneouſly, on *Wedneſday*, that an Opinion, which they had formed on *Tueſday*, after long Conſideration and Debate, was erroneous? How ſhall we account for Reſolutions diametrically oppoſite, paſſed in the ſame Houſe, and, by the ſame Members, within four and twenty Hours of each other? Will there not be then ſufficient Reaſon to ſuſpect the Influence, the mere mention of which has given ſuch Offence? Will not our Proceedings be conſidered as a ſolemn Mummery, and ourſelves as mere Shadows, changing Place with the Light behind us, and depending, for our very Exiſtence, upon it?

it? But this, Sir, bad as it is, is not the worst; the Cause of this Inconsistency is still more alarming than the Inconsistency itself; whatever may be our Dependance, it is for the Interest of all Parties that we should, at least, appear to be free; and, there is the greatest Reason to fear that an Enquiry, which such extraordinary Methods are taken to prevent, would disclose Abuses, and Enormities, which it is of the last Importance on one Side to conceal, and, consequently, on the other to discover. If the Pensions are not a Grievance, why should an Enquiry be prevented, that will shew us our mistake? If they are a Grievance, why should an Enquiry be prevented that will lead to Redress? We are told, indeed, that such an Enquiry is precluded, by an Assurance that his Majesty will grant no more Pensions for Lives, or Years, except upon extraordinary Occasion; but, if we acquiesce in this Assurance, and if the Promise should be fulfilled, we shall tacitly acknowledge a Power, to the mere forbearance of which we owe our Exemption from Ruin, and, under which, we must acquiesce with silent sufferance, whenever it shall be exerted over us. Though we may depend upon the exemplary Virtues of that most

amiable

amiable Sovereign, whom Providence has, at prefent, fet over us, it would be romantic to hope that they will be tranfmitted to all who fhall fucceed him. It behoves us to do for our Pofterity, what our Anceftors did for us; and, if it is poffible, fecure, as a Right, what as a Favour muft be precarious; and proceed to an Enquiry, which we cannot now relinquifh, without the Proftitution both of our Intereft and our Honour; an Enquiry which cannot but gratify a Prince, whofe Happinefs is our Profperity, and which may reftrain any, who may hereafter delight only in the Difplay of their own Power, and fondly endeavour to derive Glory from Oppreffion.

Mr *M— P—*.

Mr S——,

I am extreamly furprized, Sir, to hear Gentlemen indulge themfelves in Declamations, only to repeat what has been faid already, and advance Principles that have been fhewn to be erroneous: It is, furely, taking up Time to very little Purpofe, that might be improved to the Advantage of ourfelves, and the Public: It is making a Debate, once commenmenced, endless; and puts the best Reasoner, in the Condition of *Hercules*, striving with *Anteus*, who, the Moment he was thrown to the Ground, started up again with new Vigour, and gave his Antagonist the Labour of perpetual Conquest, without gaining the least Advantage from his Superiority. It was irrefragably proved, in this House, but a few Days ago, that the Crown had a Power of granting Pensions, without the Violation of any Law; that this Power was, therefore, constitutional; and so united with other Parts of the Constitution, that, to subvert it, would endanger the whole Chain, of which it was a Link. It was proved, from our Statutes, from History, from immemorial Custom, from the Journals of this House, not only that the granting of Pensions was legal, but that the Legality of it had never been called in Question; and yet Gentlemen still talk of exempting the Revenue from such Grants, as a Matter of Right, and affect to talk as if nothing more was necessary to redress a Grievance, supposed to arise from these Grants, than to enforce Laws that have been broken, and assert Powers that have lain dormant. We have no Way, Sir, of preventing more Pensions from being granted, but that of prevailing upon his Majesty

jesty not to do, what might be legally done; in other Words, by soliciting as a Favour, what we cannot claim as a Right: This Favour, Sir, without Solicitation, is already offered us, and, it may reasonably be expected, that those Gentlemen who are inclined not to accept it, should justify their Principles, so extraordinary and so new, by some Arguments equally new and extraordinary; that they would, at least, get forward in the Dispute, and not, like a Horse in a Mill, exhaust their Strength, by trotting in a Circle; a Drudgery which the poor Beast is always hood-winked to perform, and, in which, it is impossible for us to imitate him, without shutting our Eyes. Give me now leave, Sir, to observe, that several Things have, in the Course of this Debate, been taken for granted, which still remain to be proved. We have been told that Pensions are greatly encreased, which is a Fact not to be denied; but it has been taken for granted, that Pensions are a Grievance, in Proportion to this Encrease, which is a Fallacy: Under the Protection of those very Sovereigns who have encreased our Pensions, our Wealth is increased in at least an equal Degree. If, in the Year 1703, our Pensions amounted to 42,000 *l*,

and

and if, at prefent, they amount to 70,000*l.* it does not follow, that we are now in a worfe Condition than we were then, in the Proportion of 42 to 70: Has not every Revenue, both public and private, encreafed in the fame Proportion? Nay, have not the Fortunes of private Gentlemen been doubled? Befides, Sir, Money has, fince that Time, leffened near one Half in its Value; fo that, although the Sum granted in Penfions is larger, the Gratification is not equal; and, what the King now gives is lefs in Value than it was when we fuppofe that Grievance to have been tolerable, which we now alledge to be ruinous. There can be no Time more proper for the Difplay of Royal Munificence than the prefent; great Opportunities for Diftinction have offered during a War now at an End; and great Merit has been difplayed; befides, Sir, our King is young; he is juft afcended the Throne; his Heart overflows with Benevolence and Liberality; and what Wonder is it, that, with fuch Claims upon his Bounty, and fuch a Difpofition to beftow, he fhould have made fome Additions to the Penfions, which, yet, as I have obferved, do not exceed in Reality, whatever they may do in Appearance, the Gratuities beftowed by his Royal Predeceffors, in Circumſtances which leſs required them: Yet, even at this Time, and in theſe Circumſtances, his Majeſty is inclined to reſtrain his own Diſpoſition, that he may gratify ours; and what farther can be propoſed by the Enquiry, it is impoſſible for me to imagine.

Mr *R— F—* ſaid, in reply, that he was ſorry to hear the Name of his Majeſty ſo frequently made Uſe of in the Houſe; that it could not fail having an Influence, from which the Houſe, as a third Part of the Legiſlature, independant on the other two, ought always to be free: That it was the more dangerous, in Proportion as his Majeſty was the more amiable, and would more effectually ſcreen a Miniſter who had oppoſite Qualities. He ſaid, alſo, that the mention of a Letter ſaid to be written by the Secretary to the Viceroy, was irregular, and of pernicious Tendency; and that, if it had come properly before them, it could be conſidered only as the Letter of a Secretary, written to excuſe or palliate the Advice of an unpopular and deſtructive Meaſure, and to prevent a conſtitutional Enquiry into a Grievance, of which he had been the Cauſe; it was known, he ſaid, that ſuch an Enquiry was about to be ſet

on

on Foot, fo early as the second Day of the Seffions, and that the Letter was written in Confequence of that Knowledge, and with a View to effect what was now doing, the poftponing the dreaded Enquiry to a long Day.

The R—t H—ble Mr *P— T—*, the A. G. in anfwer to this, faid, that the Affair of the Letter was intirely mif-reprefented; that it was not written, in confequence of Intelligence received that an Enquiry into Penfions would be fet on foot: But that the Lord Lieutenant, upon his firft coming into the Adminiftration, had applied to the King upon that Subject, with a View of doing an acceptable Service to this Country, and had obtained a Promife from his Majefty, that no more Penfions fhould be granted for Lives, or Years, except on extraordinary Occafions; that he communicated this Promife to the Gentlemen here, immediately upon his coming into this Kingdom, and that to confirm the Promife, and give Weight to his Excellency's Report, his Majefty had been gracioufly pleafed to repeat it in a Letter, which he ordered his Secretary to write for that Purpofe.

The

The Order for the Day being read, upon the Motion of Sir *R— C—*, he fpoke to the following Effect:

Sir *R— C—*.

Mr S—,

I hope, Sir, it will not be fuppofed, that what I may offer upon this Occafion, proceeds from any partiality, either on one fide or the other: I am not inclined to fay any Thing againft Penfioners, becaufe I was formerly upon that Lift myfelf; nor am I inclined to fay any Thing for them, becaufe I confider my Efcape from among them as one of the moft fortunate Circumftances of my Life. I muft confefs, Sir, that every Thing that has been faid to Day, upon the Queftion now in Difpute, appears to me to be foreign to the Purpofe. The firft Thing propofed, by the Appointment of a Committee, is, an Enquiry into the State of Penfions; but, I think, the State of Penfions is perfectly known already: What have we been doing, Sir, in our former Debates on this Subject, but making an Enquiry that is now propofed to be made again; and, what is there to be difcovered, that is

not

not difcovered already? The next thing propofed, is, to feek Remedy for the Grievance which Penfions are fuppofed to produce; but, furely, this is no more than a Search for what is already found. The Remedy is an Act of Refumption, a Remedy that has been applied before, particularly in the Reign of King *William*, and this may be properly done in the Committee of Supplies, if we find that the public Money has been mif-applied, and that Penfions have been granted to unworthy Objects, which will be the proper Subject of Enquiry there. If we find that 75,000 *l.* is granted in Penfions, and that this is a Load which we cannot bear, let the Supplies be 75,000 *l.* lefs. I am, however, an Enemy to Heat and Animofity, and to the Relation of any Converfations that tend to produce either, and to the Reports of popular Clamour, by which the Deliberations of this Houfe fhould never be influenced; let us act, not under the Direction of Paffion, but Reafon; not under the Influence of Power, but of Judgment; let us confider Grievances, and redrefs them the fhorteft Way, and, that we may do fo, let us adjourn unneceffary Enquiries to a long Day.

Mr A— M.

Mr S——,

I think, Sir, with the honourable Gentleman who spoke last, that our Grievances should be redressed the shortest Way; but the shortest Way to redress Grievances will not be to embarrass and distress the Government, under the Protection of which we can alone enjoy any national Advantages: To cut off 75,000 *l.* of our Supplies, because we think 75,000 *l.* too much to grant in Pensions, seems to me to be a desperate and violent Remedy, much worse than the Disease: It seems to me to be as rash, inconsiderate, and injudicious, as it would be for a Man to burn his House that he might destroy the Fleas; but I am of Opinion, that we may still do something that we have not done, and something which the Letter that has been so often mentioned has not precluded. We do not only want the Encrease of Pensions to be stopped, but we want some already granted to be resumed; and, before we can specify such as we think improperly bestowed, we must enquire into the Merits and Characters of those that re-

receive them, and select the worthy from the unworthy, and represent the whole in a proper Manner to his Majesty. A Remedy we know we have; but it is proper to enquire, in the Committee proposed, what is the most eligible Remedy, and to report it, in a parliamentary Manner, to the House: And whatever the honourable Gentleman, who spoke last, may say, he must be conscious, that, if this is not done, nothing will be done. Some Gentlemen have told us, that the Encrease of Pensions is not a proportional Encrease of our Burthen; or, at least, that our Strength is proportionably increased with it; but they seem to forget, what may be seen with half an Eye, that our Strength is exhausted by other Labour, and that we have other Burthens, still encreasing, to sustain. The military and civil Lists were never so high as they are at present. We have contracted a Debt, from which we have hitherto been free; our Taxes are more numerous and more heavy, and our Absentees are multiplied. Let me only add, that we are now at Peace; and, that if we are now taxed at our utmost Ability, we shall be able to afford no auxilliary Assistance to our Sister Country, in a Time of War, nor even so much as to defend ourselves.

Colonel J— G—.

Mr S——,

It has been juftly obferved, by the honourable Gentleman who fpoke laft, that the Meafure propofed has two Objects; the preventing the Encreafe of Penfions, and the Reduction of thofe already granted: We have the Royal Promife, that they fhall not be encreafed, and Time will, without any Trouble of ours, decreafe them every Day. It is this Gentleman's Opinion, that the proper Object of the Committee's Enquiry will be, which of the Perfons, who now receive his Majefty's Bounty, as Penfioners, are worthy, and which are otherwife; but a Moment's Reflection will, I dare fay, convince him, that fuch an Enquiry will be attended with infuperable Difficulties. It is very poffible, nay certain, that his Majefty might have very juft Motives for granting Penfions to many Perfons, who, with Refpect to all that we can know about them, will appear to be unworthy of the Favour. The fecret Springs of Government cannot be laid open, and it is effentially neceffary to truft a difcretionary Power fomewhere. According to our Confitustitution it in his Majesty, with Respect to this Method of rewarding Services, either directly or indirectly, which he only can, and he only ought to know: It does not follow, that, because a certain Person receives a Pension, that Person does, or was even thought to deserve it by personal Merit, or personal Services; but it might be very fit to reward the personal Merit, or personal Services of one Man, by granting a Pension, at his Request, to another. His Majesty, who does know, and who only can know, what we should seek to discover in vain, has taken our Circumstanstances into Consideration, which none of his Predecessors have ever done; and the wisest Thing we can do, is, certainly, to avail ourselves of his gracious Disposition, and rely upon the Assurance which he has, unsollicited, been pleased to make us. Let us, at least, stay till this Assurance shall be violated, before we take a Measure which cannot fail to grieve and to provoke him; which will betray our Want of Confidence in him, and Attachment to him, and cannot fail of rendering him less inclined to concur with our Desires, and lessen his Complacency in our Prosperity. Upon the whole, I think we can gain nothing by the Enquiry proposed, and that we may lose much;

much; I shall, therefore, give my Voice for putting it off to a long Day.

Mr *T— Le H—* made use of many Arguments, to shew the Impropriety of making Use of his Majesty's Name in the Debates of the House; and said, he should be very much shocked and surprized, if, after an unanimous Resolution of the House, for an Enquiry into so alarming a Grievance, a contrary Resolution should take Place, and no Enquiry should be made. He said, such a Change of Conduct could not possibly be imputed to a Change of Opinion, and must, therefore, give Occasion to Surmises highly detrimental to the Honour and Dignity of the House, wholly incompatible with the Independance of its Members, and the true Interest of the Country they had been chosen to represent.

The Question being then put, whether the Enquiry should, or should not, be put off for a long Day, it was carried in the Affirmative, 126 to 78.

THURS-

THURSDAY, *November* 17, 1763.

NINETEENTH DAY.

Mr *E— S— P—* said, that he would beg leave to postpone the Motion he intended to make, with Respect to addressing his Majesty on the Pensions, and the Discovery which he proposed to make concerning them, till after the Supplies were granted, as he would, by no Means, delay that Business.

Mr *R— F—*.

Mr S——,

I have the Pleasure to acquaint the House, that a Work of great Importance, at which we have been labouring six and thirty Years, is, at last, nearly compleated. The Key and Harbour of *Bally Castle* are now put into such a State, that more than fourteen thousand Ton of Coals have been shipped within the last twelve Months, from thence to *Dublin*, and other Parts of the Kingdom, which will now be provided with a Necessary of Life of universal Consumption, and the greatest Utility upon reasonable Terms. This Work was undertaken by Mr *Boyd*, who agreed to advance the Money necessary for the Purpose, out of his private Fortune; and the Committee that was appointed to enquire into the State of the Harbour, and Colleries of *Bally Castle*, have come to the following Resolutions:

1. That *Hugh Boyd*, Esq; hath built a compleat and lasting Harbour at *Bally Castle*, of hewn Stone.

2. That it has not been in the least Degree disturbed by any Storms.

3. That several Ships have been saved by the Harbour, that would otherwise have been lost.

4. That large Quantities of Coals have been exported from *Bally Castle* Colleries, since the Harbour has been built.

5. That the Harbour is a great National Benefit.

6. That

6. That 7762 *l.* 6 *s.* 3 *d.* has been expended by Mr *Boyd* in the Work.

7. That this Sum should be paid to Mr *Boyd*, to re-imburse him his Expences.

8. That 1779 *l.* 5 *s.* 9 *d.* being the Remainder of the Sum of 9541 *l.* 12 *s.* at which the Repair of the said Harbour was estimated, should be paid to Mr *Boyd* to enable him to compleat his Work.

The House agreed to the first six of these Resolutions, but, when the seventh was about to be read a second Time, Mr *J— F— G—*, got up, and spoke to the following Effect:

Mr *J— F— G—*.

Mr S———,

I perfectly concur with the House, in agreeing to the first six Resolutions of the Committee, but, I think, it would be unparliamentary, to agree to the seventh and eighth, for the Re-imbursement of Mr *Boyd* ought, by the constant Custom of the House, to be referred

ferred to the Committee of Supplies. I am alfo of Opinion, Sir, that the Houfe fhould be very cautious in granting away the public Money; for it will naturally be inferred from profufe Grants, that we have Money to fpare; and that our Complaints of the Penfions, and a heavy Civil and Military Eftablifhment, as a Burthen we cannot fuftain, are ill founded. I am forry to fay, that I have been Witnefs to many pecuniary Demands upon this Houfe, which, I think, ought to be anfwered by the Inhabitants of the feveral Diftricts that were immediately benefitted by the Works, on which the Money was expended, particularly Bridges, and Churches; and, I think, that as well on Account of the real State of the Nation, as to fave Appearances, the ftricteft Oeconomy fhould be obferved.

Mr R— F—.

Mr S———,

I am forry, Sir, that it is neceffary to obferve, that the Demand now made, with which the Houfe has, upon the Refolution of a Committee, been moved to comply, is very

very different from the Prayer of a Petition. It is the Demand of a Debt, Sir, which this House has engaged to pay, upon Conditions which the Committee has reported to be fulfilled, and, which we have just allowed to be fulfilled, by consenting to that Part of the Report. In a former Sessions, Sir, Mr *Boyd* undertook to compleat a Work, at his own Expence, upon Condition, that, when it should be compleated, he should be reimbursed by this House; this House engaged to reimburse him upon that Condition; we have just agreed that the Condition is fulfilled, and the honourable Gentleman, now insinuates, that he should not be repaid his Expences, for fear the Government should think we had Money to spare! He has, indeed, recommended Oeconomy, and against Oeconomy I have no Objection; yet, besides, that it is bad Oeconomy not to pay our Debts, I must observe, that there is no worse Oeconomy than an ill-judged Parsimony. By withholding the Sums necessary to improve our Manufactures and Trade, to facilitate the Communication of Place with Place, to supply all Ranks with the Necessaries of Life, and promote such Principles as produce good Conduct, would as effectually be our Ruin as

the

the moſt thoughtleſs Profuſion. It is good Oeconomy to lay out Money with Advantage; and Money laid out in repairing Harbours, perfecting Manufactures, facilitating Communication by Bridges, and promoting good Principles, by building Churches, will be returned in public Benefits, with an Increaſe of an hundred-fold.

The R—t H—ble Mr *A— M—*.

Mr S——,

I perfectly agree, Sir, with the honourable Gentleman, who ſpoke laſt, that no Conſiderations of Oeconomy ſhould prevent us either from paying our Debts, or procuring public Advantages; yet, I think, no Reſolution of this Houſe ſhould be made to bind the Committee of Supplies to grant a certain Sum for a certain Purpoſe. I am alſo of Opinion, Sir, that ſome farther Examination ſhould be made, whether the Condition, on which we have agreed to pay this Sum, which is upwards of ſeven thouſand Pounds, has been fulfilled. I would not be thought to bring the Report of a Committee cauſeleſsly into Queſtion, but if my Memory does not

not very much deceive me, no less than ten thousand Pounds was granted, many Years ago, for the very Purpose now said to be accomplished; and, in a subsequent Sessions, ten thousand Pounds more, and the Work was then reported to be compleated as it is now, yet, for want of sufficient Skill, in conducting so unusual an undertaking, and of sufficient Knowledge in chusing the Materials, it came to nothing; the wooden Part was in a short Time destroyed by Worms, and the Waves soon afterwards beat down the rest. The Work being then to do over again, another Application was made, and more Money was granted, which was lost like the former, though reported to have been laid out to better Purpose. I am, therefore, of Opinion, that though Mr *Boyd* undertook to compleat the Work at his own Expence, according to an Estimate, upon Condition, that he should be reimbursed when it was compleated in an effectual Manner; and, though a Committee has reported it to be effectually compleated, or nearly so; yet that it would not be prudent to grant the Money, except Mr *Boyd* will enter into such Security as shall be approved, that it shall stand

for

for a certain Number of Years, which it muſt do, if the Committee is not miſtaken in their Report. I think, therefore, that the Report with Reſpect to the 7th and 8th Reſolutions ſhould be recommitted, that the Report of the private Committee may come again in the uſual Way, before the Houſe, and that it may then, according to the conſtant Uſage of the Houſe, be referred to the Committee of Supplies.

Mr *R— F—* ſaid, in reply, that there was the greateſt Reaſon to conclude, that the Work at *Bally Caſtle* would ſtand, that moſt Part of it had already ſtood four Years, and the reſt two, and that Stone Work, when it gave way at all, generally gave way before the Cement was hardened; and, he obſerved, that as theſe Conſiderations were Inducements to pay the Money without Security, ſo they would, for the ſame Reaſon, incline Mr *Boyd* to give Security, if it ſhould be required, which he made no doubt of his being ready and willing to do.

Upon this the 7th and 8th Reſolutions, were recommitted, the Houſe not being willing to bind, or to influence the Committee

of

of Supplies, in the Grant of the Money, claimed by Mr *Boyd*.

FRIDAY, *Nov.* 18, 1763.

TWENTIETH DAY.

Mr *R— F—* reported from the Committee, to whom the 7th and 8th Resolution mentioned above were recommitted the following Resolution:

" That *Hugh Boyd*, Esq; deserves the Aid of Parliament, upon his giving Security, by Recognizance before the Chief Baron, or some other Baron of the Exchequer, to support and keep in repair, at his own Expence, the Works by him erected at *Bally Castle*, for one and twenty Years."

Dr *L——*.

Mr *S——*,

This Work at *Bally Castle*, Sir, has been made a Pretence for getting Money from the Public, ever since the Year 1721; and, Mr *Boyd*,

Boyd, upon the Payment of the laſt 10,000 *l*. gave the ſame Security that he offers now for keeping it up; yet the whole Work went to rack, and we engaged to advance him more Money. I am told, Sir, that there was a Sand-bank on the Outſide of that Harbour, which by the Surge is now carried into it, and renders the Ground there almoſt level with the reſt of the Strand, and it is well known, that there is no River or other Way by which the Sand can be carried out of the Harbour; it is certain that the Public has not profited in any Degree, by the vaſt Sums that have been laid out upon the Work, and, therefore, I ſhall not give my Vote to reward Mr *Boyd*, for having profited himſelf.

Mr *P— T—*, the S. G.

Mr S—,

As I happen to be perfectly and particularly acquainted with the whole Tranſaction concerning the Coal-Mine, and Harbour of *Bally Caſtle*, I beg the Patience of the Houſe to lay it properly before them. A Colliery was firſt diſcovered at *Bally Caſtle*, in the Year 1721, and Mr *Steward*, the Gentleman in whoſe Eſtate it lay, obtained a Grant from Par-

Parliament of 2000 *l.* to affift him in working it; he obtained 2000 *l.* more in the next Seffions, and another 2000 *l.* in the Seffions following. All this Money was expended in finking Shafts, and in other Works neceffary to open and work the Colliery, which was of very great Advantage to Mr *Steward*, and to the Neighbourhood, but no Advantage could accrue from it to the Public, except a proper Harbour could be made at *Bally Caftle*, for exporting the Coals to different Parts of the Kingdom; this being reprefented to Parliament, 5000 *l.* was granted in one Seffions, and 5000 *l.* more in another, to make fuch an Harbour; but thefe Sums being found infufficient, 10,000 *l.* was granted afterwards, at which Time Mr *Boyd,* to whom the Property of the Coal Mine had defcended, entered into Security to compleat the Work without farther Aid: But, notwithftanding this vaft Expence, amounting to no lefs than 26,000 *l.* tending principally to increafe Mr *Boyd*'s private Fortune, and, notwithftanding the Security he had given, the whole Work fell to Pieces. But, after this Difappointment of the Public, and after this Forfeiture of his Engagement, he applied again to Parliament, in the Year 1759, for

A a farther

farther Aid: It is true, indeed, that he did not defire any Money in Advance, but he defired that if he compleated the Work, he fhould be re-imburfed his Expence. It is alledged, that the Parliament yielded to this Requeft, and plighted their Faith to repay him fuch Sums as he fhould lay out in the Work, upon Conditions that are now fulfilled; but I do not find this Allegation fupported by fufficient Proof; and, I think, confidering the vaft Sums that had before been thrown away upon the fame Project, and the Inefficacy of the Security that had been given, it is not very likely to be true: However, he is now come with his Claim, and expects that the Public fhould pay for a Work, which will immenfely encreafe his Eftate; this is a Meafure, in which I can never concur, and, if I thought it reafonable, that he fhould, in any Manner be re-imburfed the Sums that he has laid out for his own Advantage, I would propofe, that the Money fhould be raifed among thofe who fhare the Advantage with him, the Neighbourhood, which would have been furnifhed with Coals from his Mine, if the Harbour had never exifted; and by a Toll to be paid by the Shipping, that come into, and go out of the Harbour.

The

The keeping the Harbour of *Dublin* clear is certainly a public Benefit, yet that is not done by an univerſal Tax, but by Methods, which, I think, may be very properly adopted in the preſent Occaſion.

Mr *J— B—,* a C——r.

Mr S——,

I very readily admit, Sir, that the Colliery at *Bally Caſtle* has been an Object of Parliamentary Attention for many Years; and, I think it is impoſſible to bring a ſtronger Proof that it is of national Importance; the only Thing to be conſidered, in my Opinion, is, whether the Harbour is, at length, what the Wiſdom of Parliament has been ſo deſirous to make it. If it is, ſcarce any Sum can be called large, that has, or ſhall be paid for that Purpoſe, compared with the immenſe Wealth that is annually drained from this Kingdom for Coals, or with the Benefit the Public will derive from our ſupplying that Commodity to ourſelves. By the Account of Coals brought from *Bally Caſtle,* the laſt Year, it appears that there was a ſaving to the Nation of at leaſt 10,000 *l.* and it may eaſily

easily be demonstrated, that the Trade must encrease every Day. It is true, that the Work has not proceeded with an uninterrupted Success, and, considering its Nature, it would have been a Miracle if it had; building a Harbour is an undertaking that is not executed twice in an Age, and those concerned in it, having, consequently, no experiental Knowledge, mistake and miscarriage are almost inevitable; the Loss, however, that has accrued in carrying on the Works of *Bally Castle*, arose neither from mismanagement nor mistake; but from an Event which no Sagacity could foresee, and which neither Diligence, nor Skill could remedy. The Worm, common in the *West Indies*, but hitherto unknown in *Europe*, got into, and destroyed the Wooden Frame, on which the Masonry was constructed in the same Manner as it is in all Works of the like Kind; if it had not been for this Accident the Work would, in the Opinion of unexceptionable Judges, have stood for Ages; and, by the Accounts that have from Time to Time been given into this House, by the Persons intrusted with the Money that has been granted to carry on the Work, they appear to have laid it out with Integrity and Oeconomy. I will not

not deny, that the Work is of Advantage to the Undertaker; but it is of much greater Advantage to the Public; and, surely, it would be unjust, that the Public should withold from him a Reward for the Service he has rendered it, merely because a private Advantage accrues to him from the same Act: It is the great Art, and the great Duty of Government, to make Duty co-incide with Interest, and thus unite the Advantage of the Individual with that of the Community. The Government has very wisely allotted a Reward for apprehending Robbers; and if a Man should seize a Thief as he was going off with his Booty, and thus recover what he had stolen, would it not be very injurious to deny this Man the Reward, upon Pretence that he was a sufficient Gainer by the Act already, in recovering the Property that he would otherwise have lost? It is certainly our Interest to encourage those, who risk their private Fortune in Undertakings of public Utility, independant of the private Advantage they may obtain by their Success; and, I am, therefore, of Opinion, that Mr *Boyd*, having succeeded, should be re-imbursed his Expences, which, if he had not succeeded, would have fallen upon himself.

Mr *R— F—*, in reply to Dr *L—*, said, that he was surprized to hear one of the Representatives of the Capital object, to the Reimbursing of Mr *Boyd*, as that City profited more by the Work than any other Part of the Kingdom; he was sure, he said, that the Price of Coals was already reduced by it, as several Ships from *Bally Castle*, had arrived with Coals but a few Days ago.

Dr *L—* replied, that though he thought himself under the greatest Obligation to the City of *Dublin*, for making Choice of him for one of its Representatives, yet he should be very sory to have it thought that he would shew any Partiality to it, at the Expence of the Rest of the Kingdom; he added, that for his Part, he had as yet experienced none of the good Effects of the Harbour, and Colliery at *Bally Castle*, for, that Coals were as dear as ever; and he thought it time enough to pay for public Service, when the Public experienced that they had been served.

It was then urged, that the private Committee was impowered only to enquire into, and report the State of the Harbour of *Bally Castle*

Caſtle, and not to report that Mr *Boyd* deſerved the Aid of Parliament. That it would, therefore, be irregular, and a bad Precedent for the Houſe to agree to that Reſolution, beſides having an undue Influence on the Committee of Supplies.

It was, therefore, propoſed, that the Reſolution ſhould be recommitted.

And it was ordered to be recommitted accordingly.

SATURDAY, *Nov.* 19, 1763.

TWENTY-FIRST DAY.

THE House, according to Order, resolved itself into a Committee, to consider the Supplies, and the Lord Lieutenant's Speech.

The R—t H—ble *A— M—* took the Chair as Chairman.

Mr *P— T—*, the A. G. laid before the Committee, an Account of the Supplies that would be absolutely necessary to carry on the King's Business; and he particularly distinguished the Sums necessary for the Military Establishment, for the Civil Establishment, and, for the Payment of the Interest on the National Debt: He then, said, that in consequence of the Expences, necessarily attending a burdensome though successful War, the Parliament had granted a Power to the Crown, to raise 950,000 *l.* partly by Aids, and partly by Vote of Credit, but that it had not been found necessary to raise more than 650,000 *l.*

650,000 *l.* for which Interest was agreed to be given at five *per Cent.*. He then proposed that 100,000 *l.* which had been lent free of Interest for the first Year, should stand at five *per Cent.* that the other Debentures should be thrown together; that 350,000 *l.* should be drawn at four *per Cent.* and the Rest remain at five; but, that the Debentures at four should be last paid off: He then made a Computation of the Interest, and added the Amount to the Civil and Military Establishment: He also computed the Amount of the hereditary Revenue, and the additional Duties, at a Medium for fourteen Years, and, deducting this Amount with that of the Loan Duties, from the Sum to be raised, shewed how much would remain for incidental Charges, the King's Letters, and the Improvement of the Country. He begged Leave to observe, that, of the Money borrowed, there remained in the Treasury 130,000 *l.* so that the National Debt could not be stated at more than 520,000 *l.* He then stated the Amount of the Military Establishment in 1754, since which Time, several Regiments had been sent from that Establishment to *America*, and, said, that, although the military Establishment did now much exceed that Amount

mount, yet that the Increase could not reasonably be objected to, if it was considered that Part of it arose from the Addition of Dragoon's Pay; that the Number of Regiments, and the Staff, were also encreased, and an useful Body of Artillery added. All these Augmentations, and Additions, he said, were absolutely necessary, and such as the Country could much better bear now, than it could bear the Establishment of 1754 at that Time, though the Amount of that Establishment was less; and in this Opinion he hoped the Committee would concur. He observed, however, that, before the Motion was made for complying with the usual Grants for the Supply, it would be necessary to put a Question on the State of the National Debt. It was, therefore, moved, that it was the Opinion of the House, that the National Debt was 520,000*l.*

To this it was objected, that, if the neat Debt was supposed to be 520,000 *l.* the Sum that remained, after deducting 130,000 *l.* the Money still in the Treasury unspent, from 650,000 *l.* the gross Debt, the Nation would not get Credit for the 5000 *l.* Poundage on the

the 200,00 *l*. borrowed by a Vote of Credit. (*See the Debates of the ninth Day*.)

Mr *M*— then said, that he must put the Question on the less Sum, and, therefore, moved, that it was the Opinion of the Committee, that the National Debt amounted to 515,000 *l*. at *Lady-Day* last.

Mr *R— Fitz-G—* replied, he was well informed, and fully persuaded, that the Vice-Treasurers had an undoubted Right, by Law, to the Poundage in Question, and had actually received it: He added, that now to deprive them of it, by a Resolution of a Committee of the whole House, would be contrary to all Justice: That if their Right was doubtful, it should be tried in a Court of Law, and left to the Determination of such Court.

Mr *J— Fitz-G—*, and Mr *P— T—*, the A. G. declared themselves to be of the same Opinion. Mr *F— G—* said, that, as the House had not only acquiesced in the Vice-Treasurer's appropriating the 5000 *l*. but confirmed it, he thought that the setting aside by a subsequent Law, what a prior Law had carried into Execution, would be attended with

much

much worſe Conſequences than the Loſs of the Money. And the A. G. ſaid, that as he had not the leaſt Doubt of the Vice-Treaſurers' being entitled to the Money which had been allowed them, he could not think it prudent to put the Public to the Expence of a Suit.

The Queſtion being then put on the leſs Sum, it paſſed in the Negative, 85 againſt 57.

And the Queſtion being then put on the larger Sum, it paſſed in the Affirmative, *Nemine Contradicente*.

A Motion was then made, that the Committee ſhould agree to grant the *uſual* Supplies, which produced the following Debate:

Mr *E— S— P—*.

I think, Sir, that our agreeing to grant a groſs Sum, under the Denomination of *uſual* Supplies, will preclude us from the Advantages of objecting to the Grant of Money for any particular Purpoſe. It is the Cuſtom, Sir, of another Country, to mention every Eſtab-

Eſtabliſhment particularly, and provide for it as the Houſe thinks proper, after a ſeparate Conſideration; and I therefore intend to move for an Amendment in the Motion, and that the Word *neceſſary* ſhould be inſerted, inſtead of the Word *uſual*; and then, whatever Sums may not be thought *neceſſary*, and whatever Modes may not be thought proper, may admit of Debate; Gentlemen will have an Opportunity to offer their Thoughts upon the Subject, and a better Regulation may take Place. As to what the honourable Gentleman on the Floor has ſaid, with Reſpect to ſtating the military Eſtabliſhment, I ſhall beg Leave to obſerve, that, I think, the laſt military Eſtabliſhment, for a time of Peace, ſhould not have been ſtated from any particular Year; if it is ſtated for the two Years 1752 and 1753, and for the two Years 1754 and 1755, and ſo, at a medium, it will be found leſs than the preſent Eſtabliſhment, which is alſo a military Eſtabliſhment in Time of Peace, by a much more confiderable Sum. Now, Sir, I ſhall endeavour to ſhew that the preſent Eſtabliſhment is not neceſſary for any good Purpoſe, either to us, or our ſiſter Country, for I ſhall always conſider our Intereſts as united, and I ſhall alſo endeavour to

ſhew

shew, that, whatever useful Purpose it may be supposed to answer, it must incur Disadvantages much more than equivalent, by taxing us above our Ability. In the first Place, it will, I suppose, be readily granted, that the Military Establishment, during the Peace that was concluded at *Aix-la-Chapelle*, was sufficient for that Time; and I should be glad to know why the same Establishment is not sufficient for this. Has this Peace left us in less Security, or is it likely to be of less Duration? As we have been lately taught to think the contrary, by Assurances of the highest Authority, this cannot be supposed; and, if any Gentleman present, can suggest another Reason, why the Military Establishment, that was sufficient then, is not sufficient now, I should be glad to hear it. But it has been said, Sir, that we are now better able to bear the present Establishment, than we were to bear an Establishment so much less, when it took place. Now I must, in the first place, beg leave to observe, that, allowing this to be true, it cannot be supposed to justify the Exceedings of the present Establishment, if such Exceedings cannot be proved to be necessary; for I should be very sorry to think any Gentleman in this House imagined that our mere Ability to sustain

tain a Burthen, was a sufficient Reason for laying it on. But, by what Powers of Eloquence are we to be persuaded that our Ability is greater? At the Conclusion of the Peace of *Aix-La-Chapelle*, in the Year 1749, Money was accumulating in the Treasury, as appeared from a Surplus that will not easily be forgotten: The hereditary Revenues, as well as the additional Duties, were encreasing; the Article of Management was much lower; and the List of Pensions was comparatively small; Employments, and their Salaries, were within narrower Bounds; there were no Exceedings in the Concordatum, and extraordinary secret Services were not thought necessary. But, at present, Sir, our Treasury is not only exhausted, but we are encumbered with a Debt of 520,000 *l.* the Interest of which our best Calculators have been extremely puzzled in contriving to pay; the List of Pensions is enormous; many new and useless Employments have been created, and the Salaries of the old ones greatly encreased; many more Persons, of great Property, are become Absentees; the Revenues of the Crown, during the last Year, have decreased more than 40,000 *l.* and will, probably, decrease still more; and the Management of them is, not-

with-

withstanding, regulated upon a larger Scale. We have read, Sir, very extraordinary Accounts of Eloquence, and Accounts still more extraordinary of Music: We have read, Sir, that *Amphion*'s Music influenced the Stones to dance into a Wall; and this Feat, I believe, stands hitherto unrivalled by any Powers of Eloquence; yet, I think, he that can persuade us that we are richer, when we are not only without Money, but in Debt, than we were when we were not only out of Debt, but had a considerable Sum lying by us, will fairly turn the Scale in favour of Eloquence against Music, and effect a greater Wonder than *Amphion,* who built *Thebes* with his Harp. The military Establishment is said, Sir, to be a necessary Preparative for War; but can that prepare us for War, which tends to destroy our Existence? Are we to be prepared for War by a Drain of Taxes, which will exhaust, and more than exhaust us, during Peace? The best Way of improving Peace into an Ability for War, is the Cultivation of Arts, the Extent of Trade, and the Practice of Oeconomy; for this only can invigorate the Root, of which all the Modes of national Defence are Branches. I am ashamed, Sir, to descend to Particulars, after so general

neral a Confutation of what has been said in favour of our present Establishment; and yet, lest it should be pretended that Particulars were passed over, because they were not understood, I shall beg leave to observe, that, as Matters are now managed, the usual Establishment of 12,000 Men will cost us considerably more than formerly, without producing one single Advantage. These 12,000 Men, Sir, are now formed into six more Regiments than they used to be, and the Number of Officers is, consequently, greatly increased; this increases Expence, and it also increases Dependants, which cannot be pretended, I think, to be national Benefits: It is, however, pretended, that, when a War shall break out, these Regiments may be easily recruited, and a necessary Number of Men raised without forming new ones; and that the Officers, which are now said to be supernumerary, will be better able to discipline the Men, than young Gentlemen just taken into the Service: But, if the Peace continues long, the Expence of these Officers, till they can be useful, will be more than equivalent to the Use they will be of on the Approach of a War, even supposing they will then be as useful as is pretended; but I think it is easy to shew that this will not be the Case: Officers that have grown old in a State of listless Inactivity, during a long Peace, who have been used only to lounge about at Country Quarters, without any Thing either to think of, or to practise, but Expedients to kill Time, naturally grow dissatisfied with their Profession, and get a Habit of neglecting the Duties of it, by having little Duty to do; and it is not reasonable to believe, that, upon an Augmentation, Gentlemen in these Circumstances, and under these Habits, will exert themselves with so much Zeal and Activity, as young Men, warmed with a Spirit of Enterprize, new to the Profession, and pleased with the Splendor and Parade of it, when their Service is required: and, as to the Ability of disciplining the new Troops, every Gentleman, who has the least Acquaintance with military Affairs, knows, that the disciplining Recruits generally falls to the Share of non-commissioned Officers, and, therefore, that there is no need of an expensive Train of commissioned Officers for that Purpose. Let me also, upon this Occasion, observe, that, during the last War, the new raised Regiments distinguished themselves as nobly as any of the Veterans of the Field, and that the *English* Militia were remarkably well disciplined. I come, now, to consider the Staff, and, as that seems to have been enormously encreased, without any Pretence of Advantage, the Trouble of shewing such Pretences to be fallacious, is precluded. I shall only observe, that the Establishment in *England* is 17,600 Men, and the Establishment here but 12,000, but yet that the Staff here is double to the Staff in *England*: If in *England* the Staff is sufficient, I should be glad to know why it is to be so much more here; the Disproportion is immense; if the Staff upon 12,000 was only equal to that upon 17,600, the Disproportion would be great; but, if the Staff upon 12,000, is double to that upon 17,600, there must certainly be some Reason for it, very different from mere military Advantage. I am unwilling to suggest that Reason, and, indeed, it is so obvious, that it need not be suggested; especially as most, if not all the general Officers, are Absentees. As to the Ordnance, which is another heavy Article of our Expence, having encreased no less than 26,000 *l*. I confess myself wholly unable to conceive what End it can answer: We have no Fortifications, as I know of, to defend; and, I am informed, upon very good Authority, that all this Ordnance does not include as many Cannon as would mount a thirty-Gun Ship: There are, however, no less than twelve Clerks belonging to that Board, and it has, in every Respect, the same Establishment, as to Officers, with that in *England*; with all this it is liable to no Check, nor is it included in the Muster-Office: At present, I confess, this is not much to be regretted, for, I am persuaded, the noble Earl, who now presides in this Department, will take Care to have the Duty effectually done, and the Corps kept complete. It is, indeed, a happy Circumstance for us, that he has been appointed to this Station, as well on Account of the Integrity and Uprightness of his Character, as on Account of his residing and spending his Fortune among us: But if the Corps should go into the Hands of another Commander, who may, probably, be of another Country, the Difference will be very much to our Disadvantage. The Commander has a Power of filling up all the Employments, except six, which will then, probably, be given to Persons who reside on the other Side of the Water, and the whole Corps, being subject to no Check, might do what they pleased. As the military Establishment, therefore, appears to me to be be, in every Respect, inconsistent with the National Interest, and to be equally absurd and pernicious, both in a general and particular View, I must beg leave to move, that the Word *necessary* may be inserted instead of the Word *usual*.

Mr P— T—, the A. G.

To the Amendment now proposed by the Honourable Member, I have two Objections; I think it is, in itself, improper; and, I confess, I cannot conceive that it can answer any End. It is certain, that, in a neighbouring Country, a Supply is separately voted for every particular Part of the Establishment, and there it seems to be very proper, because the Supplies are granted every Year: But here the hereditary Revenue is a standing Fund for the Exigencies of Government, whatever they may be; and the additional Duties are voted only as an Aid to that Fund, and are, therefore, considered as included in it: The Supplies, therefore, are always voted in one Aggregate, and I do not see how they can be voted otherwise. I cannot, however, comprehend how this Mode of granting the Supplies, can deprive us of the Advantage of objecting

jecting to particular Parts of the Eſtabliſhment, which may be thought improper or unneceſſary. If the honourable Gentleman thinks 12,000 Men too many, he may object to the Sum appropriated to the Payment of them; and, if it be the Senſe of the Houſe, that a ſmaller Number of Men will be ſufficient, a leſs Sum will, conſequently, be voted. The ſame Thing may be done with Reſpect to the Officers, the Ordnance, and every other Part of the Eſtabliſhment; nor does the Motion already made, in any Degree preclude it. The Amendment propoſed, I think, is alſo improper in itſelf; for, if the Word *neceſſary* is ſubſtituted inſtead of the Word *uſual*, it will imply that ſomething *unneceſſary* had been propoſed. As to my making Choice of the Year 1754, in ſtating the Difference between the preſent Peace Eſtabliſhment, and that ſubſequent to the Treaty of *Aix-la-Chapelle*, I thought myſelf warranted in it, as that Year was, very nearly, a Medium between the Concluſion of the Treaty, and the breaking out of the laſt War. I muſt alſo beg leave to obſerve, that there are ſeveral unavoidable Cauſes of the Increaſe of the preſent Eſtabliſhment, which he has not conſidered. The Pay of the Dragoons was increaſed by a

Vote

Vote of this House; there is a half Pay List which amounts to 32,000 *l.* a Year, and an additional Staff was added to the Regiment of Dragoons; if these Sums are deducted, he will find the Encrease of the Establishment by no means so large as he would suggest. As to the Mode of fixing the Establishment, it has, upon very mature Consideration, been adopted by a neighbouring Country; and, as I am informed, approved by Persons of the greatest military Experience. As the Increase of our Expence, therefore, is not so unaccountable as he supposes, neither is it so burthensome: Let us consider the Amount of the Sums which we have voted for interior Improvements, and, from that, infer our pecuniary Ability. In the two Sessions before the Year 1753, 400*l.* in each Sessions was thought a sufficient Bounty for public Works: In the Year 1753, when there was a Surplus in the Treasury, no less than 30,000 *l.* was granted in such Bounty, and 40,000 *l.* more the Sessions afterwards, so that from that Time to this, I cannot think there has been less than 400,000 *l.* granted for the Improvement of this Country, which, perhaps, is more than any other Nation in *Europe* has allotted to the same Purpose, considering the Difference of

Extent and Revenue. Now, Sir, if we are able to expend such Sums upon other Objects, of National Advantage, how comes it that we are crushed at once by the Increase of our military Establishment? As this Increase arises from the Execution of a Plan that has been approved by the best Judges, as most effectual for our Defence, it should, in my Opinion be considered as necessary to a Scheme for promoting National Advantages, and come in for its Share of the Sums allotted to public Works: Besides, Sir, as I would not suppose that the vast Sums granted for the Improvement of this Country have been expended without improving it, I must conclude, that our Abilities, after Improvements adequate to such Sums, are proportionably greater than they were before, and that our Country is at once better worth defending, and more capable to provide for its Defence. I will add, Sir, that in Proportion as it is better worth defending, it is more likely to be attacked, and, for that Reason, a more effectual Defence is necessary; what is worth keeping, is worth taking away, and our Danger from without, increasing in Proportion to our interior Prosperity, our Preparations for Defence should also proportionally encrease,

crease, and the same Circumstances that furnish the Reasons for these Preparations, will also abundantly furnish the Power. To conclude, Sir, let me appeal from Argument to Experience; every Gentleman present, has a pleasing Demonstration of the Encrease of our public Wealth, by the Encrease of his private Fortune, and, I call upon all that hear me, to declare whether, in general, it is not more than equivalent to the increased Expence of our Military Establishment, which has, with all the Pathos of Exaggeration, been represented as an Inundation, or an Earthquake, that was to sweep us from the Face of the Earth, or to bury us in its Bowels; for these Reasons, I shall Vote to have the Question put, as I proposed it.

   The R—t H—ble *W— G— H—*.

I am very sorry, Sir, to find myself under a Necessity of differing, as well from my honourable Friend near me, as from the honourable Gentleman on the Floor, who spoke last: In my Opinion, Sir, the present Peace-Establishment should be compared with that of the Year 1751, as that Year and the present are the Years immediately subsequent to the

the Treaties of Peace, and, I muſt obſerve, that particular Circumſtances, or Exigencies, peculiar to either Year, are not to be conſidered as Parts of the general Plan, nor is the Expence which they might make neceſſary, to be conſidered as an Expence eſſential to ſuch Plan. Now, I do not find that the Expence of the preſent Peace-Eſtabliſhment, exceeds that of the Peace-Eſtabliſhment, in the Year 1751, more than 111,000 *l.* Out of the Staff which makes part of that Sum, we muſt firſt deduct the Sum of 5500 *l.* an addition to the Salary of the Lord Lieutenant; and the Sum of 4000 *l.* an addition to the Salary of the Secretaries, making together 9500*l.* we muſt deduct the half-pay Liſt which amounts to 32,000 *l.* and the additional Pay to the Dragoons, which amounts to 20,000 *l.* more, with the increaſed pay to the Deputy Quarter-Maſter, Adjutant-General, and other neceſſary Staff Officers, ſo that the Encreaſe of the Eſtabliſhment cannot be reckoned at quite 50,000 *l.* As to the Staff, I muſt acknowledge, that it is heavier here than in *England*; but, I think, it is eaſy to convince every candid and diſpaſſionate Mind, that it muſt be ſo; there is not a ſufficient Number of Gentlemen reſident in *Ireland,* and properly quali-

qualified to furnish the Staff; as a Staff, therefore, is essentially necessary, it must be formed of Gentlemen who have Regiments in *England*, and Seats in the Parliament there, with other Appointments, which make their Attendance in that Kingdom indispensibly necessary; so that if the Staff consisted only of the necessary Number, supposing the whole to be resident, the Business could never go on, some being always unavoidably absent; that a sufficient Number, therefore, may be resident, to transact the Business here, it is necessary that the Staff should consist of Super-numeraries. I must now observe, that though the constitutional Establishment, in the Year 1751, was 12,000 Men, yet there was at that Time but 11,500 Effectives kept up; but as we now keep up the whole Number, the Expence of 500 Men must be deducted from the 50,000 *l.* which the present Establishment is supposed to exceed the Establishment of 1751. But it is objected, that, in the present Establishment, there is a great Increase of Officers; I admit the Fact, but, I think it by noMeans unjustifiable; Gentlemen, that are not experimentally acquainted with military Affairs, may suggest what they please, but those that are, know that an Army my receives very great Advantages from a numerous Commiſſion. Officers that have been trained in the Service muſt have a Skill that young Officers cannot have, and, allowing that Recruits are diſciplined, chiefly, by non-commiſſioned Officers, it is neceſſary that the commiſſioned Officer ſhould have ſome Experience, in order to ſee the non-commiſſioned Officers do their Duty, and to know when it has effectually been done. Beſides the Gentlemen who have Commiſſions under the preſent Eſtabliſhment, were before in the Service, and, if they had not been taken into the Forces that were kept on Foot at the Concluſion of the Peace, when their own Corps were diſbanded, they muſt have received Half-pay; ſo that we have the whole Advantage of their Service for the additional Half-pay, which they receive upon being employed; neither is the Diſproportion between the Officers and private Men ſo great as appears at firſt Sight, when Allowance is made for the Reduction of a Company from every Regiment, and a Man from every Company and Troop, which Allowance will reduce our Commiſſion, nearly, to the ſame Plan that has been adopted in *England*. From this exceeding of 50,000 *l*,

we

we must also deduct the Increase of the Artillery, and the only Question will be, whether that Increase is necessary. Now, Sir, the State of the Artillery, before the present Regulation took place was wretched in the highest Degree. Upon the little Alarm that was spread by the rash and hopeless Attempt of *Thurot*, a Train of Artillery was marched to *Newry*, and another was sent to *Clonmel*; but, neither of those Trains had fifty Men with them as a Guard, nor was there one of those that were with them, that knew how to fire a Gun; it is, therefore, very clear that some Regulation was necessary, and that which has been so much complained of, scarce makes our Artillery proportionate to our Establishment of 12,000 Men. The Artillery Company consists of 400 Men, which cost 26,000 *l.* a Year; now in *England*, where the Army consists of 17,600; the Train of Artillery consists of 1500 Men, which costs 150,000 *l.* a Year; so that consider this Establishment as you please, it will be found neither disproportionate in itself, with Respect to its several Parts, nor to the Ability of the Country, nor to the Service it is to perform; it has been said, indeed, not to be adequate to the Service, and that it could

not

not furnish Cannon to a thirty-gun Ship, and this I am willing to admit, at present, because it is in its Infancy, but the very Objection shews a better State to be desirable, and it is making its Progress towards a better State every Day. Upon the whole, Sir, I am persuaded that 12,000 Men cannot reasonable be thought too many, and that 12,000 Men could not possibly be put under a better Regulation.

Mr H— F—.

I observe, Sir, that the honourable Gentleman, who spoke last, among other Expedients to reconcile us to the enormous Expence of our military Establishment, has observed, that, in many Instances, it is the same as in *Great Britain*; but, surely, if we take him at his Word there needs no other Proof that it is an Expence which we cannot possible sustain; how is it possible, Sir, that this miserable Country, precluded from every advantageous Branch of Trade, small in extent, and three fourths of it unpeopled, a Country that feels itself sinking under a Debt of 600,000 *l*. the mere Interest of which it has puzzled our most able Calculator's to pay,

how

how is it poffible, Sir, that this Country fhould keep pace with *Great Britain*, the moft flourifhing and moft opulent Nation under Heaven, with a Trade that covers the Sea, and bufies the moft diftant Parts of the Earth; of great extent in comparifon with this inferior Spot, fwarming with Inhabitants, and abounding with Money; a Nation that fuftains a Debt of 150,000,000 *l.* of which it pays the Intereft without giving up one Luxury, or neglecting one interior Improvement? That we fhould be expected to pay for public Eftablifhments, after the fame Rate as this mighty Nation is furely unreafonable in the higheft Degree; but the honourable Gentleman has gone farther, Sir, he has allowed that in fome Articles we pay after a ftill dearer Rate, even than *Great Britain*; he has allowed, Sir, that our Staff is fuperior, and he has alledged that it ought to be fo, for a Reafon that exhibits our Situation in the moft mortifying and alarming View. Deplorable, indeed, is the Condition of that Country, which is under the unhappy Neceffity of paying twenty Servants, that it may be ferved by ten, at the fame Time that the Wages even of the ten, amounts to more than it can afford to pay. We have been told,

told, Sir, that we muſt pay a numerous Staff, becauſe ſome will be always abſent, and becauſe it is neceſſary that a certain Number ſhould reſide; now, Sir, it will appear, that after an unreaſonable Sum has been exacted from us to pay many, as the only Condition upon which we can be ſerved by few, thoſe few render us no Service at all; it is well known, Sir, that our whole Staff is abſent, notwithſtanding the Reſidence of a certain Part is ſuppoſed to be indiſpenſibly neceſſary, and, notwithſtanding, we are to pay for the Reſidence of that Part at ſo enormous a Price: The Injury, therefore, that we ſuffer by this Meaſure, is the moſt complicated and aggravated that can be imagined; we pay a double Number, that we may have the Service of half; the Service of half is abſolutely neceſſary, but the Service of half is not rendered us, and it is not rendered, becauſe thoſe whom we pay for it are, with others, whom we alſo pay for doing nothing, ſpending our Money in another Country! I would not be thought, Sir, to exaggerate Facts by imaginary Circumſtances, or give them a more formidable appearance by Rhetorical Flouriſhes; when General Officers on the Staff were wanted here at the Reduction of the Troops,

Troops, there was not one to be found, and we were under a Neceffity of hiring other Generals to do their Bufinefs; and fhall we tamely confent to continue in a Situation at once fo oppreffive and ridiculous? Shall we contract Debts of which we can neither pay Principal, nor Intereft, that we may maintain a Number of Servants, whom we never fee, in Idlenefs and Luxury, and, at the fame Time, hire Men by the Day to wait at our Table?

There is one Article, indeed, in which the honourable Gentleman has told us, we are not rated equal to the Proportion obferved in *England*, that of our Artillery; but, though our Artillery may be lefs in Proportion to our 12,000 Men, than the Artillery of *England*, in Proportion to 17,600, yet it does not follow that we are under-rated in that Article, for the Artillery of *England* muft be confidered as relative, not only to the 17,600 Men, which he has mentioned, but to a vaft Marine, of which he has taken no Notice; and to feveral Forts, which it is there thought neceffary to keep up; whereas it is well known that we have neither Forts nor Marine. As I am now following the honourable Gentleman in a Comparison that he has drawn between this Country and *England*, I cannot omit to observe, that our Military Establishment includes four Regiments of heavy Horse; that, in *England*, heavy Horse have been laid aside, as well because they are more expensive, as because they are less useful than other Troops; in this Article certainly, the Disadvantage is on our Side, and I should be glad to know upon what Pretence we are loaded with an useless Expence from which our Neighbours are set free.

I think, Sir, that we have some Reason to complain of the Manner in which our Regiments have been multiplied, even supposing the Multiplication of them to be an eligible Measure simply considered; all our old Regiments, Sir, suffered a Reduction of one Company to make room for the new favorite Regiments that were to be placed upon this Establishment; now, Sir, the Officers of these reduced Companies, had, surely, a right to consider themselves as intitled to their Commissions, and the full Advantage of them, at least, while the Regiments to which they belonged should be kept up; the public Faith was pledged to them for this, and,

upon

upon their Confidence in the public Faith, they had formed their Habits of Life; no Man can be blamed for not providing againſt Contingencies, to which he has no Reaſon to ſuppoſe himſelf liable; and it is very injurious to ſubject a Man to Evils, which he has neither deſerved nor foreſeen; the Gentlemen, Sir, that have thus been turned out of their Appointments have Wives, Families, Creditors, or Dependants of ſome Kind, who muſt ſuffer with them; and the Injury to Individuals, muſt, therefore, extend to a very large Circle; the Miſchief, however, does not ſtop here, for the Public is equally injured as a collective Body. The Increaſe of Regiments and Officers, for which the Reduction of theſe Companies has made room, muſt encreaſe the Power of the Miniſtry, by encreaſing the Number of its Dependants; our Army is indeed, rather an Army of Officers than Men; and the Influence of the Miniſter extends as well to thoſe who are in expectancy as to thoſe that are in Poſſeſſion of Commiſſions; and this Diſadvantage alone is, in my Opinion, much more than a Counter-ballance to any Advantage, either real or pretended, in the raiſing Recruits, or diſciplining the Men. But whatever may be the Utility of the Eſtabliſhment

ment proposed, I am sure it will be too dearly purchased by this Country, for the Expence can never be defrayed but by a Tax upon Land, and, as this Country is circumstanced, a Tax upon Land must be its Ruin. I, therefore, shall give my Vote for the Amendment, that we may, at all Events, secure to ourselves the Power of objecting to those Parts of the Establishment which shall appear to be Grievances, and, from which, notwithstanding what has been suggested to the contrary, many Gentlemen think we shall be precluded, if the Resolution passes in its present Form.

M—j—r W— B—.

After making several Calculations, and considering the Establishment in all its Branches, concluded, that the additional Pay of the Officers, deducting the Half-pay, which they must have received, if they had been dismissed, did not amount to more than 4000 *l.* a Year. He said, that the honourable Gentleman, who spoke last, had insinuated that some Regiments were *Favourites*: Favourites, he said, was an opprobrious Name, because it had been generally applied to those who did

not

not deferve Favour; but that we fhould confider whofe Favourite a Perfon was before we determined the Senfe of the Word; to be the Favourite of a refpectable Character, faid he, certainly implies Merit; and thefe Regiments are the Favourites of the Public, the moft refpectable Character upon Earth; thefe Regiments moft glorioufly diftinguifhed themfelves in the Service of their Country, on the Plains of *Minden*, and have purchafed the Favour of their Country with their Blood; the Word Favourite, therefore, can be no Difgrace to them, nor to favour them a Difgrace to us. The honourable Gentlemen, he alfo obferved, had hinted that heavy Horfe were not ufeful in Proportion to their Expence; but this, he faid, he apprehended not to be univerfally, though, perhaps, generally true; becaufe the heavy Horfe, by their Weight, performed fuch Service at *Marbourg*, as no other Troops could perform. In anfwer to what had been alledged, with Refpect to the Increafe of Minifterial Influence, by the Increafe of Regiments on the Eftablifhment, he obferved, that the Influence arifing from the Dependance and Expectation of Officers upon Half-pay, would be much greater,

greater, and, for thefe Reafons, he declared himfelf againft the Amendment.

Mr *H— T—*, got up to anfwer Mr *B—*, but Mr *H— H—*, the P. S. having been up before him, he fat down.

Mr *H——* then repeated, and inforced the Arguments that had been before urged in favour of the Neceffity and Propriety of the prefent Civil and Military Eftablifhments; and he added, that there was not a Kingdom in the World that had lefs Reafon to complain of public Taxes, and that its Difadvantages, with Refpect to Trade, arofe rather from the Extravagance and Folly of its Inhabitants, than from any Reftraints that were impofed by Government; no check could be pretended he faid, except upon the Manufactures of Woollen and Silk; and this would be attended with no National Difadvantage, if the Natives would contribute to the home Confumption of thefe Manufactures, by wearing them themfelves; which a fenfelefs Vanity prevented them from doing, at the fame Time that they were clamouring againft Government, upon Pretence that the Manufactories, thus languifhing by their own Folly, were not encouracouraged: He added, that *Ireland* suffered much more from the Conduct of its Inhabitants, by wearing foreign Manufactures, and spending their Money in another Country, than by any Demands of Government; and that whatever Outcry had been made against the Supplies, as exorbitant and oppressive, it was certain that no Necessary of Life had yet been taxed; and that, even the Superfluities of Life, were enjoyed upon easier Terms in *Ireland*, than elsewhere. He observed, that Money was never scarce, where Interest was low; and that, in *Ireland*, Money might be had, upon public Security, at four *per Cent.* and upon private Security at four and an half. He therefore concluded, that the vehement Complaints of Grievances, arising from the Supplies granted to Government, were without Foundation; and directly contradicted by the general Conduct of the People; that they could answer no End but the fomenting causeless Discontent at Home, and encouraging hostile Attempts from abroad; and that the most effectual Way of cultivating the Arts of Peace, and putting a Stop to the licentious Riots of the lower Class of People, was to concur unanimously in the Support of Government and the Laws.

Mr *H— F—* then got up, and proceeded to anſwer Major *W— B—*, to the following Effect:

Mr *H— F—*.

I ſhall not attempt, Sir, to follow the honourable Gentleman below me, on the Floor, from Plain to Plain, and from Battle to Battle, in Order to diſcover which of our Regiments diſtinguiſhed themſelves moſt; for I have always underſtood, that, during the laſt War, all the *Britiſh* Forces behaved ſo as equally to deſerve the Affection and Eſteem of their Country. I therefore, Sir, ſee no Reaſon to change my Opinion, that it was a very cruel and injurious Meaſure to break one Company, in each of the old Regiments, to make room for new Corps: The old Corps had a Right to be continued by their Seniority and Situation, according to all Rules of Juſtice, and by their Experience and habitual Service, according to all Rules of Prudence: Their Diſmiſſion, Sir, was repugnant to the very Conditions upon which they held their Poſts, and contrary to the known and eſtabliſhed Rules of all the Countries in the World. Some of the new Regiments that were thus eſtabliſhed,

upon

upon the Ruins of the old, had no Service to plead; and others were kept on Foot, contrary to the very Conditions under which they were raifed, for they were raifed only during the War, or for a certain Time. The Injury, therefore, of continuing thefe, and difbanding the Veterans, was double; the Veteran, the Soldier I mean, for they are Men as well as their Officers, were, by long military Service, difqualified for any other; and the new Men, who were not perfectly broken to military Subordination and Fatigue, wifhed to obtain their Difcharge; fo that we have contrived our Difmiffion and Eftablifhment in fuch a Manner, as to punifh equally thofe whom we difband, and thofe whom we keep on foot, to fay nothing of the Injury done to the Public. The honourable Gentleman, Sir, has amufed us with very minute and elaborate Calculations, but, I am of Opinion, they will convince very few that the Increafe of our Eftablifhment, with Refpect to our Officers, amounts to no more than 4000 *l.* We have heard many Diftinctions concerning the Sum of 111,000 *l.* which the prefent Military Eftablifhment is allowed to exceed the Eftablifhment immediately fubfequent to the laft War; I fhall not enquire, Sir, into what Parts this

Sum

Sum may be divided, or examine the several Modes, Times, and Purposes, of laying it on; all that I think necessary to observe is, that it is a neat Increase of our Expence, and that it is beyond our Ability to pay, which, I think, is an insuperable Objection against it. The honourable and learned Gentleman who spoke last, has, indeed, inferred our pecuniary Ability from the low Interest of Money; but though, in general, this Inference may be just, it is not so with Respect to us, and, I think, I can easily shew that the low Interest of Money in *Ireland*, is the Effect of Poverty, not of Wealth: Our Securities are generally bad, and our Trade is under great Restraints and Discouragements; the few, therefore, who have Money to lend, are at a Loss how to employ it. As we are an Island governed by our own Laws, and not connected with other States in commercial Interest, we are still desirous of laying out our Money at Home, and, as good Security is rare, we are tempted to lend our Money on such Security, when it can be found at a low Interest, not because Money is plenty among us, but because we have no Opportunity of disposing of it better; and, if the honourable Gentleman will recollect, I am sure he must acknowledge, that,

except

except on public Security, and such private Security as is very rare, Money is not to be had here for less than six *per Cent.* besides Fees to Lawyers, and Attornies, in the very Act of borrowing. The honourable Gentleman has also mentioned the Cheapness of Provisions, and Labour, as another Instance of our Wealth; but the Cheapness of Provisions and Labour, proves, to Demonstration, that the comparative Value of Money is high, and the comparative Value of Money can never be high, but where it is scarce: Besides, Sir, Provisions and Labour are not cheap in a particular Country, in Proportion as they cost less Money, than in another Country; they are cheap and dear only with Respect to the Proportion their Value bears to the Value of Money, whatever it is. If we look into our ancient Annals, we shall find that there was a Time when a whole Sheep was sold for a Shilling, but it does not follow that Mutton was then cheaper than it is now; for it will be found that a Shilling was of the same Value then as the Sum is that will purchase a Sheep now: If this is considered, it will seem no Paradox, that though Provisions and Labour may be procured here for less Money than in another Country, yet they are equally dear; and

and if we judge of the Number that cannot procure the Provisions that the honourable Gentleman has supposed to be cheap, we must conclude that they are much dearer: I shall therefore only desire the honourable Gentleman, and every other Member of this House, to recollect the Situation of two Millions and a half, of the three Millions of Inhabitants which this Country is supposed to contain, and then lay their Hands upon their Hearts, and declare whether their Country is rich or poor. As to the Riots of the lower Class of People, which, it must be confessed, have been too frequent, I think the most effectual Way of preventing them, would be to avoid the Substitution of real Evils in the Place of those imaginary ones that have misled them; for, though we have no Reason to despair of quieting their Minds, when it may be done by dissipating an Illusion, yet there will be little room for Hope, when it can be done only by concealing a Reality.

Mr *T— Le H—* said, that he thought it very improper to anticipate a Debate, which could properly come on only upon an Enquiry into the Grievance supposed to arise from the Establishment, which was not the Subject

Subject of the Day; and, therefore, he should only say, that, in his Opinion, the Amendment ought to be admitted, as it seemed to be the prevailing Opinion, that the Motion, as it now stood, would preclude such an Enquiry, which, he was persuaded, the honourable Gentleman did not intend: He added, that he thought the Word *necessary* could be no Slur upon their Proceedings, but that they greatly exposed themselves to Censure, by objecting to so reasonable a Word.

Mr *P—T—*, the A. G. said, that, in that House, he never considered himself as a Servant to the Crown, being sensible that every Service to the Crown was a Service to the Public, their Interests being inseparably united. It was true, he said, that it fell to his Share, in Virtue of his Employment, to propose the Establishment, and made no Doubt but that his honourable Friend, who proposed the Amendment, would, upon Recollection, be of Opinion, that every proper Enquiry might be made, if the Motion should pass without Amendment, and, therefore, that he would not insist upon the Motion for Amendment, which, if agreed to, would be contrary to the immemorial Practice of that House.

Mr *E— S— P—* said, he hoped he had said nothing from which his honourable and worthy Friend could infer that he meant to recede from his Opinion, or his Purpose; and, therefore, insisted on the Question for the Amendment, adding, that, if it passed in the Negative, he would trouble the House no more, as he should be convinced it would be to no Purpose.

The Question was then put, and it passed *against* the Amendment, 122 against 74.

After this, many Petitions, which had been referred to the Committee of Supplies, in Favour of new Works, were rejected, it being alledged that considerable Sums were necessary for carrying on Works already begun, which would otherwise be absolutely lost to the Public, and that the Finances of the Country would not admit of the large Grants that were sollicited to begin others: But, notwithstanding this, a Petition for an Aid of 4000 *l.* to make the River *Bandon* navigable, was preferred, and granted, upon the Question, by a small Majority.

Sir

Sir *A— A—* then said, that he had a Petition in his Hand, for an Aid of 4000 *l.* to make a River near *Armagh* navigable, but that, being convinced by what had been just said, he would withdraw it, notwithstanding a Petition of the same Kind had been just granted; upon which many Gentlemen said, that they would oppose the Resolution of the Committee with Respect to that Petition in the House, and with Respect to the granting pecuniary Aids for any new Work.

Mr *E— S— P—* offered a Resolution to the Committee, that 8000 *l.* should be deposited in Trust with the *Dublin* Society, or any other Body of Men, that should be thought proper, to be distributed in Premiums for the Encouragement of several Manufactories, adding, that he thought himself under an indispensible Necessity of urging this Deposit, as he was the Means of preventing Parliamentary Aid from being granted to particular Persons, upon Petitions, and as the House had expressed its Approbation of encouraging Arts and Manufactures in this Way.

The R—t H—ble Mr *A— M—* said, that,
in

in his Opinion, this Motion should be deferred till all other Grants, which the Committee should approve, should be made, because it would then appear, whether such a Sum could be spared for that Use.

Mr *P*— replied, that his Health would not permit him to stay till all the Grants were made, and earnestly recommended the Resolution to the Care of the House in his Absence; upon which Mr *M*—, the Chairman, promised that he would give a proper Attention to it.

Sir *W*— *O*— recommended a Petition for an Aid of 2,600 *l.* to repair the Archiepiscopal and Parochial Church of *Cashell*, the Parishioners not being able to repair it themselves.

The H—ble Mr *B*— *M*— objected to it, as a bad Precedent, and said it would encourage Parishioners to suffer their Churches to run out of Repair, in Hopes of Parliamentary Aid.

Sir *W*— *O*— replied, that if the Assistance of Parliament should be thus abused, the Evil would be less than a public Neglect of an Object

Object immediately connected with Religion, and essential to the public Exercise of it; and that the Archiepiscopal Church, once a splendid and spacious Edifice, was now in so ruinous a Condition, that the Archbishop and his Clergy assembled for divine Worship in a Barn; he added, that while the Mass-Houses in many Places made a better Appearance than the Churches, the People, who could not be supposed to extract the Essentials from the external Circumstances of Religion, would be in Danger of Seduction, by the Arts of Priests and Missionaries, who were watchful to improve every Incident to their Advantage: As a Proof of the Effect that a proper Regard to the Rituals of Religion produces on the Mind, he told a Story of a Gentleman of *Ireland*, who, having carried his Servant with him into *Flanders*, and taken him to high Mass at a great Church, asked him, as they were coming out, what he thought of the Church and the Ceremony? " Think, " Sir, says the Fellow, why I think I never " saw God Almighty served like a Gentleman " before."

An Amendment was then made in the Motion, by inserting 1000*l*. instead of 2,600*l*.

and the Committee resolved that that Sum should be granted.

"Many other Sums were also granted, as it was said, in Consequence of a Determination previously made, notwithstanding all the Objections that could be urged against it; the Committee being small, and it growing late, Mr *W— B—* said, that it seemed to him that Time was more precious than Money, and that as he perceived it was to no Purpose to oppose the Grants of Money for particular Purposes, he moved, that the Committee should report that they had made some Progress, and that they should have Leave to sit again.

Dr *L—* seconded Mr *B—*, and said, that Health should no more be lavished by late Hours, than Money by Jobbs; and the Motion being put, was agreed to.

The Speaker then resuming the Chair, the Report was made accordingly; and it was resolved that the House would, next *Monday* Morning, resolve itself into a Committee, to consider farther of the Supplies, and the Lord Lieutenant's Speech:

The End of VOL. I.

The Gentleman who took these DEBATES, *being in a distant Part of the Continent while they were printing, a Speech of the R. H. G. H. which will be found in* p. 640, *was, by Mistake, imputed to J. H. H. the P. S. And the following Errors also escaped the Press, which the Reader is requested to correct.*

Page 1, for *March* 10, read *October* 11.
37, line last but one, instead of *for life*, read *at Will*.
51. line 1. for Mr *R. F.* read Mr *R. Fitz*.
59. line 1. for *keep*, read, *help*.
62. line 7. for *prevented*, read, *pretended*.
68. line 13. for *the*, read, *a*.
70. line 13. for *opinions*, read, *opinion*.
71. line 7. for *precept*, read, *precepts*.
79. line 20. for *Charity*, read, *Christianity*.
95. line 16. for *Wrong*, read, *no Wrong*.
120. line 4. for *Examination*, read, *Examinations*.
136. line 1. for *R. F.* read *R. Fitz*.
143. line last but one, for the *R. H.* read, the *H.*
172. line 20. for *T. H.* read *W. H.*
180. 2d paragraph, line 1, for *was*, read, *is*. line 3, for *was*, read, *is*. line 4. for *gave*, read *gives*. line 5. for *were*, read, *are*.
185. line last but one, for *dear*, read, *good*.
202. line the last, for Mr *B.* read Mr *W. B.*
208. line 4, for *Command*, read, *Commissions*.
221. line 23. for *Laws of Kingdom*, read, *Laws of the Kingdom*.
231. line 19. for *sacred*, read, *secure*.
254. line 4. for *to*, read, *in*.
308. line 6. for Mr *A. M.* read, the R. H. Mr *A. M.*
328. line 12. for *set*, read, *sat*.
340. line 8. for Mr *A. M.* read Mr *A. M.*
392. line 3. for *H. T.* read, *H. F.*
427. line 16. for *Brandon*, read, *Bandon*.
429. line 14. for Rt H—ble *W. B.* read Rt H—ble *B. B.*
448. line last, for *H. T.* read, *H. F.*
475. line 12. for *Verois*, read, *Viris*.
476. line 3. for *Verois*, read, *Viris*.
499. line 15. for *brutish*, read, *British*.
523. line 2. for *W. P.* read, *W. C.*
640. line 40. for *J. H. H. the P. S.* read, the R. H. G. H.
662. line 5. for *non residenced*, read, *non resident*.
702. line 4. for *the Serjeant*, read, *of the Servant*.
737. line 13. for *Deliberation*, read, *Deliberations*.

www.ingramcontent.com/pod-product-compliance
Lightning Source LLC
Chambersburg PA
CBHW030551300426
44111CB00009B/938